ISLE OF RUM

KINLOCH
GLEN

THE GAMEKEEPER

THE GAMEKEEPER

PORTIA SIMPSON

**SIMON &
SCHUSTER**

London · New York · Sydney · Toronto · New Delhi

A CBS COMPANY

First published in Great Britain by Simon & Schuster UK Ltd, 2017
A CBS COMPANY

3 5 7 9 10 8 6 4 2

Simon & Schuster UK Ltd
1st Floor
222 Gray's Inn Road
London WC1X 8HB

www.simonandschuster.co.uk
www.simonandschuster.com.au
www.simonandschuster.co.in

Simon & Schuster Australia, Sydney
Simon & Schuster India, New Delhi

A CIP catalogue record for this book
is available from the British Library

Hardback ISBN: 978-1-4711-5924-4
eBook ISBN: 978-1-4711-5926-8

Typeset in the UK by M Rules
Printed in the UK by CPI Group (UK) Ltd, Croydon, CR0 4YY

MIX
Paper from
responsible sources
FSC® C020471

Simon & Schuster UK Ltd are committed to sourcing paper
that is made from wood grown in sustainable forests and support the Forest
Stewardship Council, the leading international forest certification organisation.
Our books displaying the FSC logo are printed on FSC certified paper.

To Norman and my long-suffering parents,
and with thanks to all the keepers
and folk who helped me

CONTENTS

Prologue   1

1   An Outdoor Life   5
2   Monarch of the Glen   49
3   The Rut   75
4   Wildfires   113
5   The Last Great Wilderness   147
6   The Trustafarian   169
7   The Isle of Rum   195
8   The Eagle with the Sunlit Eye   217
9   Davy Chainsaw   247
10   Ravens and Eagles   273
11   The Minke Whale   311
12   The End of the Dream   343

PROLOGUE

Towards the end of September 2007, I took a client over to the hills above the sea cliffs on the west coast of the Isle of Rum, where he shot an eight-pointer stag. It was warm and sunny, extremely unusual weather for September, and the cloudless sky gave views up to Bloodstone Hill to the north and right out across the sea to the islands of the Outer Hebrides. We had managed to shoot the stag early in the day and I knew it would be at least two hours before the ghillies turned up with the ponies.

I gralloched – disembowelled – the beast, slitting its hide from sternum to groin and pulling out the spleen, stomach bag and intestines which lay steaming in the heather while my client studied the view out to sea. I wiped the blood from my arms with a handful of damp sphagnum moss, its coolness on my skin as refreshing as a drink from a mountain burn.

Having bagged his trophy, the stalking guest decided he

was going to walk back along the path and spend the rest of the day exploring the beach, so all I now had to do was drag the stag a couple of hundred yards down the hill and wait for the ghillies to turn up.

The gamey smell of the carcass filled my nostrils as I dragged it down the hillside, bumping and jolting over the projecting rocks and clumps of heather. Years of doing it had hardened my muscles but it was never less than tough work, especially on a day as hot as this, and it was a relief when I reached the path at the bottom of the hill, little more than a faint animal track across the hillside.

I radioed back and reported my location, then sat down in the heather and ate my packed lunch, gazing out over the calm, sparkling sea, with the sunbeams dancing on the surface of the water. It was a big change to see it so flat calm, because normally it was a maelstrom of clashing and churning waters as the ferocious currents and tidal rip of the Minch battled the huge Atlantic waves. Sometimes the wind even whipped up a waterspout, twisting and turning like a mini-tornado over the surface of the sea, but today the weather was perfect and I intended to make the most of it. I finished my lunch and, lying back, I closed my eyes. I could feel the warmth on my face as the sunlight glowed brightly through my eyelids. Shifting slightly to a more comfortable position among the dry heather strands, I drifted off to sleep.

I don't know how long I lay there before something – a movement, a change in the light or maybe just an instinctive sense of danger – dragged me back to consciousness. Suddenly everything went dark. Still half-asleep, I became aware of a black shadow blocking out the sunlight and felt a sudden rush of cooler air. As my eyes flickered open, I was greeted by the sight of a large golden eagle swooping down, its talons outstretched towards my torso. I screamed and jerked my arms upwards, trying to ward off the impact, and the sudden movement and the noise of my piercing scream startled the eagle. It was so close that I felt the rush of air from its wing-beats and could almost have plucked a tail feather from it as it swerved away at the very last moment and soared back into the sky.

I jumped to my feet, still in shock, sweat prickling my brow and my heart pounding so hard it felt like it was bursting out of my chest. Circling overhead, the eagle had seen what must have looked like a three-course banquet laid out before it: the entrails from the gralloch of the stag a few hundred yards up the hill, the bloody carcass of the stag twenty feet away from me and an apparently dead young woman as well, lying spreadeagled and motionless on the hillside, her long blonde hair tangled among the heather. The eagle had obviously decided to have me as its starter before moving on to the deer for its main course. Had I woken up a second later, I would have found its talons embedded in my chest and its cruel, hooked beak poised above my face. It was the first and last time that I ever fell asleep out on the heather.

1

An Outdoor Life

I didn't grow up with a burning desire to be a gamekeeper. There were none among our family and friends, and in fact I had no real idea what gamekeeping was until I was an adult. But from the time I could crawl, I've always been a real nature-loving, outdoor girl. My mother can still recall me as a three-year-old toddler out in the garden in the summer of 1982, picking up slugs, snails, worms and woodlice in my pudgy little hands, and that fascination with nature in all its forms has never left me. When I was a bit older I had scores of pet snails that I fed on cucumbers and carrots. I gave every one of them a name and could tell them apart by the different markings on their shells, but my favourite was a huge snail I called Rover. His shell was beautiful. He had hardly any pale amber whorls like the others; most of his were dark brown with a purple tinge that made them shine like jewels in the sunlight. I imagined him as the emperor of all the other snails, the one the whole tribe looked up to. I don't know how it became so intense but I swear I could tell when he was happy or sad.

Just at the point where my friends were starting to feel that my close relationship with slime had gone far enough, my indulgent dad built me a wooden 'snail hutch' in the garden. Of course the snails then laid thousands of eggs and the baby snails escaped the hutch for the garden, where my dad soon regretted his kindness.

Meanwhile my friends and I were holding races with the larger snails. I drew a large circle about a metre in diameter on the paving slabs and placed the snails in the middle. To encourage them to race to the edge of the circle, I sprayed a fine mist of water onto the slabs and then placed cucumber slices around the outer ring. I always let my friends choose their snails first, and took whichever one was left over. Usually the last one was a very small snail I called Band. As snails are hermaphrodite, they are both male and female, but I was unaware of such things then and guessed the snails' sex according to how attractive the shells were. Apart from Rover, who as emperor was allowed to be the exception to the rule, I assumed the plainer ones were male, so in my eyes Band was definitely a boy. No one wanted him because he was the smallest, and they assumed he was therefore the weakest and slowest, but I knew differently.

My friends chose their snails and I feigned disappointment at being left with the smallest one, but inside I was extremely happy because Band almost always won. His super-sleek little body slimed along the paving slabs in record time, much to the surprise of my friends who were expecting Rover to win. Although Rover was unnaturally large for a garden snail and quite fast, Band almost always managed to cross the line first and was rewarded with his very own slice of cucumber.

I grew up in Stonehaven, an old fishing village across the River Dee from Aberdeen, and throughout my childhood, first at primary school, while my classmates played with Barbies and dreamed of fairytale princesses and Prince Charmings, and then in my teens, when my friends were obsessed with fashion, pop music and boys – not necessarily in that order – I was always out of doors, climbing trees, building shelters in the woods out of branches and bracken, hunting for birds' nests and fishing in the river. Best of all was going down to the seashore and scouring the rock pools for shells, little crabs and all the other natural treasures they contained. My dad used to take me fishing too, in the river or out in a boat sea-fishing, and back then there seemed to be hundreds of fish just queuing up to be caught.

As we bobbed on the waves, on clear days I could see all the way north to the cranes on the Aberdeen docks. One day I saw a massive oil rig – much to my dad's amusement, I thought it was the Eiffel Tower on its side – being towed out to the North Sea oilfields. Out at sea, the sky was always full of buzzing helicopters flying to and from the rigs. Around Stonehaven the air was abundant with seabirds, not helicopters. I could look south to the ruins of Dunnottar Castle just outside the town, a fortress on a flat-topped crag that was almost completely surrounded by the sea. My dad would always recite its history – it was the last place in Britain to hold out against Cromwell's forces during the Civil War, only surrendering after an eight-month siege – but I was more interested in the sheer cliffs that surrounded it, the nesting site of thousands of guillemots, razorbills, kittiwakes, fulmars, shags and puffins.

We were riding the waves in a dinghy one day, fishing for mackerel, when a movement caught my eye and I saw a plume of spray a little further out to sea. 'What's that?' I said.

My father followed my gaze. 'We're in luck, Portia,' he said. 'That's a whale sounding.'

I froze, heart thumping, almost beside myself with excitement and not even daring to breathe in case I broke the spell. Then I glimpsed the glistening, grey-black hump of the whale's back as it broke surface again and a few moments later, its massive tail flukes, outlined against the clouds for a second before it dived below the surface again. That was a thrilling, never-to-be-repeated moment, but the regular sights and events of the turning year were wonderful too. In late autumn every year we could see thousands of pink-footed geese, greylags, whooper swans and goldeneyes darkening the sky like a murmuration of starlings as they took off from Loch Skene at dawn, returning to their roosts there a few hours later as dusk fell.

At times my mum must have despaired of her tomboy daughter and, as I grew older, she did her best to steer me back onto the path of womanly righteousness. One day when I was about eight, I was mooching about the kitchen while my tired-looking mother stood over the ironing board, with piles of clothes on either side of her. The iron hissed as she pressed it down on the laundry, sending a hot jet of steam into the air, and she brushed a strand of hair away from her face as she worked the iron over a small square of cotton.

'What are you doing, Mum?' I said, edging closer.

'I'm ironing your father's pants,' she said, pointing to a large pile of neatly pressed squares, each with a Y-shape facing the front.

'Why do you need to iron pants, Mum? It's not like anyone sees them. Or socks for that matter.' Over in the corner was another pile of perfectly pressed socks, neatly arranged in pairs.

'Oh, you should always iron your pants,' she said. 'It just looks neater that way.'

'Well, I'm never going to iron when I grow up.'

'I'm afraid you will,' she said, putting the iron down while she folded the Y-fronts. 'When you grow up and get married you'll find yourself ironing your husband's underwear, and cooking all his meals.'

'Then I'm never getting married,' I said.

'Oh, you will do, just wait until you grow up.'

'No way!' I said, warily eyeing the pants. The future was staring me in the face and it was distinctly Y-shaped. Why on earth get married anyway, if that's all you had to look forward to? As I skipped out of the back door and ran towards the woods I made a vow to myself never to get married. At eight years old I thought I had all the answers. My life was going to be different and my place in the world was among the trees, rivers and meadows, not in a kitchen with an iron in my hand.

That was many years ago now and since I grew up, I've had three proposals of marriage. But every time, as soon as I heard the words 'Will you marry me?', all I could see was a pile of Y-fronts on an ironing board and every time I said 'No'.

My childhood best friend, Gillian, was a farmer's daughter, living on an 800-acre farm outside the town, and I often went out there at weekends. It was heaven; we'd climb on the haystacks, dam streams, make dens in the woods and get covered in mud and cow-shit. I loved every moment of it. We would climb trees together, too, though I always had to be the one to go just a little bit higher or a little further out along a creaking branch. Much of the woodland was commercial forestry but there was a huge beech tree rising well above the surrounding pines and that was my favourite tree to climb. I was eleven by the time I could finally reach the first branch and it was a real effort to haul myself up onto it, but from then on the going was easier. Each time I dared myself to go a little bit higher than the time before, although there was always a prickle of fear when I looked down and saw how high I had already climbed and how small my friend seemed, standing there on the ground or clinging to a lower branch, staring up at me.

I clambered up, hand over hand, the tree bark rough beneath my fingers and the heady scent of resin from the pine trees filling the air around me. Any fear I felt as I climbed higher and higher was drowned by my mounting excitement. There was a squirrels' drey in a hollow where the tree forked and although I tried to avoid disturbing them by moving round to the other side of the trunk, I could hear them chattering angrily at me as I climbed on. A few moments later, I swung myself up onto the next branch and found that there was a gap where another branch had been torn off in a winter storm, opening up a view out through the canopy of the tree. I was now higher than all the surrounding trees and looking right out over the forest. I was probably still only fifty or sixty feet above the ground, but it felt as if I could see forever.

In the far distance to the west, I could make out the silvery glint of the cold northern light reflecting from the surface of a loch and the purpling shapes of the mountains of the Highlands merging with the clouds as the sun sank towards the horizon, and I felt an ache to be there, exploring those forests, climbing those mountains and fishing for trout in the lochs. If there was one moment in my young life that fore-shadowed what the future would hold for me, that may well have been it. I clung to the tree trunk, watching the sunset painting the clouds red and gold until it was so dark that I could barely see where to put my hands and feet as I climbed back down the tree and hurried home to a scolding from my parents both for being so late home and, yet again, for coming back with my leggings and jumper all muddied and torn.

Gillian was also with me when, aged twelve, I found a pet that was even more unusual than my collection of snails. We were walking past some tall beech trees down by the river when I spotted a baby crow that must have fallen out of its nest. I took him home and my brother and I gave him water through a straw and fed him dog food from a teaspoon. Although I hadn't realised it at first, the little crow had broken his leg in the fall from the nest, and putting it right required an expensive visit to the vet with my long-suffering dad.

We found a second-hand parrot cage which became my crow's home and being handled regularly made him become tame very quickly. Soon he was calling out for food. The calls were very loud – we christened him Tennis because he made such a racket – and he never seemed to stop; even while he was eating he was still calling out for more. As a result he was often calling and choking on his food at the same time.

I did try to teach him to perch on my shoulder, Long John Silver-style, but he kept falling off, so I had to settle for having him sit on my lap instead. Very soon all the kids in the neighbourhood were coming round to see Tennis, who had become a minor local celebrity. We took him out in the garden, talked to him and sang to him, and he would answer with calls of his own. I had become really attached to him and as soon as I got in from school every day, the first thing I did was to rush to his cage, take him out and pet him, and give him some dog food in the usually vain hope of silencing his calls for a few moments.

We had taken him back to the vet for a check-up on a couple of occasions but not long after what turned out to be his final visit there, Tennis suddenly fell ill. Whether his immune system had been permanently compromised by the fall from the nest or he had just picked up some kind of bug from somewhere, he worsened rapidly and died within twenty-four hours of first becoming ill. I was devastated. I had never experienced the death of anyone or anything I'd been close to before and it was one of the most heartbreaking moments of my young life. It took me a long time to get over it.

My parents were quite strict with me when I was young. Quite rightly, they wanted their daughter to grow up to be an upstanding citizen, respectful of her elders, but being good is so boring and being bad is so much fun, so I was a real teen-age rebel whenever I thought I could get away with it. And, with practice, I got pretty good at getting away with it. My concentration at school was quite poor and I often got into trouble for not paying attention and talking to my friends. My terrible memory also meant I frequently forgot to do my homework and I ended up with a handful of after-school detentions. To avoid further punishment at home, I was slightly economical with the truth and told my parents I was staying late to study with a friend.

Wherever my love of the great outdoors came from, it clearly wasn't genetic, because my parents and my brother were real 'townies'. They didn't really like animals and though they didn't mind the countryside, they certainly didn't go out of their way to discover it. We were a middle-class family – my dad was an engineer, working offshore, and my mum worked as a secretary – and my parents undoubtedly had hopes that I would follow in their footsteps and choose a 'respectable pro-fessional career' like being a solicitor or doctor, but I always knew that I wanted an outdoor life. When I was younger, I'd thought about being a vet or a farmer, but I was too impatient to do the five years of training to be a vet and when I asked Gillian's dad about farming, he said, 'If you own your own land, you can make a living, Portia, but if not, you'll work all the hours God sends and probably earn less than the boy who delivers the newspaper you won't have time to read.'

With that lukewarm endorsement ringing in my ears, when I left school in July 1997, I chose forestry instead. My choice horrified my parents at first, but I was unshakeable in my determination to live and work an outdoor life and, once they realised my mind was made up, they swallowed their disappointment – though I'm sure that privately they were hoping that a few months of hard physical work would make me 'see sense' and opt for a more 'ladylike' career instead. None of my friends seemed to care much about their future careers, preferring just to live in the moment, and my best friend Gillian's life took a turn she would neither have anticipated nor wanted when she became pregnant at just fifteen years old. She opted to have the baby and though the child's father played no further part in her life, Gillian raised her son on her own. She did a good job; he's now a fine young man.

I trained in forestry at a college in Suffolk. We all stayed at a large farmhouse, about two miles from the college, and the social life there was great, involving lots of drinking and trips to the pub. We usually took a shortcut home in the pitch darkness through cow pastures and woodland, which tended to get very interesting when you were drunk. I fell into a ditch more than once as I blundered my way back after closing time. We even got chased by an angry bull one night and tore our clothes jumping a barbed-wire fence to escape.

At the end of the course in the summer of 1998, I moved back to Aberdeen and completed my chainsaw training on a one-day-a-week placement at Clinterty College, about ten miles from Aberdeen. I wasn't the only woman on the course but there were only two of us, surrounded by fifteen men. The course tutor and my fellow students were all very accepting of women on the course, in sharp contrast to my previous college where, as the only woman, I experienced sarcastic comments and openly sexist behaviour. One of the tutors at my previous college clearly didn't think much of a woman joining the course, and he would sometimes look at me and just shake his head. A couple of times I also heard him say to the other men, 'We don't need women in this job.'

To make matters worse, one of my fellow students would rib me at least once a week. His favourite saying was 'Woman, know your place', and half the class would join in the laughter. I tried to shrug off the comments but inwardly I was seething. One year later, I still had a huge chip on my shoulder and although the guys on my new course were very nice, I was still quite sensitive. Things came to a head when we were taking it in turns to use a great big chainsaw to cut up a gigantic tree. When the tutor got to me and the other woman, he said, 'You girls won't be able to use the big chainsaws, because you're too small.'

I completely lost the plot at that, yelling at the tutor and calling him a 'sexist pig' and a few other things. Even while I was shouting at him, part of me was feeling sorry for him as well, because he didn't really deserve such a tirade, but I just couldn't control myself. I suppose it was the reaction to the petty, snarky, snide comments I'd been subjected to the previous year, and this particular tutor just happened to be the one who copped the backlash.

I wouldn't have liked to have been on the receiving end of it but everyone else in the class, including the other woman, thought it was hilarious. She said to me afterwards, 'When the tutor said that, I just thought, "Oh well," and sort of agreed with him and didn't bother.'

She still didn't try to handle the big chainsaw but I wasn't going to let anyone tell me I couldn't do what the men were doing, so I picked it up. One of the other guys said, 'Here, let me help you with that,' and started to reach for it, but he also got a mouthful from me for his trouble. I was young and quite hot-headed back then and overreacted, but all I wanted was to be treated as an equal and I saw the offer of help as a real slur. As I've grown older I've come to recognise that I was being much too prickly; not every offer of help was from some sexist pig trying to demean me, some were just decent people who wanted to help.

It turned out that the guy fancied me and was trying to be my hero and come to my rescue, but I didn't realise that at the time, and I still have no ability to recognise when someone is interested in me in that way. Something in my make-up means I don't read signals like that in the same way as other people. So a man has to come up to me and say, 'Portia I fancy you, will you go out with me?' before I'll realise. If he doesn't, I just don't get it at all.

When I picked up the big chainsaw it was actually a lot heavier and more unwieldy than I'd expected but there was no way I was going to put it down again. With normal-sized chainsaws, you just put it into the wood and press down slightly and I hadn't realised that with king-size ones like that one you still had to take the weight of the saw when you had the blade in the wood. So my technique was wrong at first and the chain got pinched and stopped spinning, but I soon adjusted my technique, cut a perfect slice right through the trunk and then handed the saw to the next student in line. That incident seemed to mark a turning point and from then on there were a lot fewer comments about what 'girls' could and couldn't do.

I passed all my exams at the end of the course and then began work as a fully qualified tree surgeon in Aberdeen. I rang round all of the half-dozen tree-surgery companies in the area and managed to secure a job with one of them. The boss of the company proved to be quite an open-minded character who had employed a woman tree surgeon before, so he didn't have any qualms about hiring me, though if I wasn't the only woman tree surgeon around, there certainly weren't many of us. Dressed in my climbing harness and hard hat, and toting a chainsaw, I certainly thought I looked the part but, like all women in men's worlds, I still had to prove myself to my often sceptical male workmates. There were the inevitable piss-taking comments when I started: 'Make us a cup of tea and we'll do the man's work, Portia,' and 'The job's for lumberjacks, not lumberjills.' However, this time I bit my lip and just ignored them and once I'd shown that I could shin up a tree trunk or drop a full-grown tree and turn it into logs as fast as they could, I was accepted. From then on, I was just another one of the boys.

I spent two years as a self-employed tree surgeon, mainly working on contract to two companies, but both of them then closed down in 2001 within a few weeks of each other. Many others had already gone bust in the previous few years, so it wasn't a huge shock, but it left me feeling very worried about my future.

I had to travel further afield in search of work and, having borrowed my mother's car up to then, it was high time I bought my own. I leafed through the newspaper each night, trying to find my perfect car, but nothing took my fancy until one day my father circled an advert for a second-hand Panther Kallista, a modern vehicle but styled like a 1930s sports car. It was well out of my price range and there seemed little point in viewing a car I was unable to afford, but a little voice in my head kept telling me that there was no harm in simply looking, so we arranged a viewing and set off towards Cove Bay on the south bank of the River Dee. The car was still in the lean-to garage alongside the owner's house when we arrived and as he opened the garage doors, I peered into the gloom inside, trying to catch a glimpse of it. He started the engine and reversed out slowly, and I had only seen a couple of inches of the car when I fell in love with it. It was a two-seater convertible with a long cigar-shaped body and side boards swept up over gleaming alloy wheels. The bonnet was over two metres long and painted gun-barrel blue with shining silver wings. The dashboard was made from solid walnut and all the dials and gauges looked like they were straight out of the cockpit of an air-craft in a wartime movie.

Feeling like I'd died and gone to heaven, I ran my fingers over the sparkling paintwork and then jumped in the car and we took a short test drive around Cove Bay. As we zoomed along the road, children stopped to wave and motorists beeped their horns. How I loved this car. By the end of the test drive I knew I had to have it but the price was more than I could afford and as the owner tended to address all his comments to my dad rather than me, I thought I might have more chance of success if my dad negotiated on my behalf. He offered the man the price I could afford but was promptly turned down. 'Oh well, at least we tried,' my dad said, as we drove home, but I refused to give up hope.

Over the course of the next month I added another £250 to my savings and then pestered my father incessantly to phone the car owner with a higher offer. My pleas fell on deaf ears, so I changed tactics and left little notes all over the house reading 'Phone about the car'. After this also failed to catch his attention, I decided to make one last-ditch attempt. What I really needed was a captive audience and I knew just where to find one. Grabbing some Sellotape and a pen and paper, I headed towards the bathroom and, lifting the toilet lid, I carefully taped the same message to the underside. 'Perfect,' I thought to myself as I stood back to admire my handiwork. 'The next time my dad goes for a pee, he'll have to look at it for at least thirty seconds. If this doesn't work, nothing will.'

When my dad next emerged from the bathroom, he gave a rueful smile and said, 'All right, I surrender. I'll ring him but don't get your hopes up too much. He's probably sold it by now but even if he hasn't, I'm sure he'll still be holding out for a higher price.'

One telephone call later, I was the proud owner of a Panther convertible. The owner had still wanted a few more quid than I could afford but, either taking pity on me, or perhaps just anxious to be allowed to take a pee in peace in future, my dad lent me the extra money. Looking back now, I'm not proud to have used my feminine wiles to manipulate my dad and it wasn't the first occasion when I'd acted helpless to get 'Daddyo' to do things for me, but it was to be the last one. From then on, whatever the circumstances, I decided to be master of my own destiny.

We picked up the car that evening and I instantly christened it 'Brum', after the car in the kids' TV series. Brum and I went everywhere together and never was I happier than when I was at the wheel of my little sports car, with the hood down and the wind in my hair. However, as well as having something of a short fuse, I am also enormously impatient, so poor Brum sometimes found himself crossing terrain that was more suited to a Land Rover than a Panther.

One day I was out driving with my dad when we got stuck in a queue of cars waiting at a barrier that had jammed and couldn't be raised. After sitting drumming my fingers for a few minutes, I got so frustrated that I pulled off the road and drove up over the grass verge. There was a collapsing wire fence at the edge of the field next to the road and I got my dad to stand on that and flatten it to the ground so I could drive over it. We then went cross-country, weaving in and out of the trees and, even with my wing mirrors folded in, there was sometimes no more than an inch to spare on either side as we squeezed through the gaps before emerging through a farm gateway and rejoining the road on the far side of the jammed barrier. All that because I just couldn't deal with sitting there and having to wait.

Forestry jobs – felling, thinning and 'crown-lifting' trees – continued to slow down that winter and eventually I found myself with only two or three days' work a week. Figuring that I could go back to tree surgery at any point if things improved, I thought it wouldn't hurt to add an extra string or two to my bow, but it had to be outdoor work; I wasn't going to be cooped up in an office for anything.

I was twenty-one when I first began to think seriously about a gamekeeping career. At my grandmother's ninetieth birthday party, I was chatting to my uncle Angus, who was a keen fisherman, shotgun shooter and deer-stalker. He had always wanted to become a gamekeeper, but nobody has ever become rich doing that. With two children and a large mortgage, his family and financial obligations had to take priority over his dreams and he ended up working in the offshore oil industry instead. However, on his weekends off, he regularly went away to local estates and farms to indulge his passion for shooting and he promised to take me out deer-stalking with him, to give me a flavour of what life as a gamekeeper would be like.

Uncle Angus was true to his word and one afternoon in the autumn of 2001 we went hunting with his next-door neighbour, Billy, who owned a rifle and was a keen deer-stalker. We drove out to a secluded farm on the edge of a local estate, where Billy had permission to shoot. It was a beautifully sunny day and the wildlife was out in force. Rabbits and pheasants lined the fringes of the fields, flocks of pigeons flew overhead and goldfinches were stripping the down from the thistles at the side of the lane where we parked.

When we got out of the car, Billy handed me his rifle to hold and I tried to look nonchalant about it. I knew enough to keep it pointing at the ground or the sky, not those around me, but although I'd handled shotguns before, I'd never had my hands on a rifle and I was itching to cradle it against my shoulder and squint through the telescopic sight. Billy had meanwhile picked up a pair of binoculars and begun scanning the hillsides. 'Oh, here we are now,' he said after a few minutes.

'Looks like an empty patch of heather,' I thought to myself, as I peered at the hillside with my naked eye, but as soon as he handed me the binoculars, to my surprise, I saw a group of deer ambling along the fenceline.

'Okay then,' Billy said. 'Follow me and walk in single file so there's less chance of being seen. If we all walk close together we will look like just one person rather than a big group. We've also got to walk into the wind so they don't catch our scent.'

Falling into step behind him, I kept a wary eye on the deer, whose white rumps were now clearly visible against the heather. Two broad, open fields stood between us and the animals, and we couldn't walk across them without being seen, but there was a five-foot-deep drainage ditch running between the fields, providing the perfect cover. Billy dropped into the ditch and I slithered down behind him, feeling cold, muddy water seeping over the top of my boots and into my socks. We had also disturbed the muddy sediment in the bottom of the ditch, sending bubbles of stinking methane rising to the surface.

Holding onto the long grass to keep our balance, we were edging our way along the ditch, trying to get as far as we could without being seen, when two of the deer, still not spotting us, jumped over the fence and bounded into the field directly in front of us. All we had to do now was wait for them to get a bit closer so Billy could take the shot.

Settling his rifle into position, Billy waited, motion-less, and within a few minutes a buck walked towards us. Squinting though the rifle's scope, Billy waited for it to turn sideways so he could get a clear shot and be sure of killing the animal cleanly, then squeezed the trigger. The echoes of the shot rolled around the hillside like thunder and the buck dropped, stone dead, while the rest of the deer scattered in panic. We waited a few more minutes – you always do so after shooting an animal, in case it proves to be only wounded and gets back up, in which case you need to be ready to fire again – then scrambled out of the boggy ditch and went over to inspect the kill.

As I looked down at the buck I felt mixed emotions: elation at our success, but a deep sense of pity for the death of such a beautiful animal. Its tongue lolled from its mouth and I was startled to see how quickly its eyes had lost their life spark, already becoming dull and rheumy as if a veil had been drawn across them. Flies were beginning to cluster around them, no longer dislodged by a toss of the buck's head or a flick of its tail. Denser clouds of flies explored the fresh wound in its chest, still oozing blood.

I could sense Billy watching me. 'How do you feel?' he said as he pulled out his hunting knife and began to gut the deer.

'Um, well, I feel a bit sorry for it, to be honest.'

He smiled. 'Don't worry, most people feel like that the first time, but just think of the great life that buck had led, living in complete freedom, right up until the moment it was shot. And anyway,' he said with a wink, 'it's a great source of free-range meat.'

He dragged out its steaming intestines, which landed with a squelch at my feet. 'Now think about where the meat you buy from the supermarket came from,' he said. 'Factory-farmed pigs and chickens – and even the cows and sheep don't have it easy, with their lambs and calves taken away from them early for fattening up. No, lassie, it's much kinder to eat free-range game like venison, pigeon or wild duck.'

Picking up his bloody knife he wiped it on the grass and put it back in its sheath with a metallic click, then gave me an appraising look. 'Here's something else I bet you didn't know: a deer's teeth get ground down as they grow older, to the point where they can't chew their food properly. The grass and vegetation they eat then pass through their system only partially digested and their body weight drops until they're just skin and bone. During the winter they then die a long, slow and painful death from hypothermia. Isn't it much kinder to put a bullet in them before that happens?'

'I never really thought of it like that before,' I said.

He smiled. 'Anyway, here you go.' He threw a length of rope my way. 'Make yourself useful and tie this on to its head, then you can help me drag it back to the car.'

When I got to bed that night, I was too excited to sleep and lay awake for a long time, staring at the ceiling, thinking about everything I'd seen and done that day. I'd never had a sentimental, Disney-style view of nature. I knew it could be 'red in tooth and claw', and it didn't upset me to see an osprey swoop to impale a salmon with its talons or a fox stealing away from a farmyard with a chicken in its jaws; it was just the way of the natural world. Taking part in stalking and killing that buck had crystallised everything for me. The whole experience had felt so natural that at that moment I made up my mind: this was what I wanted to do with my life.

Although I'd always loved wildlife and the open country – the wilder the better – I also knew that estate owners and their employees tended to be ultra-conservative types, and I had never imagined that they would dream of employing a woman in a traditionally male job like gamekeeper or stalker. However, this was now 2001, not 1901, so perhaps it was worth a try. I phoned the North Highland College at Thurso the next morning to ask about the gamekeeping courses they ran and then applied for the following year's course: a Higher National Certificate in Gamekeeping with Wildlife Management. To my delight I was accepted, subject to my finding a satisfactory work placement to complement the theoretical side of the course. When I told my parents about it, they were horrified at first and they actually didn't want to sign the permission forms to allow me to go to college, but in the end they relented because they saw how much I really wanted to do it.

The college had told me that it was up to me to gain as much experience as possible before starting there, so over the next few weeks Angus and I went shooting on a regular basis, which only increased my desire to become a game-keeper. However, there was still almost a year ahead of me before the start of the course and my tree-surgery jobs had almost dried up. After scouring the local newspaper and finding nothing, I decided to pay a visit to the job centre, even though I wasn't technically unemployed. Searching around in the miscellaneous section, an advert caught my eye: 'Grouse beaters wanted for an eight-week period starting 1 August, working for Invercauld and Braemar Crown Estate. Accommodation and food provided.'

'Perfect,' I thought, printing off my CV.

Within two weeks I had been interviewed and hired on the spot. Packing up my belongings, I threw my bags into the back of Brum and headed up Royal Deeside. A few hours later, I was driving up the private track towards Invercauld House, deep in the heart of the Cairngorms National Park. Owned by the same family, the Farquharsons, for centuries, Invercauld House was a spectacular, towered and turreted granite mansion, surrounded by 200 square miles of magnificent forests, moors, lochs and mountains.

Although the grouse-shooting season lasted from 'the Glorious Twelfth' of August until the tenth of December, most shoots, including Invercauld's, finished well before that, so I and the fifteen other beaters had only been hired until the end of September. The beaters' accommodation was an open-plan log cabin set back into the forest, a few hundred yards from the big house. However, as I was the only woman, they had decided to put me in Invercauld House itself, in a small but cosy attic room, with a cast-iron bed, a walnut wardrobe and a chest of drawers that smelled faintly of mothballs.

I quickly unpacked my belongings and then set off up the track towards the log cabin, eager to meet my new workmates, but it was still quite early in the day and only six people had turned up when I got there. There were rows of pine bunk beds on each side of the cabin and in the centre of the room was a large pot-bellied stove that one of the game-keepers had lit for us, sending the scent of burning peat and pine logs drifting through the room.

The first person I met was a boy called Graham and we became instant friends. He was my height – five foot six – blond-haired and solidly built, and like me he had never done grouse beating before and was feeling a bit nervous. Throughout the course of the day, more and more men turned up but the last one to arrive was a formidable sight. Wearing a white vest and tight-fitting, ripped jeans, he was tattooed from head to foot and his dirty blond hair was tied back in a ponytail, showing off the hardest, meanest-looking face I had ever seen. I could also see the hilt of a large hunt-ing knife protruding from the top of one of his Doc Marten boots. As the door banged shut behind him, he fixed each of us in turn with a menacing stare from his piercing blue eyes.

Graham and I exchanged nervous looks. 'I wouldn't like to meet him down a dark alley,' I whispered.

He nodded. 'Hope he doesn't kill us in our sleep.'

However, when I got talking to the new arrival, Paddy, I discovered that, despite his intimidating looks, he was one of the nicest men on our team. Reliable and trustworthy, he soon became my first port of call whenever I had a problem of any sort, and he also kept us all entertained with a constant round of jokes and rude insults.

At eight o'clock that night the local gamekeepers arrived to give us a briefing. They ranged in age from sixteen to sixty but were all wearing identical tweed suits, with plus fours, waistcoats and flat caps. It made me smile to see even the boys dressed up like old men.

The briefing took ages, but boiled down to:

1) Do as you're told.
2) Walk across the moor waving a flag.
3) If in any doubt, see 1) above.

By the time it was over, it was pitch dark and as it was a cloudy, moonless night and I didn't have a torch, I had to grope my way back through the woods to the big house by Braille.

The following morning we were all herded into the back of an old ex-army Unimog, ready for our first day's work. Unfortunately, as there were now twenty-five of us, including all the beaters and gamekeepers, there weren't enough seats for everyone. All the estate gun dogs were piled in on top of us as well and very soon there was a heaving mass of crushed bodies – human and canine – all jostling for a better position. As there was no room left inside, the gamekeepers had to hold on to the back door or the anti-roll bar and as we set off up the track towards the first drive, they kept themselves entertained by punching and kicking each other and trying to uncurl each other's fingers so they could push them off the moving vehicle. It was becoming clear that Health and Safety considerations were not necessarily uppermost in the keepers' minds . . .

As if to prove it, the gamekeeper at the wheel drove as fast as he could along the bumpy track, so by the time we arrived at our destination, we were all covered in bruises and cuts. The Unimog had an anti-roll cage on the back with big metal bars around us and over our heads. That caused most of the problems because the bars were sharp and had been left uncovered. Having been flung from side to side for half an hour, most people's heads had been bashed on the exposed bars at least once.

Before the first grouse drive began, we were lined out over the course of a couple of miles, roughly 200 yards from each other, in a massive horseshoe shape. It took almost half an hour to get us all in position and the beaters who were dropped off first had a very long wait until the last person was placed up to two miles away. So on this and every subsequent day, I tried to make sure I was one of the last to be dropped off. That way there was only a few minutes' wait before starting, not long enough for hypothermia to set in. Since we were all newcomers and the gamekeeper didn't know our names, he kept choosing the first person who made eye contact with him. To avoid being chosen, every time we were getting ready to drop off another beater, I turned my back and pretended to be studying the lie of the land.

Once I had been dropped off, waiting for the grouse drives to start was quite eerie, as I was unable to see the beaters on either side because of the slope of the hillside and the hill fog that descended without warning, blanketing the moor, and calling to each other was the only way to navigate. The gamekeepers had hand-held radios to help keep the line in order and stop people from straying too far in front or behind, but most of them ignored those and just bellowed their instructions across the hillside.

Each drive took up to an hour. We walked miles through the heather waving big white flags to scare up the grouse. They were so beautifully camouflaged, with even the red wattle over their eyes blending into the tapestry of moorland colours, that I would almost jump out of my skin every time an unseen grouse burst from beneath my feet, giving its gabbling alarm call as it flew away, inches above the moor.

The ground was constantly rising and falling, and we also had to negotiate bogs of cotton grass, sphagnum moss and wet peat that sucked at our boots, and clamber up and over peat hags – pillars of peat, capped with clumps of heather – that rose several feet above the eroded peat-beds surrounding them. Even more gruelling were the belts of old heather. The tangled, woody stems formed a dense mass, two, three or even four feet high, and the only way through them was to adopt a high-stepping gait, bringing your knees up to your chest at each step. A few hundred yards would have been tiring and several miles was absolutely exhausting. My legs were a mass of scratches from the sharp, woody stems and my boots were brimful of heather seeds.

Waving our flags and with gun dogs running out in front of us, we set the grouse skimming over the moor towards the stone-built butts, where the 'guns', who had each paid a four- or even five-figure sum, were crouching, ready to shoot. Somehow the gamekeepers managed to keep us all in line and towards the end of the drive we got closer and closer to each other, forming an almost solid wall of bodies and white flags.

I'd never seen a drive at such close quarters before and the end of it was a real spectacle. Stretched across the hillside, the wall of beaters with white flags flapping and cracking in the wind sent coveys of grouse soaring over the butts. The hillside erupted with the sounds of gunfire, shouting and dogs barking. The speed the grouse flew and the way they hugged the contours of the land – not for nothing are they nicknamed 'low flyers' – saw a large proportion of the birds survive and escape back into the hills.

The shot grouse folded their wings and plummeted to earth; most were dead before they hit the ground. All around us, dogs raced through the heather to retrieve the birds. At the end of the day, the gamekeepers sorted out the birds, placing each brace of grouse on a hanger. Young birds were put on one side of the game larder and the old birds on the other side, ready for the game dealer to pick up later.

Grouse beating might have sounded like a country stroll but walking up to ten miles each day over such punishing terrain, up and down hills, over uneven ground and through dense heather, while waving a big white flag overhead, was simply too much for many of the original beaters. After a couple of weeks most of them had quit. At the end of each day my muscles still ached so much they felt like they were on fire, but I was revelling in it and had no intention of giving up. As our numbers kept dwindling, more and more beaters were recruited from the surrounding area to replace them. Most of them came from the local school or were the wives, girlfriends and family members of the gamekeepers. I was no longer the only woman out on the moor during the day but it didn't really change the group dynamic because they all lived locally and went back to their own homes at night, so the only time we saw them was the short time before we set off in the morning, or while waiting for our transport at the end of the day.

By now, living at the big house no longer seemed such a good idea. By the time I got in at night, muddy and sweaty from the day's work, there was never any hot water left as the guests and house servants had used it all, and as the nights were drawing in, I found myself having to grope my way back through the dark, eerie forest alone every night. Since I spent most of my time at the log cabin with my friends anyway, it made sense for me to live up there as well. There were now only ten of us, once the beaters had headed home, so the cabin was half-empty, leaving me with plenty of beds to choose from. Although there was a television in the cabin, mostly we just sat around the log-stove in the evenings, talking and swapping stories. No one batted an eyelid about having a woman living and sleeping under the same roof and they all still wandered round in their pants or long johns. I think they saw me as asexual, if they thought about it at all. We'd go on the town on Saturday nights and when the boys were getting ready to go out, they'd all be talking to each other about the women they were going to chat up that night. I remember thinking 'I'm a woman, anyone want to chat me up?' but they never did; I was definitely just one of the boys to them.

After three weeks at Invercauld, we switched to Balmoral, where the Royal Family had just arrived for two weeks' shooting, and we were given a strict briefing on how to behave. Cameras were not allowed and bad language was forbidden, though even the threat of execution for treason could not have stopped some of the keepers and beaters from swearing. We were also told not to talk to the Royals unless spoken to first. We were all excited about it, apart from Paddy, who was very anti-establishment and a diehard republican.

The next day we took the long bus ride to Balmoral, but to my disappointment I didn't even glimpse the Royal Family on the first drive. However, on the second one, the keepers placed me halfway along the line and as we reached the top of the hill above the butts, I had a perfect bird's-eye view of the Royals. Princes Harry and William were in the middle butt, Prince Charles was on one side with a group of friends and the Queen was on the other. Each had a loader beside them with a bag of cartridges.

As I approached the butts, despite the strict instructions we'd been given, I decided that it was too good a chance to miss so, picking up one of the shot grouse, I walked over and presented it to Prince Harry. Smiling, he took the bird from me and we chatted for a few minutes. We hunted around in the heather with the gun dogs as we were talking and found several more birds that we stacked in a neat pile. Sadly, he didn't ask me for a date and when I looked round, I realised that the rest of the beaters had disappeared. Luckily Prince Harry pointed me in the right direction and, saying goodbye to him, I took off up the hill at a jog.

After twenty minutes I caught up with the other beaters, who were all sitting down munching sandwiches. Panting and out of breath, I dragged myself over the brow of the hill, more than ready for my own lunch. The only problem was the river between the beaters and myself. It was about fifteen feet wide and five feet deep and very fast-flowing. I really didn't fancy falling in and getting drenched but the alternative was not getting any lunch.

Walking up and down the river bank, I came to a place where three boulders, widely set apart from each other, rose out of the water. That would just have to do as a crossing point; it would certainly be better than swimming across. Taking a run, I sprinted to the bank, jumped from boulder to boulder and threw myself onto the opposite bank. My left boot splashed down in the water and my foot got a bit wet, but that aside, I was quite dry and pleased to have made it across safely. Looking around me, I noticed everyone else appeared to have crossed without getting even slightly wet.

'How come you lot are so dry?' I said.

Paddy grinned. 'Probably because most people just use the bridge, Portia.'

Turning around, I noticed an iron bridge which I'd completely failed to spot, spanning the river about thirty feet from where I stood. 'Eyes of a hawk,' I said, going red with embarrassment.

Being late for lunch was never a good thing, as all the good sandwiches had already been taken. I stared disenchantedly at what was left, then settled for a Scotch egg instead, and sat down with my friends in the heather. Before long, a convoy of Land Rovers pulled up alongside us; to my surprise the

Royal Family were joining us for lunch. The Queen sat down with her lunchbox about five yards from us and began to eat her sandwiches – crusts cut off, as far as I could see. In her wax jacket, green wellies and headscarf she could easily have passed for one of us.

Paddy remained unimpressed and, taking off his shirt to show off his tattoos, he started telling jokes in a voice that must easily have carried to the Queen's ears. A throwback to the 1960s, he often smoked a joint after work but now, grinning away to himself, he said, 'Time for my pudding,' and, rummaging in his pocket, he produced the longest, fattest joint I had ever seen. He lit it with his Zippo lighter, took a long drag and then slowly blew out a plume of sweet-smelling smoke. We stared at each other in disbelief as it drifted towards the Queen.

'I think you have an audience,' I said, pointing at her two police bodyguards with rifles slung across their chests, who were giving Paddy menacing stares.

Completely unfazed, he was revelling in the attention and just blew out another plume of smoke, saying, 'Mmmm, this is nice,' even louder.

The Queen continued to eat her lunch in silence, either ignoring him or oblivious to him.

'Shall I go and offer her a smoke?' Paddy said.

'Yeah, go on,' I said. 'I'll just stay here and watch for the bullet exiting the back of your head.'

In the end he decided not to push his luck and we headed up the hill for the start of the next drive. We didn't see the Royals at such close quarters again, but I can now quite truthfully say that not only have I chatted up Prince Harry, but I also once had lunch with his grandmother.

By the time we reached the last week of the grouse season, there were only eight beaters left and our cabin was starting to look pretty empty. Saying goodbye to my friends on the last day was sad, but my time at Invercauld had been a fantastic experience and had only increased my desire to become a gamekeeper. However, there were still nine months to go before the start of my course and since tree-surgery work remained in very short supply around Aberdeenshire and it was the wrong time of year for gamekeeping jobs, I was forced to look further afield.

A few years earlier, I had worked with a tree surgeon, Nick, who had become a very good friend. He had since moved to the south of England to set up his own firm, and when I called him to see if he needed any extra staff, my luck was in and he offered me a job on the spot.

A couple of days later I hugged my parents goodbye, loaded my bags into Brum and set off on the long journey south to Farnborough in Surrey. I'd been to London before but this was my first time in the South-East commuter belt and I was shocked to see how built-up the whole of it was. Towns and villages seemed to merge into each other and even the countryside was more like farmland or parkland, with barely a wild area to be seen. Almost everyone I met sounded terribly posh, making me very aware of my own Scots accent but, barring the odd dialect word, most people seemed to understand me well enough, not that I met that many, because

Nick handled all the dealings with the clients, so I just turned up, chopped the trees down and went away again.

My initial plan had been to rent my own place but once I discovered how extortionate the local property market was, I took up Nick's offer to spread my sleeping bag on his office floor. I got down to work straight away and took all the overtime and weekend work that was going. Nick was a total workaholic as well, so we did 8 a.m. to 6 p.m., six days a week.

My previous tree-surgery jobs had mostly been on younger trees, but many of the ones I was now working on were over 100 feet tall and hundreds of years old, so my climbing and chainsaw skills improved greatly and I took a real pride in the work. Between the two of us, we lifted tonnes of wood and branches each day. My muscles tightened all over my body, my arms were lean and powerful, and my stomach was as flat as a washboard.

One day while cutting down a tree, Nick disturbed a drey containing three baby squirrels. They were about a week old and each one was only the size of a house mouse. Since we could not put the tree back up, we adopted them as company pets. Deciding that I would be their new mother, I rushed to the pet shop and bought a small bottle, a nest box and some goat's milk to feed them on; no one sells squirrel milk, so goat was the closest match I could find. Every hour or two I gave the squirrels a feed, followed by a quick wash as they usually spilt the milk all over themselves. They were incredibly cute, tame and full of beans and I couldn't help but fall in love with them – I told myself that I would definitely have to toughen up before I became a gamekeeper. The squirrels thrived and very soon started crawling all over the office floor, much to Nick's anxiety as he had just bought a new computer and was worried they might chew through the cables.

I'd been working with Nick for three months when the North Highland College phoned to tell me that the interviews for student work placements were to be held in two weeks. The gamekeeping course was a two-year, 'block release' course, with eight one-week blocks in the first year and seven two-week blocks in the second. Since gamekeeping is a hands-on job and college could only provide us with small amounts of practical work, the rest of our time had to be spent working on a Highland estate gaining practical experience. It was a straightforward equation: no work placement equalled no college place.

Going up north on such a long journey – it was almost 700 miles from Farnborough to Thurso – meant I couldn't take my baby squirrels with me. They would have got car-sick and anyway, I knew my mother, who did not share my love of wild animals, would never allow them into the house. So, giving Nick strict instructions to feed them every couple of hours and keep them warm, I packed my bags, kissed my squirrels goodbye and headed north.

I was still pretty young at the time, just twenty-two, and had never been to a formal interview before. I had no one to tell me how to do it and no idea what an interview for a gamekeeper's job would involve. Now, older and wiser, I'd have done much more legwork and sought out a gamekeeper for advice beforehand, but back then, I pretty much closed my eyes and hoped for the best.

I was so nervous that I turned up at the college well ahead of my interview time and was only slightly reassured to see a couple of other potential students wandering around, looking equally lost. A friendly middle-aged lady named Iris eventually greeted me. 'Before you go into the interview,' she said, 'you have to fill in a mission statement to explain why you want to be a gamekeeper.' She steered me to a table and told me she would be back in half an hour to collect me. I sat down and began writing as though my life depended on it. By the time Iris came back, a few more students had turned up and I couldn't help but notice that they were all men. As she led me to the interview room, she said, 'Now don't worry, try not to be frightened.'

'Frightened?' I thought. 'Why should I be frightened?' Not knowing what to expect, I had naively imagined an informal interview, laughing and chatting over a cup of tea.

'There are about thirty head keepers in there, waiting to talk to you,' she said, and if I wasn't scared before, I certainly was now. In my naivety and ignorance, I hadn't even worn the appropriate clothing. Instead of a gamekeeper's traditional garb – stout boots, tweed or moleskin trousers, Viyella shirt and Barbour or similar jacket to keep the Highland weather at bay – I was wearing trainers, a pale-blue sweater and a pair of black trousers.

As I stepped through the door my heart nearly stopped. Thirty solemn-looking, leathery-faced gamekeepers were sitting at a horseshoe-shaped formation of tables, facing a small chair about fifteen feet away. Most of them had bushy beards, they were all dressed in traditional tweed suits and looked like hulking brutes to me. 'Take a seat, Miss Simpson,' the college tutor, John Waters, boomed. Feeling like a rabbit caught in the headlights, I sat down on the small chair and shot a glance at the crescent of gamekeepers facing me. Most of them seemed shocked to be confronted by a woman, and even worse, a woman wearing an outfit that she might have chosen for a night on the town, not a day on the moors, and they hastily looked away, as if they were embarrassed by me. Whatever faint shreds of confidence I'd been clinging to now disappeared without trace. I felt myself shrinking inwardly and suddenly became very conscious of my glittery, candy-floss lip balm. I could guess the thoughts of this dour Caledonian gathering: 'What on earth do we have here? What's this wee lassie doing at the interview?'

The room was so quiet that I could hear a fly buzzing against a window pane as it tried in vain to find a way out; I knew exactly how it felt. I scanned the room for a friendly face. Unable to find one, I could only wait for my trial by ordeal to start.

John Waters eventually broke the silence. 'So, Miss Simpson, tell us why you would like to become a gamekeeper.'

I started to speak, dry-swallowed and tried again, stumbling through some sort of answer. I felt like I was reliving Spud's job interview in *Trainspotting*, with similarly disastrous results, except that he hadn't wanted the job anyway and I really did. I could hear my words echoing from the walls in the empty space between the gamekeepers and me, and the gap between us seemed to be growing wider and wider with each hesitant or fluffed answer. While John Waters took charge of the interview, asking me some questions and telling me a few things that I needed to know, the vast majority of the gamekeepers stared into space and said nothing at all, as if praying for the ordeal to be over as soon as possible. That was one thing – probably the only one – on which we could all agree.

Even when he invited them to ask me questions, most of them still looked down at their hands and said nothing, apart from one guy who seemed a little less hostile. When he asked me what I wanted to work with, I said, 'Grouse and deer.' I found out later that he'd actually been thinking of offering me a placement but decided against it because he only had deer on his estate.

I kept doing my best to stammer out answers to the questions I was being asked but when another gamekeeper at last broke his silence to ask me if I'd be able to lift a red deer stag on to a pony or a quad bike, I could only answer, 'I don't know, I've never tried.'

By the time John Waters called a merciful halt to the interview about twenty minutes after it had begun, I was such a bag of nerves I could hardly trust my legs to propel me out of the room.

Iris was waiting outside and she steered me back to the entrance. 'Well, how did it go then?' she said kindly.

I practically burst into tears. 'Oh, it was terrible. I was so nervous and I'm sure they all hated me.'

'Don't worry, dear,' she said, giving me a reassuring pat

on the arm. 'I'm sure you did just fine. It's very difficult for all the students and some of the others will have done a lot worse, believe me. Now, the college will phone you within two weeks to let you know if you've been successful.'

I thanked her and set off on my long journey back to Surrey. When I got there, I discovered that my poor baby squirrels hadn't fared very well in my absence. Their fur was matted and dirty and they looked scrawny and malnourished, because Nick had forgotten to feed them half the time, though to be fair, he did have a lot else on his mind. I cursed myself for leaving them and wished I had taken them with me after all. I fed them as much as possible and kept them warm with a hot-water bottle, but it was to no avail and they all died the next day. I was heartbroken, but threw myself back into my work to help me avoid thinking both about my poor baby squirrels and my disastrous college interview.

When the call from the college finally came, John Waters got straight to the point. 'I have some bad news for you, Portia. I'm afraid you didn't manage to get a placement from any of the keepers.'

I was distraught. This wasn't supposed to happen. It was not part of the grand plan at all.

'Don't worry too much though,' he said, 'because we forgot to invite two head keepers to the interview and since there were twelve students, including yourself, who didn't get a place, we're sending out your CVs to them. The interviews will be within the next two weeks and if you get one, you must be available for it.'

'I'll be there in a flash,' I said, though I was thinking to myself, 'Twelve students for only two placements? I'll have to be incredibly lucky to get one.'

For days afterwards I was subdued and moody, and poor Nick could hardly get a word out of me. I'd set my heart on the gamekeeping course; if I didn't succeed, what else could I do? Tree-surgery work was scarce around Aberdeen and I certainly didn't want to live in Surrey for the rest of my life. I had been so sure I would get a placement, what – apart from the total lack of preparation and the glitter candy-floss lip balm – could possibly have gone wrong?

A few days later, Nick and I were up early to remove a rotten oak tree that was overhanging a house. When we got there, I was very surprised to see a large set of red deer antlers and a set of pony shoes hanging on the wall near the door. For hundreds of years the traditional method of taking deer off the hills in the Highlands of Scotland had been on the back of a pony, and on some estates, ponies are still used to this day. But Scotland was the only place in the UK where such a method was used, so it was very surprising to see them on someone's wall in the south of England. Could it be a sign?

Our next job was in a nearby wood, felling fifteen huge spruce trees that a gale could easily have brought down across the power lines, cutting off the electricity supply to the town. Around lunchtime Nick was busy sharpening his big felling saw, a job that could take up to half an hour, so I went for a quick walk in the woods. I had only gone a few yards when I heard a rustling in the trees and a female roe deer jumped out of the gorse bushes in front of me. We stared at each other for a moment and then she calmly walked towards me.

As she got closer, she began running around me in circles, moving closer and closer until she was only about ten feet away. This was not natural behaviour for a deer – usually they run away from humans – but this one seemed to want to come rambling with me. She was so close I could see the individual hairs on her face and the dark pools of her eyes as she studied me intently. For a few minutes we stood staring at each other, then she tossed her head, walked back into the gorse and disappeared. 'Now if that isn't a sign,' I thought to myself, 'I don't know what is.'

It took until the Friday evening to finish felling and logging the spruce trees. It had been a gruelling week and wanting five minutes' rest before I began packing up our equipment, I dragged myself over to a bench facing the road at the edge of the wood, and flopped down. My fingers were stuck together with resin and I was covered from head to foot in sticky woodchips. My climbing harness was still around my waist and thirty feet of rope stretched out behind me; I hoped it wouldn't trip up any passing pedestrians. The traffic was getting quite heavy as the rush hour got under way and bored-looking motorists sat waiting for the traffic lights to change.

I was struggling to remove my rope and harness from around my waist when I saw the body of a red deer stag on the back of a flatbed truck, trundling along the road towards me. The truck stopped right in front of me, stuck in the traffic. The stag was a full-sized taxidermy specimen, held on the flatbed by two large ratchet straps. Its head was turned towards me, showing off its sixteen-point antlers, and its black glass eyes stared at me. 'It must have come from a local museum,' I thought to myself, 'but what a strange way to transport it. What happens if it rains?' Then the traffic lights changed and truck and deer disappeared around the corner. That was it, someone was definitely trying to tell me something.

The following day I got a telephone call. 'Hello Portia,' John Waters said. 'I have some good news for you. Ardverikie Estate want to interview you for a placement. Can you come?'

Could I? Wild horses couldn't stop me. 'How many people are being interviewed?'

'Just yourself and a guy from London.'

'Great – a 50 per cent chance.' I thanked him, hung up the phone and then danced around the room in glee.

My interview took place in the estate office of Ardverikie, between Aviemore and Fort William. I still wasn't wearing a traditional keeper's outfit because I didn't really have any country clothes at that time and since they were horrendously expensive, I was reluctant to fork out for a whole new outfit for a job that I might not get anyway. Hoping that it wouldn't count against me too much, I turned up in a pair of smart black trousers and a nice dark-red shirt, though I had at least learned enough to do without the glitter, candy-floss lip balm this time. After my previous diabolical interview, I was expecting the worst, but this time I had spent many hours preparing myself and rehearsing answers to the difficult questions that had been thrown at me last time. This was my last chance: if I didn't get this job, that would be it for me, the end of any hope of becoming a gamekeeper.

Arriving at the estate office half an hour early, I parked my car in the grounds and waited outside, a bag of nerves, shuffling the pages of my CV, but when I went into the office I felt my anxiety disappear at once. On the table was a large plate of biscuits, a teapot and several cups. This was going to be my kind of interview. The estate factor, the head keeper and under keeper interviewed me for an hour but this time the atmosphere was friendly and my preparation really paid off; I had answers for all the questions they threw at me about my previous experience and wildlife knowledge. I was taken on a quick tour of the estate to show me the cottage where I would be living if I got the job. We shared one last pot of tea before the gamekeepers had to leave. The factor saw me out. He was a friendly, handsome Englishman in his mid-thirties and to my delight, he made it very clear that he believed in equality and wasn't going to let any prejudices or old-fashioned attitudes prevent him from hiring me if he felt I was the right person for the job. He promised to let me know the outcome within the week.

After all the stress of the interview, when I got back to my parents' house in Aberdeen that night, all I wanted to do was go out on the town, have a few drinks and let my hair down. So, slipping into a skirt and high heels, I set off to walk to my cousin's flat. She greeted me with a hug. 'Your mother just phoned,' she said. 'You know that interview you went for today? You've got the job!'

I gave her another huge hug and then danced around her kitchen; it was the happiest moment of my life.

I went back to Surrey to work my notice and then say

goodbye to Nick. Working with him had been great, we'd achieved so much together and I'd earned enough money to pay for my first year of college and buy a .270 hunting rifle as well. Luckily I didn't have to worry about leaving him in the lurch because he was able to hire another young woman who had just finished a tree-surgery course at the local college.

Along with a glowing reference from Nick, I loaded my belongings into Brum and headed for Scotland, ready to start my new life. All I had to do now was work hard and pass my gamekeeping course. Even if I did, I still wasn't sure whether I'd ever be accepted as an equal by the other students, let alone the stalkers, ghillies and keepers I'd be working with, but I really wasn't bothered about that. This was what I wanted to do for a living and no one was going to change my mind. Change happens slowly, so I knew the Neanderthals and knuckle-draggers weren't going to have a sudden, dramatic change of heart about women in their workplace, but I told myself that for every ten people who wouldn't accept me, there'd be one who would. I just had to live with that and find that one person who would take me on my merits and might even give me a job. I didn't necessarily revel in being the odd one out but I was certainly a stubborn character and once I'd set my mind on something it was going to take more than a few snide or patronising comments to put me off. There was one other thing I wasn't going to change: I was still a woman, so whether felling trees, grouse beating or stalking deer across a sodden Highland hillside, I'd be doing it in full make-up.

2

MONARCH OF THE GLEN

I started my work placement at the end of June 2002, one week before the start of the stag season. It was a perfect summer morning as I drove right across the Cairngorms National Park and followed the River Pattack down towards Loch Laggan, revelling in the views of the mountains all around and the sunlight shimmering on the surface of the loch.

Ardverikie was a vast, 40,000-acre estate, an amazing sight, seeming to stretch as far as the eye could see. The conifer forests on the lower slopes gave way to wild, open moorland and rocky crags on the heights above. I could see the mountains of the Creag Meagaidh range ('bogland crag' in Gaelic) soaring to the north of Loch Laggan, with the ultra-remote Ben Alder to the south, both over 3,700 feet high. A dozen other 'Munros' (Scottish mountains over

3,000 feet high, named after Sir Hugh Munro, who compiled the first list of them) towered above me and, looking down the length of the loch to the south-west, I could also see the towering, cloud-shrouded summits of Carn Mor Dearg and Ben Nevis in the far distance.

The factor met me at the estate office and we drove to the small, whitewashed stone cottage that I'd seen at my interview and that would now be my new home. Nestling into the foot of the hillside, it had a small garden and open views to the front, with the woods cloaking the slopes behind it. I felt extremely nervous as I opened the door but also very excited. The cottage looked lovely from the outside and though it was a bit dilapidated inside with threadbare carpets and paintwork in need of a freshen up, to me it was perfect. For the first time in my life I had my own place, albeit one that I'd be sharing with the other gamekeeping student, Owen, who was in the second year of his work placement.

'Just unpack your bags,' the factor said, 'and the gamekeeper will be along in an hour or so to pick you up and show you around.'

It wasn't hard to work out which bedroom was Owen's because it was almost buried under piles of dirty clothes, damp towels and old socks. I hastily closed the door on that and unpacked my stuff in one of the other ones. It was a simple, homely room but from its windows I could look out across the sparkling river and the sandy beach at the head of the loch to the mountains rising beyond the far shore. I would see that view every morning when I opened the curtains and I doubted I would ever get tired of it.

My new home was miles from anywhere but that didn't bother me at all because I'd always felt at home in places far from 'civilisation', the farther the better. I couldn't have explained why that was but it had always seemed to be something within me. I'd been an outdoor person since I could walk but there was also a definite element of shyness about it too. I was much more comfortable around people I knew and if I was living in a small community a long way from the nearest town or city, then I wouldn't have to be dealing with loads of strangers.

Still with half an hour free, I took a stroll along the river bank to the loch. The beach seemed to stretch for miles – the gamekeeper later told me, with a touch of local pride, that it was the largest freshwater beach in Scotland. The sands were glowing in the sunshine and the only things breaking the silence were the sounds of the birdsong and the gentle lapping of water against the shore. I saw oystercatchers probing the fringes of the loch with their vivid orange beaks and a heron stalking the shallows and impaling a frog on its bayonet-like beak.

A few minutes later I saw a green Land Rover pull up outside the cottage and hurriedly retraced my steps. The gamekeeper, Dougie, was a weather-beaten man in his mid-fifties, his dark hair flecked with grey. He was wearing a deerstalker hat that never left his head; before long I began to suspect that he might even sleep in it. 'Welcome, Portia,' he said. 'We're all looking forward to working with you. We've not had a woman keeper before, although—' He gave a broad smile. 'Come to think of it, nobody has, have they?' He pointed to the tall, lanky lad with dirty blond hair who was grinning at me from the passenger seat. 'And this is Owen, who'll be sharing the cottage with you.'

I jumped into the Land Rover, which smelled strongly of deer cobs (the food given to the deer as a supplement to their winter diet), and we drove up one of the estate roads towards Ardverikie House, the owners' ancestral home. Built on a promontory overlooking Loch Laggan and King Fergus's Island, it looked like a fairytale castle, a multi-turreted granite 'Scottish baronial' building, with a saltire flying above it. There were manicured lawns to each side of the broad gravelled driveway and formal gardens leading down to a small pier on the loch, where a couple of rowing boats bobbed about on the water.

'It's beautiful, Dougie,' I said. 'I feel so lucky to be working here.'

He smiled. 'Let's hope you still feel the same way in a few weeks. But it's a lovely place right enough and there are a lot of worse ways to earn a living than this.'

'So how long have you been working here?'

'I joined the estate as a trainee when I was a teenager and I've worked here ever since. When I first started, my early-morning duty was to walk the Laird's three pointer dogs. It was a three-mile walk and the head keeper would leave an empty can at the furthest point of the trail, which I had to retrieve, just to make sure I walked the full three miles and didn't cheat by turning back before I was supposed to.'

'You could have got your own cans and saved yourself a walk,' I said.

'I could,' he said, 'except that he was wise to such tricks and had half a dozen different cans – Tennent's, McEwan's, Irn-Bru, and so on – so I never knew which one he was going to put out on any particular day.'

Over the years, Dougie had worked his way up to under keeper, in charge of two of the three different stalking areas, known as 'beats'. The head keeper, helped by Owen, was responsible for the East Beat, and I'd be working with Dougie on the Middle and West Beats.

As we drove along the miles of gravel roads spanning the estate, we passed a group of people milling around film cameras and lights set up in the grounds. 'What's going on over there?' I said.

'It's the BBC crew filming *Monarch of the Glen*,' Dougie said. 'They've been here for three years now. Have you never heard of Glenbogle?'

I watched with interest until we rounded a bend and lost sight of them. Further on, I saw something even more interesting: the sleek shape of an otter in the river, twisting and turning in the water as it chased down a fish. We also passed hundreds of deer grazing peacefully in the heather, ignoring the Land Rover as we drove by.

Dougie grinned. 'They won't be doing that before long.'

'What will they be doing?' I said.

'Running away from us, no doubt. You'll get a chance to shoot your first stag soon. We've got a cull target of 150 stags to shoot before the end of October, so we've got to get moving quickly. Then after that we have to shoot 300 hinds [female deer].' Deer did not necessarily respect estate boundaries, so Ardverikie and all the neighbouring estates did a collective annual deer count and then decided on the cull target – the percentage of stags and hinds that would be killed that year.

I'd had very few chances to get close to red deer before and I studied them with interest. Their fur was a dark reddish-brown, rather like fox fur, and they had darker legs, a paler, greyish face and neck, and a lighter patch on the rump. In summer, when food is plentiful, they rest most of the day, feeding around dawn and dusk, but in winter, they spend much of the day searching for food. They graze on moorland grasses, sedges, heather, berries, mosses and lichen, but when other food is scarce in winter, they will also eat seedlings and the bark from trees. In harsh winters, particularly if the deer herd has been allowed to grow too large for the available grazing, many will starve to death.

Wolves, lynx and bears used to prey on Scottish deer but since we hunted them to extinction we have to control deer numbers ourselves because with no other serious predators, the deer population would otherwise spiral out of control. There would be starving and dead deer all over the place in winter, many more car accidents, cereal crops decimated, forestry destroyed and moorland flattened. So shooting them is as much about conservation as it is about killing, and when we shoot an old animal, it is for the good of the whole herd.

Back at the cottage that evening, I started to get to know Owen, who turned out to be a pretty hyperactive character.

He never sat still nor stopped talking for a second. He used to stay on the telephone for a couple of hours at a time and he was always calling up to vote on television shows like *The X Factor*, running up phone bills of £300 a month. Since we shared the phone bill, we'd have an argument every month when it arrived.

'Why don't you just talk to me instead, Owen?' I said one evening. 'I'm a good listener and think of the money you'll save.'

That experiment lasted precisely one evening. After three and a half hours of Owen machine-gunning conversation at me, I had a blinding headache and had to lie down in my darkened bedroom with a damp cloth over my face. After supper the next evening, I just said, 'Sorry, Owen, maybe you'd better phone a chatline this evening,' and, avoiding his reproachful gaze, I went for a moonlit walk along the loch, revelling in the peace and quiet.

Owen could never get up in the mornings, so he was always running late and never had time to make himself sandwiches before we left. As a result, his lunch every day was a bag of crisps and a bar of chocolate, and he ate Super Noodles for dinner every single night. With that diet, it wasn't surprising that his skin was the colour of skimmed milk and he was so skinny that if he turned sideways, he almost disappeared from sight. He also smoked roll-ups, using the cheapest possible tobacco, which always stank the house out.

I had arrived before the start of the stalking season, so I had a few days to explore the estate before the serious work began. Early the next morning, Dougie and I threw our lunch bags into the Land Rover and then drove the thirteen miles to the entrance of the West Beat, containing the highest hills and some of the most dramatic upland scenery on the estate. As we travelled along the banks of Loch Laggan, the peaks of the rugged hills and Munros towered above us. Even this far into summer, there were still the last traces of the winter snowdrifts in some north-facing gullies and crevices.

We drove to where the dirt road petered out and the terrain became too rough even for the Land Rover and then set off to walk the three-mile path to the 'spy point', from where we could use our binoculars to scour the slopes of the mountains for red deer. The path was rocky and uneven, the stones mottled with patches of pale-blue lichen that had withered and dried to a crisp in the glare of the sun, and dry vegetation and heather stems crunched under our feet as we walked along. On the hillsides around us, the ling and bell heathers were bursting into bloom, their small purple flowers covering the hillside.

Jumping over small streams and skirting peat bogs, we eventually arrived at the foot of a small grassy knoll at the top of the glen. We dumped our bags, then crawled to the top and looked out. As I gazed through my binoculars, I could see a herd of stags high up on the tops, grazing peacefully. From this distance they looked like tiny brown dots, but that was very deceptive because they are actually the largest wild animals in Britain, with a mature stag measuring up to five feet at the shoulder and weighing over 400 pounds, though the Highland deer tend to be smaller than those living in lowland woods and forests. In either case, the hinds are about a third smaller than the males. 'They come down to the lower ground in the depths of winter,' Dougie said, 'but move back up to the high moors in summer. There's a bit more breeze up there, giving them a little relief from the biting insects and—' he gestured at the clouds of midges around us, 'as you can see, there's no shortage of those. It also provides safety for the hinds while they give birth.'

As we lay there watching the deer, we had been providing a smorgasbord for the hordes of midges and clegs, a species of horsefly that lives in grassland and damp woods. Like midges, only the female clegs bite and although they usually feed on the blood of horses, cows and deer, they will happily drink human blood too. After a while, the ravenous insects became too much for us and, vowing to invest in some industrial-strength insect repellent at the first opportunity, I followed Dougie back down the path.

We drove back down the dirt road towards the Middle Beat. Its gentler, rolling hills looked to be much easier stalking ground than the peaks and crags of the West Beat. Two lochs set in a broad expanse of flat bogland separated the two beats and we took a walk around one of the lochs so I could further familiarise myself with the lay of the land.

As we crossed the boggy moor, the sphagnum moss squelched underfoot. It came in three distinct shades: red, yellowish-green and a pure mint-green, and I quickly learned that the vivid mint-green moss was the most treacherous to stand on, as it invariably contained standing water underneath. Not knowing any better, I had trodden on the moss, only to find myself sinking up to my knees in cold, wet bog water, soaking my boots and socks. The red and yellow moss was much safer, especially if there were grass or heather stems growing through it, indicating firmer ground underneath. Further on, I saw what looked from a distance like white flowers growing out of the moss and water: tufts of bog cotton, also known as cotton grass, their delicate white plumes raised above the surface of the bog and waving in the summer breeze.

After a few hundred yards, we came to the head of the loch. Looking out over the expanse of water I could see brown trout creating circular ripples as they broke the surface to swallow flies and then, with a splash and a flick of their tails, returning to the murky depths of the peat-blackened loch.

By the time the stag season began the following week, I was raring to go. I just hoped my rifle shooting would be up to scratch, as I didn't want to leave any wounded deer, but I'd been practising with a target for quite a while, so I felt ready. I slung my rifle over my shoulder and, full of excitement at the thought of shooting my first stag, I set off with Dougie. Unfortunately, however, it turned out that we weren't the only ones heading for the hills that day, because the Army had just arrived as well. Short of training areas of their own, they had paid the estate to stage a week-long training exercise and a hundred soldiers were now running across the hillside, firing their rifles continuously. They were firing blanks, so we didn't need to worry about being shot, but the gunfire made a terrible racket and the terrified deer had all run away.

For two days we searched fruitlessly for deer, but they had fled over the hills to the neighbouring estate. I was beginning to take our lack of success personally and starting to think that I was cursed but on the third day, when we walked to the spy point, Dougie spotted a group of twenty stags that had returned and were grazing halfway up a steep hillside. There were some fine stags among them with imposing spreads of antlers. They can be well over four feet long in mature stags and become progressively more branched with age, with up to sixteen branches – also called 'points' or 'tines' – on each antler, though most Scottish hill stags have between eight and fourteen. The antlers are covered in velvet during spring and summer, which helps to protect them while they're growing – and they can grow as much as an inch a day. They are fully grown by early autumn, when the velvet is shed, and the stags hurry the process along by rubbing their antlers against trees, shrubs and heather. Once the velvet has gone, the antlers calcify and harden, becoming the formidable weapons they use when duelling with other stags during the rut – the mating season.

We began the hour-long climb to where they were feeding. As we got closer, we started to crawl on our bellies, flattening our bodies into the heather to avoid being seen. We eventually crawled into position on the side of a large knoll and Dougie selected a stag for me to target. 'We always choose old, ill, weak or injured stags to cull,' he explained.

'You have to look for the subtle differences in the condition of the body and the coat, and on the older deer, you need to study the antlers. If a stag has long brow tines on its antlers and has lost some of its points, like that one on the right of the group, it means it's an older stag and may be ready to be culled, but you need to assess the condition of its body before you can be sure.' 'Brow tines' are the first points on a stag's antlers above its brow, the second set are called 'bay tines' and the third ones 'trey tines'. He studied it a while longer and then nodded. 'It's ready to be culled, right enough,' he said. 'Take the shot when you're ready.'

I squinted through the telescopic sight of my rifle, studying the stag he had picked out. When it turned broadside on to me, I lined up the cross-hairs on the exact centre of the stag's chest. I took up the first pressure on the trigger, exhaled in a long, sighing breath and then squeezed the trigger home. I was so intent on making the shot count that I wasn't even aware of the recoil. The bang echoed across the hillside and the stag jumped, ran ten feet and then fell down, stone dead. With lightning speed, Dougie shot two more before the rest of the herd scattered across the hillside and disappeared from sight.

I'd imagined that I would feel a sense of sadness after shooting my first stag, just as I had when watching Billy shoot one, but when it came to it, all I actually felt was relief and a tremendous sense of accomplishment. The next step was to carry out 'the gralloch': the disembowelling of the deer. Removing the intestines and allowing the blood to drain off into the heather not only prevented the meat from spoiling but also gave the bonus of reducing the weight we'd have to lift, though not by enough to make it anything less than gruelling work. Dougie watched me closely as I went to work. Taking my knife out of my pocket, I turned the stag onto its back, as Billy and Uncle Angus had taught me, and made an incision just below the sternum. Placing my fingers inside the cut, I ran the knife down, opening up the stomach wall all the way down to the lower abdomen. I had to be really careful not to nick the stomach bag with my knife, otherwise brown, slimy stomach contents would have seeped out and tainted the meat. Once I'd made the cut, I turned the deer to lie on its right side. That gave me easy access to the stomach cavity and, rolling up my sleeves, I delved into the wet, steamy intestines. First I needed to separate the spleen, then remove the large stomach bag, and lastly the small intestines and rectum. With a loud sucking noise I pulled it all out, and it landed on the sphagnum moss with a wet plop.

I was sure Dougie had been watching for any signs of squeamishness from me, but blood and guts had never fazed me at all and I caught a slight nod of approval from him when I'd finished. The guts steamed gently in the crisp autumn air as I set about cleaning my knife and forearms. We were close to a burn so I used the water to wash myself but, as I soon discovered, in dry areas I had to resort to sphagnum moss, or if I was really desperate, crispy heather stems that very rarely cleaned me properly and also left me with scratches all over my arms.

Extracting the shot deer was the hardest part of the job

but the other ghillie, Owen, soon appeared with a large six-wheeler quad bike. Between the two of us we lifted the stags onto the back luggage rail and tied them on securely with rope. 'It won't be that easy when the shooting guests arrive,' Dougie said. 'We'll be using hill ponies then and if you think lifting a stag onto a quad is hard work, just wait until you've lifted one five feet onto the back of a pony. I hope you're feeling strong, Portia, because you'll need to be, but on what I've seen so far, you'll do just fine.'

At the end of my first month at Ardverikie, I had to go up to Thurso for my first session at college. It was a long drive – Thurso was 170 miles to the north, a handful of miles from John o' Groats – but a combination of excitement and first-day nerves saw me arrive nearly an hour early. Hiding a smile at my keenness, John Waters led me to a Portakabin where I settled down to await the arrival of the other student gamekeepers. Three-quarters of an hour later my classmates started to turn up. I expected to see at least one other woman and was disappointed when every one of them turned out to be male. Even worse, they all looked about twice my size, but though I felt quite intimidated, I was determined not to show it.

At nine o'clock a more normal-sized student peered round the door. 'Erm ... is this the gamekeeping department?' he said.

From the back of the class a voice shouted, 'No, it's the bloody hairdressing department, come in and get your highlights done.' They all erupted in laughter as the poor guy turned bright red. Head down, he shuffled in and sat down. Like the wild places and the wildlife we were here to learn about, this was clearly an environment in which only the strong would survive.

It was my turn soon afterwards. One or two Neanderthals had already wolf-whistled at me and then one guy just turned round in front of the whole class and said, 'Women shouldn't be doing this course.' Some of the others sniggered, but the rest waited with bated breath to see what I'd do. However, I was so surprised and taken aback by it that I didn't have a quick comeback. Flushing red, I tried to ignore him, though I was inwardly seething and thinking, 'You absolute bastard, I'm going to get you back for that.'

A few days later we had a practical test where we had to reverse a quad bike and trailer quite a distance, through some traffic cones and then around a corner. As a general rule, big trailers are relatively easy to reverse, but the smaller the trailer, the harder it is to reverse, and the one attached to the quad bike was very small indeed. When it came to my turn, after one false start, I did it fairly easily on my second try but then, even though I'd passed the test, I did it a couple more times just to make sure my technique was right, because I wanted it to be absolutely perfect.

Next up was the 'Women shouldn't be doing this course' guy and to my great delight and his total mortification, he simply couldn't do it at all, no matter how many times he tried. He was so crap at it that he ended up having to use his whole lunch hour, still trying to do it, while the rest of us ate our sandwiches and, in my case at least, smiled broadly as

I watched him failing, over and over again – instant karma! After that, whenever he said something sexist, I'd just say, 'Remember reversing the trailer?' and he'd fall silent straight away.

As we milled around, waiting for the start of the lesson, I did find some friendly faces and spoke to a couple of guys who seemed willing to treat me as an equal, but it seemed some of them felt threatened by my presence. That just made me all the more determined to succeed.

John Waters then appeared and gave us our induction lecture. 'There are twenty-six of you altogether,' he said. 'And since that's too many students to teach at one time, I'm splitting you into three groups of eight or nine. From now on you'll only attend college in your separate groups, so this is not only your first, but also possibly your last sighting of two-thirds of your fellow-students!'

He paused while we took that in. 'Now, next topic: working dogs. Hands up everyone who has a gun dog.'

We all looked at each other in silence and only three people put their hands up. 'Three?' John said. 'Out of twenty-six people, only three of you have gun dogs?' He gave a weary shake of his head. 'By the next time I see you, I expect you all to have dogs and if any of you don't, I'll want a good explanation as to why not.'

Until that moment it had never occurred to me that I'd need a gun dog, but when I thought about it afterwards, it was blindingly obvious; who had ever seen a gamekeeper without a dog at his side?

Back at Ardverikie at the end of the week, I began

making enquiries about buying a puppy to train and I asked Dougie for his advice. 'Spaniels, pointers, Labradors and retrievers are the most popular gun dogs,' he said. 'They're all good . . . in the right hands. I'd maybe go for a Labrador but it's not what breed it is but how well it's trained that really counts.'

I began looking around locally for a puppy but I hadn't found one by the time the stalking clients began turning up for their annual stag-shooting break, a few days later. Most of them came from the south of England, but there were clients from all over Europe and a few had travelled all the way from America. Even though they had paid a large sum of money for the privilege of shooting a stag, they were tested on their shooting ability before going out on the hill and each morning started at the target, a life-size, cast-iron cut-out of a stag. An experienced stalker was always with them on the shoot with his own rifle poised, ready to administer the *coup de grâce* if the client made a hash of his shot and only wounded the stag.

We started work at eight o'clock sharp each morning, when we had to be up at the gun room with our flasks and packed lunches. Dougie would then hand Owen and me two head collars and send us off to get the Highland garrons (the deer ponies) from the field. Those fat ponies were always reluctant to begin the hard day's work on the hillsides and I can't honestly say I blamed them. When we went to collect them, we invariably found that they were standing in the furthest corner of the sloping field, clearly hoping that if they kept very still, we might not notice them. After fitting their head collars, we dragged the unwilling ponies back down the hill and got them into the horsebox.

At nine o'clock the guests turned up with their rifles slung over their backs. Some of them were clearly on their first ever stalk and were kitted out from head to foot in absolutely brand-new gear: deerstalker hats, Barbours, tweed jackets, waistcoats, Viyella shirts, moleskin trousers, socks and gaiters, and shooting boots, and equipped with every kind of shiny new gadget you could possibly imagine. I shuddered to think how much it had cost them, given that some of them might only be wearing it this once, but I suppose that if you were going to pay a few thousand pounds to go deerstalking, then an extra few hundred pounds for some new clothes was probably neither here nor there. Many of them were 'something in the City' but though a couple of them were really arrogant and unpleasant, most of them were very nice. Whatever they were like on the trading floor or in the boardroom, there wasn't too much 'alpha male' behaviour on show at Ardverikie, because they knew that, no matter how rich or powerful they were, out on the hill the stalker was always the boss. To my surprise, about 20 per cent of the guests were women, which might also have helped to keep the larger male egos in check.

When we set off, Dougie decided which of the two beats to stalk, depending on the wind direction and weather that day. If we were lucky, it would be a nice easy day on the Middle Beat; if not, we would set off for the far corries (the armchair-shaped hollows formed in the mountains by Ice Age glaciers) on the West Beat. Dougie would scan the hillside for deer and, having identified a suitable group, he would set off in front, striding through the heather. The guests followed him in single file, while I was at the back, carrying the estate rifle. We always formed a straight line behind Dougie, or at least that was what we were supposed to do, but I was fascinated by hairy caterpillars and whenever I saw one, I just had to go and grab it for a closer look. As a result I was regularly told off by Dougie for being out of line.

Apart from carrying the rifle, my main job was to walk in Dougie's footsteps, learning how to be a stalker. The job sounded straightforward: lead a client to a stag he could shoot. However, the skills needed to identify and stalk a suitable animal, and bring a client who might not be the healthiest physical specimen over the gruelling terrain – rock, forest, peat bog and heather moorland – to a point from which he was close enough to take the shot, were not acquired overnight.

Once the guest had taken the shot, the next job was the gralloch and Dougie usually made me do it as I needed the experience. Whether or not he was watching me, I took pride in doing it well. When I'd finished and was wiping down my arms, Dougie set off to carry on stalking with the clients, leaving me to drag the dead stag down the hill and find a good place to load it onto the pony. Ali, who worked as a forester most of the year but doubled as a ghillie during the stalking season, had already put deer-saddles on the two ponies and was waiting back at the Land Rover for the summons to the site of the kill by a call on his walkie-talkie. He always arrived within the hour with the two reluctant ponies.

The Highland garrons were strong and powerfully built, purpose-bred for carrying deer back from the hills, but no one had ever managed to breed any enthusiasm for the task into them and it was always a struggle to get a stag loaded on to the deer-saddle. The first job was to tighten the girths. Having done that, the pony was always loaded from the left-hand side. Lifting the deer onto its back wasn't quite as hard as I had thought it would be, but it still required a huge effort, and being shorter than the men was a disadvantage, so I usually dragged the deer onto a slope or small hill, and positioned the pony below it, giving me a one- or two-foot height advantage.

Using this method, Ali and I managed the job with relative ease. Picking up one end of the stag each, we lifted it up onto the pony, a mare, and tied it on with the strong leather straps, making sure it was correctly balanced, otherwise we would end up with a saddle slip. If the girth was loose, or if the pony jumped over a small burn, an unbalanced stag would slip down underneath it. If that happened, both stag and saddle would have to be removed and the whole laborious process started again.

Having loaded the stag onto the pony and made as sure as possible that the saddle would not slip, Ali handed me the reins and set off after Dougie and the stalking clients with the remaining unloaded pony, in case they shot a second stag. I coaxed the laden mare back down the hill, talking to her constantly, woman to woman. 'Come on, girl, you've carried bigger stags than this before. Don't let the boys see you're struggling, or you'll never hear the end of it.' As I was saying it, I ruefully reflected that it might have been nice if there'd been someone around to give me the same sort of encouragement sometimes. Dougie did support me but he was pretty much the only keeper or ghillie I'd met who ever did. When I'd led the now exhausted mare back to the Land Rover, I removed the stag and took off the saddle. I dragged the bloodied deer into one side of the horsebox and then had to coax the nervous pony into the other side. Slamming the back door, I watched it sniff the dead deer, obviously wondering what on earth it was. All I had to do then was wait for the others to return with the second stag.

I was lucky that during my first few attempts we were working with reasonably docile ponies because not all of them were quite so well behaved, especially a four-year-old mare that we unkindly named 'Loony', after an incident the first time we ever loaded her. To keep her calm and stop her running off, she was blindfolded while a twenty-three-stone stag was placed on her back and two fully grown men – Ali and Dougie – hung onto the lead rope dangling from her head collar, but when the blindfold was removed, the poor mare whinnied in fright, reared up, and dragged both men and stag for a mile down the glen. I probably should have been concerned for their wellbeing, but the sight of them being dragged along by a psychotic pony was so funny that I was far too busy laughing.

For most of the year Dougie wore jeans, but in the stalking season he donned the traditional plus fours, hill boots and tweed jacket, and when the guests arrived, he wore a smart shirt and tie that made him look quite dashing. He was great with the stalking clients, some of whom had come every season for years and who all loved him, and in the time they were there, Dougie never let a single swear word pass his lips. I was amazed by his self-control because, although we had already been pre-warned about our language, on several occasions the other ghillies and I let slip with the F-word, purely by accident of course and under extreme stress. Dougie gave us a hard stare each time we slipped up; I got a lot of hard stares from him . . .

However, when the stalking season ended and the last of the clients had departed, Dougie reverted to type, becoming much more relaxed, laughing, joking and really letting rip with the swearing himself, as if making up for lost time. One day, we were having our lunch in the Land Rover with two of the foresters, Ali and his father Jimmy. Like Dougie, they had worked on the estate their whole adult lives and, like Dougie, they both punctuated every sentence with swear words. I amused myself by trying to keep count. Within three minutes I had registered seventy-six F-words before I lost count and gave up.

At the end of their week's shooting, the stalking guests often invited the keepers and ghillies up to the hunting lodge, where we were served a delicious three-course meal, courtesy of the hired chef who accompanied the shooting party. Afterwards we sat in front of the open log fire, sipping drams of malt whisky and swapping hunting stories, with the guests often going into great detail of how they'd walked for miles, crawling through the heather and getting soaked to the skin in muddy peat bogs before shooting their stag. It was a new experience for many of them and although it was very familiar to us – after all, it was what we did every day – we hung on every word. That was not just out of respect for the guests but also, I have to confess, because we were hoping for a decent tip from them.

We could never drink too much because there was always the final job of the day to be done: larder work. Owen and I had to climb back into the Land Rover, bid farewell to the guests and drive to the deer larder. Almost all the carcasses were sold to a game dealer who came to pick them up at the end of the week, so we were expected to 'dress' the carcasses, which involved cutting off the heads, legs and all the other inedible bits.

I found it hard, clumsy work at first, but with a cull target of so many stags and hinds to fulfil, by the end of my first deer season at Ardverikie, I had become quite skilled with a knife and both Owen and I could get a deer dressed and hanging up within five minutes. However, the cleaning up and paperwork took much longer and we were often in the larder for up to an hour.

Once a week Owen and I were also expected to empty the larder bins. At eight in the morning, we would drive up in the Land Rover and load three or four heavy bins into the back. Occasionally one of the bin lids would spring open and stags' heads and legs would roll all over the floor, while blood dripped out of the back of the vehicle, laying a trail that you could follow all the way to the 'drop-hole': the pit where we buried the offal and unwanted body parts.

Ali had dug the drop-hole using the 'forwarder' – a

forestry vehicle fitted with a grab and normally used for carrying felled trees and large logs out of the forest to a point where they could be loaded onto a truck. When needed, the grab could be replaced by a digging bucket which made light work of excavating the drop-hole. The hole was about twelve feet square and ten feet deep, covered by long wooden planks fixed together with battens, and it was accessed by a trap door in the middle. When we opened the door after the drop-hole had been in use for a few weeks, the stench almost knocked us unconscious. We always gave the air a few minutes to clear before dragging the bins out and dumping the contents. If it was my turn to open it, I always took a huge lungful of air and held my breath before heaving it open and retreating as fast as possible, but I always ran out of breath before I got out of range and had to take another gulp of air that was so rancid I could taste it at the back of my throat ten minutes later.

Pulling the bins into the centre, we emptied them into the hole with a series of wet thuds. Clouds of flies buzzed around our ears as we did so and we could hear the hissing noise from the millions of maggots beneath us. Although that writhing mound of maggots made me shudder whenever I caught sight of it, they did us a big favour by keeping the pile of deer remains from growing so high that they spilled out of the top of the drop-hole.

Once we'd finished emptying the bins, we had to clean them thoroughly and then get back to the gun room for the next task. When the drop-hole was full or the deer season was over, we'd remove the wooden 'lid' and Ali would use the forwarder to bulldoze earth back into the hole, before digging a new drop-hole a safe distance away, preferably upwind. Vegetation soon regrew over the earth of the old drop-hole, but the smell – and the flies – took a lot longer to dissipate.

3

THE RUT

The year was now well on the turn. Autumn had come slightly earlier than usual and the leaves had already changed colour, painting the slopes in russet, amber and red, before falling and littering the forest floor. The heather dropped its purple blooms and changed back to a dull brownish-green, and the grasses faded from the green of summer to pale yellows and browns, making the hillsides look desolate and barren. The last of the summer migrant birds – dotterels, swallows, ring ouzels, warblers, wheatears, terns and ospreys – had departed, but skeins of wild geese were still passing high overhead, honking softly to each other as they disappeared into the darkness, heading south from their Arctic breeding grounds to the gentler climes where they would overwinter.

Although I loved all the seasons in turn, I always had a

slight feeling of desolation at the sight of those Vs of geese flying south, or the swallows lining up on the telegraph wires, chattering to each other before beginning their own long migration. That was the sure sign that summer was over and when I was a kid I can remember fantasising about keeping the swallows here somehow because if they didn't fly south, summer might never end.

For most of the year, the red deer stags and hinds had lived in separate herds, but they came together in autumn in preparation for the rut. The males had now moved into the areas of good grazing where the females were usually found and the first cold snap of the season coincided with the start of the rut. As I walked across the hillside one morning, I could hear the distant roaring of several stags. During the rut, which ran from mid-September to mid-November, the males that roared loudest and longest and had the most imposing bodies and antler spreads established harems of up to twenty hinds and mated with them as they came into season.

Stags demonstrated their dominance first by bellowing and walking in parallel with potential rivals, strutting up and down like a pair of street toughs checking each other out before starting a punch-up. That allowed them to assess each other and at that point the weaker one would usually back down. They only locked antlers and fought when facing an opponent of similar size and strength. The noise of thundering hooves and clashing antlers as the rival stags battled it out usually ended in nothing worse than an undignified retreat for the loser, but the sharp-pointed tines of the antlers could cause serious injuries and sometimes even fatalities.

The bellowing of the stags reached a crescendo twice a day, around dawn and in the late evening, and during the rut I didn't need an alarm clock to wake me because the stags had already done the job. Only a few dominant stags established harems and they expended such enormous amounts of time and energy on roaring, fighting or chasing off challengers, and herding in and mating with the hinds, there was little or no time to graze. So they rarely, if ever, ate during the rut and lost up to 20 per cent of their body weight.

Out on the hill one day, keeping well away from two stags that were circling each other and preparing to fight, I found a well-worn deer path snaking away between the large boulders and scree slopes towards a series of rock outcrops. As I rounded one of them, picking my way carefully as there was a steep drop to one side of the narrow path, I spotted feathers and droppings spread over the ground. Picking up one of the feathers to examine it, I realised I had stumbled across a golden eagle's eyrie (nest), sited on the rocky ledge high above my head.

I could see the nest, an untidy collection of twigs, heather stems and pieces of rope that had probably been scavenged from the shores of the lochs and local farms, all piled together in a heap about three feet high. The chicks had already fledged and the eyrie was empty – perhaps fortunately for me, as the adult eagles would not have taken kindly to any intruder straying too close to their nest – but judging by the quantity of droppings still littering the ground, they had clearly been there until quite recently. Like most birds, golden eagles go through a moult in late summer through to early autumn, and their feathers lay scattered along the path for twenty feet in either direction.

As I made my way back down the hillside, a mountain blackbird alighted on a rock close to the track. Puffing out its white chest, it studied me inquisitively with its dark eyes, before popping up into a rowan tree to pluck off the plump red berries. A few yards further on, as I rounded a bend in the track above a scree slope, I noticed a young fox slowly ambling away from me. Every so often it stopped to sniff between the large boulders, searching for prey. It looked sleek and well fed, so it was obviously doing well for itself. Had I been carrying my rifle, I would have felt honour-bound to shoot it – foxes were the natural predators of the estate's lambs and deer calves – but I had no weapon with me and on this crisp, sunlit autumn day I was happy to live and let live, and stood watching the fox until it disappeared among the rocks lower down the slope.

A mile or so further on, the path curved downhill towards an expanse of open moorland. Even from a distance, I could see a large group of hinds pacing around in circles as they were herded by a large stag. The stag paused, scratching at the ground with his hooves. Then he thrust his antlers down into the peat he had exposed and thrashed them around furiously. When he lifted his head again, I could see his peat-blackened antlers, now draped with heather stems and grasses that must have made him look even larger to a potential rival. As he paced back and forth, hot plumes of breath escaped from his nostrils.

High on the hillside above me I heard a clash of antlers as

two more stags battled for control of another harem of hinds. Again and again they locked horns, using their body weight to try to overthrow their opponent. Dislodged by the force of the fight, rocks came crashing down the hillside, gathering momentum as they fell and bouncing high into the air around me. I decided now might be a good time to leave.

As the top stags became exhausted, they moved away from the rutting areas and reformed their bachelor herds. That sometimes allowed younger males a chance to mate with females that had come into season late and by the end of the rut, many but by no means all of the mature females (aged three or more) were pregnant. Red deer hinds carry a single offspring – twins are extremely rare – through the winter and the calves (not 'fawns', which is the name given to baby fallow deer), are born from mid-May to mid-July. They have white spots in their fur, just like Bambi, which help to camouflage them. They can stand within half an hour of being born but for the first few weeks of their lives, they stay with their mothers away from the herd, and when not being suckled, they remain hidden in the longer vegetation while the hinds graze. After that, they follow their mothers closely and continue to take milk until at least the beginning of the next rut.

By the end of the stag season in late October, the coats of the deer were beginning to change to their winter colouring, the dark-red fur growing greyer and thicker and the mane lengthening around their necks as protection against the cold. The heavy dews of autumn were now giving way to sharp frosts and on several mornings as I opened the curtains at dawn, ready to go to work, the ground was dusted with white and the shallow waters at the edge of the river were glazed with a thin coating of ice. One still, icy morning, a mist hung over the valley, so dense that even the nearby river was invisible from my window. By the time I went outside, the mist was beginning to lift and the pale, low sunlight revealed a magical sight: every blade of grass, every twig, every pine needle, had been painted with hoar frost. With not a breath of breeze to ruffle the waters of the loch, every detail was perfectly reflected in its mirrored surface. I stood there open-mouthed, drinking in the sight until Dougie's Land Rover rumbled into view along the road, breaking the spell.

One dark, cloudless night, with the frost biting my skin, I stood outside the cottage watching the stars wheel overhead and the Milky Way shimmering across the sky, in a silence broken only by the hoot of an owl hunting over the frozen ground and the eerie, scream-like call of a vixen somewhere in the dark forest behind me. Over the years that sound has fooled many people into thinking they're hearing a child or woman being attacked, but it's just a vixen calling her mate to find out his whereabouts. It's one of a number of curious sounds that foxes make, including the alarm call that sounds like a dry cough if you're close to it, but more like a terrier's short, sharp bark if you're further away, and 'gekkering' – an aggressive, almost metallic-sounding 'ack-ack-ack' noise, interspersed with yelps and barks, which they make when play-fighting or when warning off another dog fox from entering their territory.

When I looked up, I stood transfixed as first one, then

another and then a flurry of fiercely bright specks arrowed across the sky above me as the shooting stars of a meteor shower passed through. Barely had the last of those faded from sight, when a pale-green glow began to light up the northern horizon. At first I did not realise what it was, but then I stared, spellbound, as the Northern Lights danced across the sky for a few minutes, before fading back into blackness.

The first snow started to fall in late November, pushing the deer down from the hilltops towards lower ground. The winter months are tough times for red deer. Males must recover body condition lost during the rut and pregnant females have to support themselves and their growing foetuses throughout the winter when food is scarce. Lowland hinds can calve every year, but the strains of carrying a calf through the bitter winters up on the hills meant that our hinds only calved once every two years.

Within a few weeks of the first flurries of snow, we had a two-foot covering, which lasted through until the end of January. Although the red deer stag season had ended, the hind season had opened the next day, continuing until mid-February, and the snow not only pushed the hinds lower on the hillsides, making them easier to reach when stalking, but also made dragging the carcasses much less strenuous. Highland ponies were not used to extract the deer in winter as the ground was usually too wet or snow-covered for their short legs, and instead we used a quad bike, or just dragged the hinds down to the roadside by hand, pulling them like sledges over the snow.

The hinds were culled when many of them were in the first stages of pregnancy, but there was no other time when it could be done because during the rest of the year they were either too heavily pregnant or still had the previous year's calf 'at foot' with them. Although the hind season still had another seven weeks to run, we tried to get the majority culled before Christmas. That left January and February free for counting deer and checking the six-foot deer fences around the forests. Deer heading down off the hills in winter would try to push past the fences to hide in the forest. If they did, they would usually be trapped there, unable to find a way out again and would browse and damage the young saplings, so our job was to ensure that deer were discouraged from entering in the first place by repairing any holes in the fence line and removing trees that had fallen across the fences.

There were wildcats at Ardverikie and after the snows came, I often saw their footprints among the trees, but they seemed to stick to the higher ground in areas where there was the least human disturbance, and I only saw a wildcat in the flesh a handful of times. I had to look twice to be sure it wasn't just a feral domestic cat, but it was bigger than a normal cat and its thick fur, with markings a bit like a tabby cat, and a thick tail, ringed with alternating brown and black bands and ending in a black tip, made it seem even larger. The way it moved was also much more like a big cat's prowling gait than a domestic cat's, and it had a broader face and jaw. They are ferocious hunters with powerful jaws and needle-sharp teeth. I've heard that zoologists trying to catch them to weigh or study them often use tranquilising darts because wildcats have been known to bite right through even the thickest leather gauntlets.

As winter deepened, our stone-walled cottage grew steadily colder. In the Highlands, the summer was always a month shorter than in the Lowlands and it was not unusual for winter temperatures to drop as low as -20°C. When we came in from our day's work, with our breath fogging the air even inside the cottage, the first job was always to get the log fire blazing. At bedtime, going from the warmth of the living room to my ice-cold bedroom was a shock, but I had a small, two-bar electric fire that took the chill from the air. I always took great care to leave it in the middle of the room, so there was no chance of it setting fire to the furniture if I fell asleep and left it burning all night.

I was still keeping an eye out for a puppy to train as a gun dog but, hampered by my heavy workload during the stag and hind seasons, I hadn't been able to find one as yet and I was dreading having to explain that to John Waters at my next session at college. One night, I had a vivid dream that I was on my way to pick up a gun-dog puppy from a farm. As I entered the kennels, I saw six little black Labradors, wrapped up in a pink blanket. One of them pushed its way out of the blanket and crawled over to inspect me. It was so small and cute that I couldn't help but pick it up and give it a cuddle. Setting the puppy back down, I really felt this was the dog for me. Placing its fat little black paws on my knee, it wagged its tail as I stroked its head, but all of a sudden, the dream changed and the puppy began growling at me, baring its teeth and then barking and snarling. I backed away, starting to feel frightened. 'What's wrong?' I asked the little dog. It opened its mouth and I heard it growl, 'Wake up!'

I woke with a start and at once began coughing and choking. The room was filled with thick black smoke and flames were licking at the ceiling in the centre of the room. Then I noticed the electric fire. I must have had a fight with a pillow in my sleep and thrown it across the room. It had landed right on top of the fire and caught alight. Choking and spluttering, I staggered across to the window and threw it open. With no fire extinguisher and the nearest fire station fifteen miles away, I knew I had to deal with it myself and I didn't have much time; the only other option was to let my cottage burn down. I yanked the plug from the socket and, grabbing two towels from the shelf, I wrapped them round my hands to protect them from the heat. I then lifted the fire, complete with burning pillow, and threw the whole lot out of the window. It landed with a crash on the road below as I slumped across the window sill, taking great gulps of fresh air.

As I opened all the other windows and doors to clear the smoke, I sent up a silent prayer of thanks – saved by my gun dog and I hadn't even bought it yet. The smell of the smoke was still so terrible in my room that I grabbed a spare duvet and headed downstairs to get what sleep I could on our lumpy couch. In his downstairs bedroom, Owen had managed to sleep through the whole drama and knew nothing about it until I woke him up. Cleaning up my smoke-blackened room was a filthy job and even after I'd redecorated, it was weeks before the smell faded completely.

The week after the fire, I heard about a farmer in Perth who had a litter of black Labrador puppies for sale. Both parents were working dogs and the pups came with all the correct papers. Very excited, I arranged an appointment to view them the following weekend and when Saturday finally arrived I jumped into the car and made the ninety-minute journey down to Perth.

The farmer led me to a barn and as I opened the pen where they were kept, I saw six little black puppies, wrapped up in a pink blanket, just like in my dream. The pups all jumped up at once and bounded over to me, climbing on my knee and wagging their stumpy tails. They were so adorable that I wasn't sure how I would manage to choose one, so placing all the puppies back in the blanket, I moved away from them and sat down, deciding that the first pup to reach me would be my dog. I called out loudly, 'Come on pups,' and, while the others held back, one of them bounded over and leapt on me. That was the one!

Three hundred pounds poorer, I drove back to Ardverikie with my new gun dog. I christened her 'Mint', not because she'd cost that much, but because I liked the name. As I tried to concentrate on the road, Mint did her very best to distract me by first peeing on my lap and then getting herself stuck under the foot pedals. I reluctantly put her in the back where she eventually settled.

I kept her in the cottage with me to start with, but after a month of Mint peeing and pooping on my carpet, and chewing my shoes and any letters the postman delivered, I moved her to the kennels at the back of the house, allowing me to go to work for the day and come home to a house that had not been torn apart. In the early mornings before I went to work, I'd take her for a walk along the river bank and around the shore of the loch, and often there would be something that would make me catch my breath, like a glimpse of an eagle circling high in the sky over the mountains, a pair of pure-white swans drifting together on the current or the vivid flash of electric blue I saw one morning as a kingfisher arrowed down into the water and emerged a fraction of a second later with a minnow flapping in its beak. When I got home at night I'd take the dog back down to the loch, picking my way by starlight or moonlight as the frozen sand crunched under my boots, while Mint tracked intriguing scents or chased sleepy ducks out into the middle of the loch.

In my spare time, I spent hours training her, first teaching her the basic commands that any dog owner would use: 'Heel', 'Sit', 'Stay', 'Lie down', and so on. She learned so fast that by the time she was three months old, she would walk at my heel in the fields and woods or along the road without any need for a lead, even while traffic was thundering past. I also taught her to sit and wait for her food, not touching it until I said, 'Go ahead.' Soon I had a well-trained, skilful and obedient dog that I could take anywhere without fear that she would do anything to embarrass me in front of the guns, stalkers, keepers or anyone else.

At this stage she was still too young to learn how to be a gun dog; that would come later, when I could teach her to work a field or section of forest, flushing out the game, and retrieve shot birds and bring them back undamaged in her soft mouth, rather than running off and settling down to eat them herself, as would be a dog's natural instinct.

I was still learning myself, of course, and as the season progressed, I learned much more about how to stalk deer, work hill ponies and the myriad tasks that went to make up the gamekeeper's and deer-stalker's year.

The deer season lasted from July right through to February, with 14 February – Valentine's Day – the official end of the season. When not out stalking, and during the spring and early summer months after the end of the season, we turned our hands to a whole host of other duties around the estate.

At the end of the deer season, we tidied up the larder and oiled up all the ponies' tack – the saddles, bridles and reins – and released the ponies for their annual holiday; they roamed free during the summer but were rounded up again when the next stag season began. We then started the main period of vermin control, trapping stoats, weasels and mink, and we also did a bit of work with the sheep during lambing time and clipping time, and repairs to the fencing. The estate was cut in two by a public road and for some reason people driving along it were always coming off the road and flying through the fences into the fields, so it was a never-ending job repairing them. Despite the dismissive looks I got from some of the male keepers on other estates, I was never afraid to get my hands dirty and I never dodged any task or asked for any favours because of my sex.

Heather burning was always done between the end of the

deer season and the end of March. All the sporting estates did it, with the aim of burning off the old woody stems, stimulating new growth from the existing plants and helping to 'chit' (germinate) the heather seeds in the upper layers of peat to create new plants with the green shoots on which grouse love to feed – at some times of the year, heather forms 99 per cent of a grouse's diet. Heather regenerates from its roots and its seed can survive the heat of all but the most intense moorland blazes, so it regrows quickly after a fire, while many other plants and weeds are destroyed.

As spring progressed, the burns (streams) swelled with the volume of meltwater, turning into torrents that tumbled down the hillsides into the loch below. The deer shed their winter coats, rubbing themselves against the trees to remove the excess hair. Their new coats were a deep-red colour, replacing the dark browny-grey of their winter coats. New grass shoots pushed their way up through the withered ground cover, a rich diet for the deer after the lean pickings of the winter months. New growth appeared on the Scots pines and the deciduous trees burst into leaf, the birds began nesting and the trout became active after a long, dormant winter. As the first flies appeared, the fish jumped and splashed in the lochs, relieving their hunger after months of fasting.

Another sure sign of spring was the stags shedding their antlers. The mature stags always shed first, in late winter every year, but by early springtime, all the younger stags had also dropped their antlers. As soon as they had been cast, the stags – the hinds don't have antlers – immediately started to grow a new set, which continued to grow during the spring and summer. All the deer chewed the shed antlers as a source of phosphorous and calcium. The estate also collected the antlers and they were sold to stick makers for handles for walking sticks and shepherds' crooks. April was the best time to find them as they had only recently been shed, and had not been lying around long enough to be chewed by the deer. The best places were usually around the feeding grounds and low-lying areas and the creamy-white antlers were relatively easy to spot. Each time I went out, I collected up to twenty, tying them roughly to my backpack with a drag rope.

We also conducted a winter mortality search. Any deer not strong enough to last the winter had perished and their carcasses were now being uncovered as the snows melted. The youngest and oldest deer were always the most likely to succumb to cold and lack of food, and the harshness of the winters and the shortage of grazing in the Highlands meant that we lost a lot of red deer calves every winter, particularly in wet and cold years, along with any males that had failed to recover condition from the rut. Many calves died during their first or second winter; only half of them made it to their second birthday. Foxes and golden eagles sometimes took young deer calves but the adult red deer had no natural pred-ators – other than man – because the wolves, bears and lynx that once preyed on them have long been extinct in Britain. In exceptional circumstances, red deer can live to twenty years old but their lifespan is usually much shorter and on Highland estates like Ardverikie, the average lifespan of the females is just over ten years and the males just less than nine.

The pine plantations around the feeding grounds were the

best places to search for deer carcasses because sick and weak deer headed down into areas of heavy cover to shelter during the long winter months and inevitably many died there, so the majority of the carcasses were found within a few small areas. They were always crawling with ticks and keds (also known as deer flies) and as I sawed away at the antlers, I could feel them marching slowly up my arm. Keds can only fly for short distances and once they land on a deer, they shed their wings and start burrowing through the fur to suck their blood. Although they only reproduce on deer, they can give humans a painful bite that can cause an allergic reaction. After recording the sex and estimating the age of each dead deer, I removed the antlers – I carried a small saw in my backpack for that – picked the ticks and keds off my arms and then carried on across the hillside, searching for more unfortunate deer. I was terrified of keds because they always made a beeline for my long hair and as I walked across the hillside, I could feel them crawling through it, which drove me absolutely mad. Owen was no keener on them and, without a hairbrush, we would resort to pulling them out of each other's hair, like a pair of baboons grooming each other.

As well as ticks and keds, deer are also plagued by warble flies. They lay their eggs on the tips of grass stems and the deer ingest the eggs when eating the grass. They then migrate through the body before hatching out into grubs. The warble grubs live on the deer's back, just under the skin, eating the poor deer from the inside. During springtime, the fat warble maggot bores its way out of the deer's back, leaving a hole the size of a bullet. The maggot drops to the ground, pupates and then hatches out into a fly so the painful cycle begins again. The deer are driven to distraction by them, scratching them-selves against trees to try and relieve the irritation and pain.

Among our other seasonal jobs, we worked closely with the estate shepherd in spring. The estate had around 800 black-faced sheep and in every lambing season the shepherd was keen for the gamekeepers to keep the fox and hooded crow numbers down to stop lambs being killed. The two stalkers would often go out with a lamp at night and wait for Mr Fox to put in an appearance. If he did, it was usually his last.

Killing foxes was a year-round activity, whenever time permitted, but usually came to a peak in April. January was the height of the mating season for foxes and the month when the previous year's cubs were chased away by their parents to stop them competing for food and breeding rights. So it was a time when a lot of young foxes were roaming around in search of a new territory and a mate, but we were normally still too busy with the stag season to have much time to spare for trapping foxes then. Meanwhile the adult foxes were busy defending their territories against all-comers, marking their borders with urine and droppings, barking and yelping to deter intruders, and fighting any that came too close.

In February the pregnant vixens largely remained hidden in their earths, ready to give birth in March, the peak cubbing season, after a gestation of fifty-one to fifty-three days. The typical litter was five cubs, which were born blind, deaf and unable to regulate their own body heat, so the vixen stayed at their side for about the first ten days of their lives, relying on her mate to bring food. If the dog fox was slow to do so, the vixen would go to the mouth of the earth and bark to summon him. By April the vixen was beginning to wean her cubs and that was also the time when we were out searching for fox earths and dens, hoping to trap the cubs before they left the den behind and began to hunt on their own account.

As well as keeping an eye out for foxes, I had to run a daily 'trap round', checking the vermin traps. These were large 'letterbox traps' all around the estate. Approximately twelve foot by six and made of chicken wire, supported by wooden posts sunk into the ground, they were used to catch hooded crows, which peck out the eyes of young lambs, and so are understandably less than popular with shepherds. The best time to catch them was during the heavy snows of the winter. The traps were baited with deer offal and there were perches, a good supply of food and water and a small shelter inside them, plus a decoy bird that had been trapped earlier.

Hooded crows flying past would be reassured by the sight of a crow already inside and would be lured in by the prospect of an easy meal. The trap worked in a similar way to a lobster pot: the crows could enter from the top and squeeze down through the entrance, but once inside, they were unable to get back out again. We checked the traps every day and managed to catch lots of crows which were quickly dispatched and the trap re-baited, but however many we trapped, more always seemed to turn up.

Although the traps were set all year round, in the winter we were able to catch large numbers of crows at once; during one heavy snowfall, we caught eighteen in one twenty-four-hour period. A buzzard had also squeezed through the top and had then set about killing all the crows, saving us a job. As we approached the trap, I could see it on the perch looking extremely pleased with itself. We released it back into the wild, but removing birds of prey from the traps was always difficult as they never wanted to fly out through the door once we'd opened it. Instead we had to catch the bird with our bare hands and carry it out before releasing it. It inevitably tried to peck and claw us, so we had to be very careful how we handled it.

I also ran a mile-long trap line for vermin on the north-western side of the estate, where there was a large, fenced-off area which marched (bordered) with the Creag Meagaidh nature reserve and had a population of around fifty black grouse. The males were magnificent-looking birds with blue-black bodies, a vivid red wattle and lyre-shaped white tail feathers that they raised and fanned out when displaying to females in the mating season. They were increasingly rare and it was my job to protect them. They had a lecking site (the place where the males display) just over the border in Creag Meagaidh. Black grouse were popular with the conserva-tionists and tourists too, so that gave me an added incentive to help them out.

The line consisted of snares and Fenn traps (spring-loaded traps activated by a pressure plate or sometimes a wire trigger), which were used to humanely kill pests like grey squirrels and rabbits, and predators on game birds like rats, stoats and weasels, but were powerful enough to break the bones in your hand if you were careless when setting them. By law, Fenn traps and other spring-traps had to be of a specified design and set in a burrow or a natural or artificial tunnel. Above-ground traps were banned not only because they could be a hazard to livestock, walkers and their dogs, but also because unscrupulous gamekeepers could use them to trap protected species like birds of prey.

When I first started, Owen showed me the best places to position the Fenn traps and very soon I was catching quite a lot of vermin. I experimented with every kind of bait, but strangely I found cheap dog food was the best lure. Stoats that would turn up their noses at fresh quail or rabbit were mad for Bounce Meaty Chunks; as one of our American stalking clients liked to say: 'Go figure,' though since there are plenty of humans who prefer McDonald's to fillet steak, maybe it isn't so surprising that stoats like junk food too.

When the stalking season was over, Dougie and I spent many an afternoon driving round checking the crow traps. It was miles between the crow cages and with the estate Land Rover only able to do fifteen miles an hour over the rough tracks, it took us a few hours to make the circuit. Dougie was a talkative and entertaining chap, and as we drove along, he told me lots of stories about things that had happened to him over the years. Smoke rising from a patch of heather being burned on the neighbouring estate was enough to start him reminiscing. 'I was once burning patches of rank heather on the north side of the estate,' he said. 'This was in the days before students came to work at Ardverikie, so keepers had to do everything for ourselves. I'd burned a large area of ling and bell heather, using the streams as natural barriers to stop the flames, when suddenly an angry-looking tourist came running up to me, shouting about his bike. It turned out that he'd cycled up the glen on his brand-new, £2,000 mountain bike and hidden it in the heather while he climbed to the top of the hill. When he spotted the smoke and flames from the burning heather, he'd rushed back down the slope to try and save his bike, but he was a wee bit too late for that, because it had already been burned to a crisp. The seat, handlebars and tyres had melted and the frame was blackened, so his precious bike was now just a pile of melted plastic and rubber, and charred and twisted metal.

'Naturally he was hopping mad. "You're going to give me £2,000 for my bike," he said, but I shook my head. "I don't think so, pal. I'll not be giving you two grand, in fact I'll not be giving you any money at all. I'd have to be an idiot to do that and there's already one of those here, because only an idiot would have wandered off after hiding his very expensive bike in the heather during the heather-burning season."' Dougie smiled to himself at the memory. 'Anyway, things got a bit heated after that but when we'd been arguing for about ten minutes, I'd had enough so I told him "Fuck off", and drove off in the Land Rover. I never saw him again, but I bet it was the last time he left his bike in the heather while he went for a country stroll.'

One of the trap lines Dougie had given me to run was on the north side of the estate, behind a large forestry plantation block. To reach it, I got a lift in the Land Rover with Dougie up to the march between Creag Meagaidh and Ardverikie. He dropped me off at the side of the road and I took my bait bag and shotgun, and started the long trek up the steep hill. Opening the deer gate, I made my way upwards over the boggy, uneven ground and rounded the edge of the plantation, picking my way through long, rank heather and birch scrub. An animal track ran through the undergrowth along the fenceline, made by badgers, foxes and deer. Footprints and droppings littered the pathway, letting me know not only which animals had been past but, from the look of the prints and the decomposition of the droppings, how long ago.

When he gave me the trap line to run, Dougie had handed me six brand-new Mark IV Fenn traps and four rusty old ones. A lot of gamekeepers preferred older, rusty traps, claiming that the bright, shiny metal of new ones could be off-putting to animals. Some keepers even buried new traps in the peat to 'season them' and get rid of the shine. Personally I thought it was a bit of an old wives' tale. I preferred the gleaming new metal traps and caught more animals with them than I did with the old ones, which often had stiff, rusted mechanisms that made them less reliable.

One of the traps I had been given was particularly battered and rusty, although it still seemed to work reasonably well. As the weather had been quite hot, the meat I had used as bait had gone rotten and needed replacing. I'd placed each of the Fenn traps inside a tunnel that I'd purpose-built from large, heavy stones. Limiting the size of the entrance stopped larger animals like badgers and cats from getting inside the traps, and ensured I only caught my target species: mink, stoats, weasels and rats.

Reaching inside my game bag, I took out my tin of Bounce Meaty Chunks dog food – still the stoats' favourite – and a large spoon. If I was very careful, I could place the meat into the back of the trap without springing the mechanism. I'd done this many times before quite safely, although on two occasions I had sprung the trap which had then snapped shut on the back of my hand with enough force to break the skin and leave an ugly bruise that took over a week to heal.

Everything was going well until I came to the rusty, bent trap. It had already sprung but nothing was inside it, so I carefully prized the bars apart and reset it, but as I was reaching in with my spoonful of dog food, disaster struck. The trap sprang shut again, right on my hand. Cursing, I dropped the bait and did my best to prize the trap off with my left hand but it remained clamped shut and refused to budge. The bars on top of the trap were slightly bent and for some reason it just wouldn't open. For fifteen minutes I struggled, shouting, cursing and strangely enough, trying to reason with the trap. However, it just wasn't listening and continued to refuse to open.

There was nothing for it; I would have to walk the two miles back home with the Fenn trap still on my hand. I felt like a right ninny trudging back with a lump of metal clamped to my hand but one thing was for sure, there was no way I was going to ask Dougie for help as he would never have let me live it down. By the time I'd walked the two miles, my hand had gone completely numb and I had lost all feeling in my fingers. Feeling more foolish by the minute, I realised that I would have to get the trap off quickly to restore the blood supply to my hand before I did some permanent damage to it.

The estate cook, Mary, who was in her late seventies and had worked at Ardverikie her whole life, tending to the shooting guests, lived in a small cottage near the Lodge with her forty-year-old son, Hamish. A big bear of a man, Hamish looked like a true Highlander. He had a dark, bushy beard, unkempt hair and weighed about fifteen stone, but he was a kind and gentle man who I was sure would help me out. I made one last vain attempt to dislodge the trap myself, then knocked on the door and heard his answering shout from inside, 'Just come in.'

Hamish was eating soup in the kitchen. I held up my arm and showed him the Fenn trap and to give him his due, he never laughed or even cracked a smile, though he would have been perfectly within his rights to do so. Instead, he placed his bowl of soup on the sideboard and tried to force the bars of the trap apart. To my surprise, even Hamish couldn't shift them and after a few minutes of struggling, he gave up and went off to look for a tool to prise the trap open. Meanwhile his mother also made an attempt to help me but she too had to admit defeat.

Hamish eventually came back with a garden fork, which he jammed between the plates of the trap to try to lever them apart. For a few moments they still remained clamped shut, but then with a squeal of tortured metal, they began to open. When he had made enough room to get his fingers between the bars, Hamish forced them wider apart and I was finally able to pull my hand out of it. The sense of relief was enormous as I felt life flooding back into my throbbing fingers. There was a deep purple weal on the back of my hand where the bar had dug into me.

Shaking my arm to get the blood flowing again, I thanked Hamish profusely. 'But promise me you won't tell anyone,' I said. 'If anyone finds out, I'll be the butt of everyone's jokes for the next ten years or so, or at least until someone else does something even more stupid.'

He laughed. 'I promise, though it'll cost you a dram or two to guarantee my silence.'

'Let's make it a bottle,' I said, 'just to be on the safe side.'

I put the offending trap at the bottom of my bucket and covered it with a large pile of rubbish. I didn't want Owen to find it and rescue it, so I made sure that I was the one who put out the trash that night.

True to his word, Hamish never did tell anyone, as far as I know, although I bet he and his mother had a good laugh about it after I left.

During my first year at Ardverikie, I also spent part of my spare time volunteering on several other nearby estates, learning everything I could about gamekeeping. It wasn't compulsory to do so, but I was hungry for every scrap of knowledge I could obtain. Although Dougie could teach me pretty much all there was to know about deer-stalking, by working at different estates I could also learn about grouse moor management and pheasant and partridge shoots.

I learned to detect the faint, wavering tracks of animals crossing the fields and moors, and identify what animal had made them from the tracks, trails and signs – the scat (droppings) left by different creatures. Before long, I could distinguish deer pellets from sheep droppings and identify the breed of deer that had left them. I could tell badger droppings by their sweet musky smell, and fox scat by its unmistakably 'foxy' odour and black colour, except in urban areas where their human-influenced diet made them lighter in colour. I could spot shiny black hedgehog droppings; the narrow, twisted scat of weasel and stoat, often with the fur of the rodents that were their main prey visible in them; the fruity, slightly musky scat of pine martens; and the tarry 'spraints' of otters that were readily identifiable by the fishbones and scales they contained.

I also learned to place snares, nooses of fine wire used to catch rabbits. Animal welfare and conservation laws, not to mention common sense, required all traps to be set with great care. Snares had to be non-locking types, set only in areas where you could be as certain as possible that there was no danger of snaring cats, dogs or livestock by mistake, and by law, they had to be checked a minimum of once a day, though all gamekeepers would automatically do that anyway.

An old keeper on one estate showed me how to set rabbit snares. He was already past retirement age but was in no hurry to give up the work that he loved and seemed delighted to be passing on his knowledge and skills to a new generation. 'Learn how to set snares and you'll never go hungry,' he said as we walked out over the fields early one summer morning, with the dew still heavy on the ground. 'In the lean years before the war we'd have starved if it hadn't been for the rabbits we caught and there's a knack to getting it just right. So . . . first of all let's find us a couple of rabbit runs.'

We walked along a bank of gorse bushes and he watched while I identified a few rabbit runs leading out into the field where the rabbits grazed. 'Good,' he said, 'but now look closer. You see those slightly stronger marks in the run? Those are where the rabbits are landing as they hop. You want to set your snare at the mid-point between them, so you snare your rabbit in mid-hop, which will guarantee catching it. And either wear gloves when you're setting your snares or wipe them down with a handful of grass to remove any trace of human scent.'

He showed me how to set the snare, with the bottom of the loop a hand's breadth above the ground and tethered by a stake driven into the ground or tied to a branch or tree root. 'You need a strong stake,' he said, 'particularly in soft ground, because you'd be surprised how hard a snared rabbit can pull.'

He also taught me how to hold the top of the wire loop in a split made in the top of a thin twig, and on a broad rabbit run, how to use branches and twigs to funnel the rabbits towards the snare. It took a few trial goes before I could do it to his satisfaction. 'Good enough, lassie,' he said. 'You'll do. Now if you've set your snares and the rabbits are out feeding in the field after dark you can boost your chances of a few for the pot by walking across the field from the far side making a bit of noise and waving a torch. The rabbits will bolt for the safety of their burrows among the gorse and they're more likely to be trapped when they're bolting than when they're coming out to feed and being more cautious.' He grinned. 'Oh, and if you check your snare and all you find is the head of a rabbit, then you'll know that a fox has got there first and eaten your dinner.'

Sitting around the fire or in the pub in the evening, listening to the old keepers talking, I also got a real sense of the history and traditions of gamekeeping. I'd never really thought much about it before, but they made me aware of how far back gamekeeping went, at least as far as the Norman Conquest, when the royal 'forests' (which included open spaces like heathland as well as woods and forests) were reserved for the king. Any hunting or even disturbance of the game or its habitat was forbidden and 'verderers' – the forerunners of today's gamekeepers – administered the Forest Laws and punished poachers.

An Act of Parliament in 1671 gave 'any gentleman above the rank of esquire' the right to appoint a gamekeeper but it was the development of the great sporting estates in the eighteenth and nineteenth centuries that saw a boom in gamekeeping. The number of keepers reached a peak of well over 20,000 just before the First World War but has been declining ever since to the point where there are just 3,000 employed today, and at the time I started gamekeeping, almost all of them were men. Things have changed a little, but only a little since then. Perhaps one in ten students on gamekeeping courses are now women, though most of those who last the course and qualify usually go on to work on pheasant shooting estates, where they are routinely assigned to rearing the pheasant chicks, possibly because the almost invariably male head keepers think that rearing and nurturing small creatures is what women do best.

When I looked into the history of women gamekeepers I discovered that there had been a few in the past, almost all of them the wives of keepers who were pressed into service either when their husbands fell ill or were injured, or when called up for military service, particularly during the First World War. However, there was one woman keeper from the past I would love to have met. Polly Fishburne was a keeper on the Earl of Leicester's estates in the early years of the nineteenth century. According to Lord Albemarle, who wrote about her in his memoirs, she had 'large black eyes, red cheeks and white teeth, her hair was cropped like a man's and she wore a man's hat. The rest of her attire was feminine ... Polly was the terror of poachers, with whom she had frequent encounters and would give and take hard knocks, but generally she succeeded in capturing her opponents and making them answer for their misdeeds at Petty Sessions.' There have been others, including Jill Mason, one of the first women gamekeepers of the modern era, who is also a respected writer on country matters, but no woman had ever qualified as a deer-stalker at the North Highland College, an omission I hoped soon to remedy.

The primary job of gamekeepers in previous eras was to eliminate any potential predators on the game, and in the days when the diets of most carnivores and raptors were little understood, most took it as carte blanche to kill anything and everything. The meticulous records kept by one Scottish sporting estate show that in a three-year period during the nineteenth century, its keepers killed: 246 pine martens, 106 polecats, 67 badgers, 46 otters, 301 stoats and weasels,

198 wildcats, 15 golden eagles, 27 sea eagles, 18 ospreys, 63 goshawks, 98 peregrine falcons, 285 common buzzards, 371 rough-legged buzzards, 83 hen harriers, 275 kites, 462 kestrels, 78 merlin hawks and over 100 owls, together with 1,431 hooded crows and 475 ravens. With carnage on that scale, it is not hard to understand why so many species were pushed up to – or over – the brink of extinction.

The war on poachers was similarly unrelenting. Game laws were heavily weighted in favour of landowners and punishments for poaching were savage. In the brutal old days, poachers caught by keepers were routinely flogged, imprisoned, transported to the colonies or even hanged, particularly if convicted of using a firearm or wounding a gamekeeper. Until they were banned in the 1830s it was also quite legal for gamekeepers to set spring-guns – guns triggered by a tripwire – to maim or kill poachers, and man-traps: steel spring-traps with spiked jaws powerful enough to crush a man's leg and leave him helpless, pinioned until the gamekeepers arrived, by which time some poachers had already died from shock or blood loss. However, the violence was not all one-sided and many keepers were attacked and some were killed by poachers.

Poaching continues to this day but is now much less likely to be by a local person taking 'one for the pot' than an organised gang coming from the city to steal deer, game birds, wildfowl, salmon and trout, for sale to unscrupulous game restaurants. The poachers' methods are often indiscriminate and very harmful, including netting rivers to catch fish in bulk, and if caught in the act, the poaching gangs can be armed and extremely violent.

Scotland's National Wildlife Crime Unit recently recorded 335 incidents of poaching in the space of eighteen months and many more instances must have gone unrecorded. It is not just game animals, birds and fish that are targeted. One survey team inspecting a river in a remote part of Scotland were appalled to discover that poachers hoping to find freshwater pearls had stolen a bed of highly protected freshwater mussels. Even plants are sometimes poached; 200,000 wild bluebell bulbs were recently stolen in North Wales.

I was lucky because I never actually encountered any poachers or saw any sign of poaching on the estates where I worked, but that was in very remote areas. Poaching was much more of a common problem on the estates nearer to cities, especially those with good salmon rivers or pheasant shoots. You can net salmon or catch or kill pheasants relatively easily, whereas poaching grouse or deer is a much less quick and easy business. If you've then got to transport what you've caught fifty miles to where you're going to sell it, passing through sparsely populated areas where strangers tend to be noticed, your chances of being caught are much higher. The estates where I worked also had locked gates or barriers where you had to tap in a key code to unlock them so, unless the poachers were willing to walk and carry their 'bag' out on their backs, even gaining access to them was difficult.

I was all for the 'one for the pot' poachers who just wanted a salmon or two for the dinner table – as we say in Gaelic, *'Breac à linne, slat à coille is fiadh à fireach – mèirle às nach do ghabh gàidheal riamh nàire'*: 'A fish from the river, a staff from the wood and a deer from the mountain – thefts no Gael was ever ashamed of' – but commercial poachers just killed everything that moved and were in it purely for the money. Conserving fish stocks for future generations didn't even enter their heads and they would stop at nothing to take as many salmon as they could get their hands on, even going as far as dynamiting rivers.

One West Highland river ghillie took an inventive approach to his problem with poachers. He worked on an estate with a particularly fine salmon river, but unfortunately the abundance of fish attracted a gang of local poachers who had started netting the river every night. The gang would sneak in under the cover of darkness, set their nets and then, just before sunrise, pull in literally hundreds of adult salmon on the way up the river to spawn. The gamekeeper complained bitterly to the police but they couldn't help him because the police station was woefully understaffed and in any case it was three-quarters of an hour's drive away. Even if they did manage to make their way out to the estate, by the time they got there, the poachers would have long gone.

The river ghillie didn't want to confront them – there were too many of them and they looked a real rough bunch – so he knew he would have to outwit them instead. After a lot of thought, he came up with his plan. He went to the local mechanic, borrowed a twenty-foot length of heavy chain and then waited for the poachers to turn up. Right on cue, the gang arrived about midnight and, hoping to avoid detection, parked their pick-up truck in a lane behind some bushes. However, they were out of luck because the ghillie was already lying in wait for them. As soon as the poachers went down to the river bank to spread their nets, he crept out of hiding and, crouching low, he slid underneath the pick-up truck, bolted one end of the chain to the rear axle and fixed the other end to a sturdy 'strainer post' (the heavyweight wooden posts used to brace lines of fencing) a few feet away. He coiled the rest of the chain underneath the vehicle and then hid the exposed chain from sight by scattering grass and leaves over it. Chuckling to himself, he found a nearby bush where he could hide and await the poachers' return.

Hours later the gang came back with tatty (potato) sacks filled to bursting with fresh salmon. It had been a good haul, but they had yet to get it back to town. The ghillie waited until the poachers had loaded all the fish into the back of the pick-up and then he sprang out from behind the bush, shouting angrily and waving his fists. The poachers, who just wanted to get away with their haul, jumped into the pick-up and the driver started the engine and stamped down hard on the accelerator. Engine roaring, the jeep hurtled forward with a screech of tyres and had just really started to pick up speed when it came to the end of its tether.

The heavyweight chain snapped taut and tore off the pick-up's rear axle. The rest of the pick-up, now with only two wheels, lurched forward a few more yards before slewing to a halt, buried up to the wheel arches in the soft ground. It was now a complete write-off and the poachers knew it. Not wanting to risk a confrontation, the gamekeeper had already made himself scarce but as he slipped away through the woods, he was laughing to himself.

The poachers slunk away and, facing a walk of several

hours in which there was a strong possibility of encountering the police, they had to leave all their stolen salmon behind. They never came back to net the river again, nor did they come and retrieve their vehicle and although the estate had to pay for a tow truck to remove the pick-up, they at least kept the salmon, which were loaded into large chest freezers and eaten over the course of the rest of that year. After word about the incident got around, poachers in the area tended to avoid that river from then on.

If, like the battle against poachers, some things never change, other aspects of a gamekeeper's life are now very different. We may still trap and kill predators like foxes, rats, stoats and weasels, but keepers are now far more alert to the conservation of wildlife in general and the protection of the environment. A tiny minority of keepers still seek to max-imise the number of grouse on their moor or pheasants in their woods by the indiscriminate laying of poison baits or the use of gin traps ('gin' being short for engine and meaning a mechanical trap) that catch animals by snapping shut on their legs. The traps were banned in 1958 but cases of foxes and other animals being caught in them are still reported. However, such men are now pariahs and the vast majority of keepers are as thrilled as I am by the sight of birds like the osprey, sea eagle and red kite, once hunted to extinction in Britain, but now once more flying free in the skies over the Highlands and Islands.

As well as revelling in seeing wild birds, I sometimes tried to give nature a helping hand, but the consequences were not always predictable. As I was leaving my cottage one morning,

I noticed a housemartin's nest had fallen on to the driveway. The adult birds had built the nest with beakfuls of mud collected from the side of puddles and the banks of streams. Unfortunately for them, their mud mix must have contained too much sand, a fatal error for builders of all kinds. Over time the mud and sand nest had dried out and then crumbled, and now the broken nest and its three tiny occupants were lying on the drive. Clearly only a few days old, they were still completely bald and pink. I touched one of them, but the poor little thing was cold to the touch and stiff as a board. Looking up, I could see the mark where the nest had been in the eaves above me, but the adult birds were nowhere to be seen.

My boyfriend at the time, Gary, was staying with me for the weekend, and our plan for the day was to take the dogs for a long walk and then go food shopping. By the time we got back, laden with bags, it was late afternoon. The chicks were still lying on the drive and I bent down and picked up one of them. 'What a shame,' I said, but as I turned its body over in my hand, the 'dead' chick suddenly moved. It was only a slight twinge but enough for me to realise that it was actually still alive. We hurriedly picked up all three of the bodies and took them inside. Gary lit a fire while I tried to warm the baby birds in my hands. One of them was definitely dead, but by now, the other two were moving; I couldn't believe they had survived. They had felt cold and stiff that morning and we had been out for around five hours since then.

After an hour in front of the fire they were completely back to normal, a healthy pink colour and chirping for food. That gave us a problem: housemartins eat flying insects and I knew there was no way I could collect enough to keep them alive. They needed new parents to rear them, so we went out to the barn to search for other nests. We saw half a dozen but only one of them was within reach. So Gary climbed up a ladder to the rafters and deposited the chicks in the nest with their new siblings. He assured me the chicks were all of a similar age, so the newcomers should be accepted by the parents. He climbed down from the rafters and we went back into the house feeling very pleased with ourselves.

Later that evening I went outside to check on them, only to realise that, although their adoptive parents were feeding them, we had accidentally put the baby housemartins into a swallow's nest. When the housemartin chicks finally opened their eyes, they would imprint on the swallow parents and grow up thinking they were swallows. That meant that even if they survived to adulthood, they would never breed because they would try to pair off with swallows and would no doubt be rebuffed. Feeling guilty, I slunk into the house. We had tried our best but we really shouldn't have interfered with nature. Weeks later, I came out of the front door to find eight young birds lined up on the roof, chirping for food. There were six swallows and two housemartins, all being fed by two very worn-out looking parents.

The housemartins had at least lasted longer than my relationship with Gary, though that was really neither his fault nor mine. Most of my boyfriends, including Gary, were gamekeepers on other estates, but it's the kind of job where you have to work long hours and if both of you are doing that, you hardly ever get to see each other. I'd met Gary on the gamekeeping course – he was one of the non-sexist students – but our work placements were a long way away apart and even getting to each other was quite difficult. He was working down near Perth so it was an hour's drive to see him and an hour's drive back again afterwards. Working long and often unpredictable hours, especially during the stag season, meant that we didn't really see much of each other and because of that, the relationship eventually fizzled out.

It was the same story with several subsequent boyfriends and the long hours we worked were always my biggest problem. I genuinely didn't have enough time to make a relationship work. However, apart from that problem, social life on those remote estates wasn't quite as limited as I had imagined before I started work there. At Ardverikie my friends and I would either go over to each other's houses, or go pubbing or even clubbing, because Aviemore wasn't too far away and it had a pretty lively nightlife even when the ski season was not in full swing.

4

WILDFIRES

At the start of my second year at Ardverikie, the estate took on another student gamekeeper, John, who was in his first year at college. We didn't get off to the most promising of starts because when he was introduced to me, he was really taken aback to find a woman working as a ghillie and blurted out, 'Women shouldn't have jobs. They should be schoolteachers and nurses, and that should be it.' It was hard to imagine that anyone would actually have come out with a remark like that in the twenty-first century, but he really did think that way. I stared at him for a moment, thinking 'How can anyone possibly be that thick?' and a year or so earlier I would have torn him apart, but now I just laughed it off, though I was definitely laughing at him, not with him, and thinking to myself, 'What an absolute complete and utter knuckle-dragger.' However, he turned out to be basically a nice guy, just a little bit intellectually challenged.

Owen had now finished his placement and qualified as a gamekeeper, but he had been kept on as an extra ghillie and to drive the snow-track machine on the East Beat. Resembling a small green tank, the snow-track rumbled along on caterpillar tracks and was able to cross wide ditches, rivers and peat hags. It worked well in snow, but it could also be used on boggy ground. However, the trail of destruction it left behind was a bone of contention with local conservationists, who complained bitterly about habitat damage. They claimed that the tracks it made could be seen from space – I wasn't quite sure how they knew that – but after taking a look for myself, I could see why it might have been possible. The broad caterpillar tracks had dug a deep trench through the peat, uprooting the plants and leaving a black scar on the hillside. Water from the surrounding bog had then seeped into the tracks, turning them into quagmires.

Ali had now taken a back seat with the ponies, choosing instead to spend more time in the sawmill. That left John and I to act as ghillies with the ponies, week and week about. At six foot tall, with dark hair and blue eyes, John was a strapping lad who always had a smile on his face, and all the local girls promptly fell in love with him. I was rather less impressed because, quite apart from his 'Women shouldn't have jobs' comment, I'd seen the state he left the house in, which put me right off him.

When it had only been Owen and me living together, the housework had been just about manageable. Throughout the week we let the cottage get quite messy as we worked long hours and by the time we had come home, bathed, cooked dinner and walked the dogs, it was very late in the evening. So the housework was pushed on to the back burner and done at the weekend. Owen usually left on the Friday night to stay with his mother, but was always back by Sunday afternoon. That gave me the opportunity to clean the kitchen and bathroom and hoover the house. Owen rarely helped, but at least when he did, he made a decent job of it, though unfortunately those occasions were few and far between. However, he was usually on hand for an even more vital job: evicting big scary spiders from my bedroom. To my shame, while I can face fierce dogs, rutting stags, angry bulls and even snakes with equanimity, show me a spider and I at once dissolve into a jelly. So I would always send Owen into action with a cup to catch and remove the spider, while I kept well back, watching in horror from the doorway, poised for flight if the spider scuttled my way.

If Owen was pretty messy, John proved to be even worse and did no housework at all. He also regularly stole my fireside chair in the living room (a serious offence). Even after I had cleaned the whole house at the weekend, the place would always be a wreck again by Monday. The boys left plates of food lying around, trod crisps and dog food into the carpet and blocked the toilet with piles of paper. Not only was I doing the housework, I was also in charge of clearing the ashes from the grate, cutting the logs, chopping up the kindling and lighting the fire. I was sitting on the bathroom floor, Marigolds on and with my arm round the U-bend, trying to unblock the toilet again, when I came to an abrupt decision: enough was enough. I was sick to death of everyone presuming I should be the one to do the cleaning up, just because I was a woman, so I decided to go on strike.

The weekend came and went and I left everything exactly as it was. Henry the Hoover sat ignored in the corner, his happy face gazing reproachfully at me as I walked through the mess. Dirty dishes were piled at the side of the sink, the waste bucket was overflowing and the living room carpet was barely visible under the volume of rubbish. When the boys came back they glared at me as if all this was somehow my fault for shirking my duty.

By the end of the second week, the house was a bomb site with rubbish strewn everywhere. Every dish in the house had now been used and the sink had become blocked. Owen had eaten a curry the week before and the dishwater had now turned dark red with globules of fat bobbing around on the surface. A bowl of cornflakes lay abandoned on the sideboard, its curdled milk attracting flies. The whole place stank. 'Perfect!' I thought to myself. 'Not long now and the boys will finally see the error of their ways and help me clean up.' Of course I was completely wrong. They didn't even think twice about the housework. Instead, ignoring the mess, they simply plonked themselves down on the living-room chairs and played their PlayStations while I looked on in disgust.

As the third week drew to a close, I was beginning to despair. No one had lifted a finger and I was seriously considering going to live in a tent in the adjacent field. Doing the work myself was not an option. I was trying to prove a point and if I gave in now, I'd be stuck with cleaning up their rubbish for the rest of the year, so I was determined not to fold, even though by now the cereal bowl had grown its own supply of maggots, wriggling and squirming inside the bowl.

At eight o'clock on the Friday morning, there was a loud rap on the door. When I opened it, Dougie was standing there with a stern look on his face. 'The factor wants to see all three of you in the office right now.'

John appeared, bleary-eyed and half-dressed, as Owen and I put on our shoes. Throwing on a shirt, he jumped into the Land Rover beside us and we drove to the office in silence. We filed sheepishly into the office where the factor, Peter, was waiting for us. His normally ruddy complexion was now several shades further towards the puce end of the spectrum and it was clear that he was barely suppressing his fury about something. 'What the hell is this?' he boomed, pointing at a large wooden board he'd set up, on which were a number of photographs of the interior of our cottage, including close-ups of the rotten food in various stages of decomposition. The prints were very good quality; he had clearly used an expensive camera and had even zoomed in on the cereal bowl to show the fat white maggots crawling over what was left of the cornflakes.

Peter was a top wildlife artist, who sold his paintings in London for £25,000, and I did wonder if we were to be part of his next exhibition. He had obviously spent all of the previous afternoon creating this masterpiece and I have to say I was quite impressed. His display would not have looked out of place in an art gallery; he could have titled it 'Urban Decay' and charged people to come and view it.

'Well?' Peter said, folding his arms across his chest. 'I'm waiting for an explanation.'

Now was my great opportunity to explain the unfairness of the situation; the boys had been using me as their skivvy but I was no longer going to stand for it. Unfortunately I can be a bit of a giggler, especially when nervous, and as I opened my mouth to explain, a burst of laughter escaped from me instead. Once I'd started, I simply couldn't stop. Personally, I blamed his display board. So much effort had gone into this artistic masterpiece that I couldn't help but laugh. Did the factor of a large estate not have better things to do than make collages of filthy houses? At thirty-seven grand a year, it was a well-paid job and if this was all he had to do for it, perhaps I should consider a career change.

This was clearly not the reaction that Peter had been expecting and it merely fuelled his already considerable anger. He proceeded to let rip, shouting and cursing at us, although to be honest it was mostly at me, since I'd been the only one to burst out laughing. He ordered us to go back to the house immediately and clean it up. 'And if it gets in anything like that state again,' he said, 'you'll all be sacked on the spot.'

So Owen hoovered the house from top to bottom, John cleaned the living room and I was on kitchen duty, though I left the maggots for Owen to deal with; it had been his cereal after all, so I wasn't going to be touching it. Very soon the place was back to normal and I felt much better, breathing in the fresh scent of pine floor cleaner. The place did get messy again but at least the boys started to pull their weight a bit more and never again did we leave it to get into that awful state, though the weekly inspections that Peter made from then on may have had something to do with that. Even John managed to stir himself to tidy up and actually went as far as decorating his room, so perhaps my efforts had not been entirely in vain.

When I started my second year of college, I discovered that the original twenty-six students had now dwindled to just fourteen. The rest of them, including all of my closest friends from my group of eight, had either given up because they didn't like gamekeeping or found it too taxing, or else had already left to take on full-time jobs. As we had been split into three separate groups, I had never really got to know the people from the other groups, so now I hardly recognised anyone and suddenly felt even more isolated, but it did not lessen my determination to become the first woman to successfully complete the course. When I wasn't at college studying, I was back at the estate, working hard and gaining more experience.

I still worked as a ghillie during the deer-culling season, saddling up and leading the two awkward ponies up the hillside every morning. The long walk out from the stables to the remote parts of the estate where the stags tended to gather was hard for them and the weather that year didn't help, because almost every day was wet and blowing a gale. Sometimes I had to literally drag them for miles up the hill and by the end of each day my arms were like jelly. Going home was a different story. The reward for their day's work was a large dish of pony nuts and they couldn't wait to get at them, so despite the fourteen-stone stag on their backs, they ran down the path, barging and pushing to hurry me up.

At the start of the stag season and throughout the hind season we had plenty of opportunity to go out alone to practise our stalking. Without the presence of shooting guests, we left the ponies at home and took the quad bikes instead. Stalking alone was a great experience and a good chance for me to learn. Slowly but surely I learned to distinguish between the stronger and weaker animals, so that I could target old or sick deer or, when culling the hinds, those without calves. Dougie taught me to look for subtle differences in the condition of the body and the coat, and on the older deer, I learned to pay close attention to the antlers. The differences were far from obvious to a casual glance and it was difficult to distinguish them at first, but I gradually got the hang of it.

To prevent high winter mortality, from November to March we supplemented the deers' grazing with cobnuts. Hundreds of deer came down to the feeding grounds from miles around to await our arrival each morning. Dougie drove the Land Rover slowly along the road, while I sat in the back and poured the nuts onto the ground. As soon as we had passed, the deer would jostle and barge each other out of the way to get at the nuts. March was the best time to watch them at the feeding ground as that was the month when they cast their antlers. Without any other weapons, the stags then had to resort to boxing. Standing on their hind legs and rearing up to their full height, they would thump each other with their front legs until one of them gave way.

No sooner had the stags finished their bouts than the hares on the high pastures and moorland started boxing as well. It used to be thought that male hares did this to establish dominance and impress watching females. However, more recently it's been discovered that one of the boxers is always a female hare, either rebuffing the amorous advances of an overeager male or testing his suitability as a potential mate by his strength in a boxing match.

Early spring also marked the start of the heather burning, which had to be completed by mid-April to avoid risk to nesting birds, though we always finished well before that. The estate didn't have many grouse on the Middle or West beats, but we did have small populations of red and black grouse north of the Old Military Road – the A93 – that bisected the estate, and that was where most of the burning took place. Some estates took the greatest care when burning, creating perfect, blackened squares and rectangles on the hillsides by following the fire with water sprayers or fire beaters. However, Dougie didn't care much for perfect symmetry and often just let the fires burn themselves out, making use of the burns and water-filled ditches to naturally stop the blazes from spreading too far.

Dougie showed Owen and me how to do a controlled burn, though he warned us that there was always an element of risk, because if the wind got up unexpectedly, it could whip up a controlled fire into a raging inferno engulfing half the hillside. Controlled burning was done in the winter and early spring, when fires blazing out of control were much less likely, and fires were carefully planned, tended and watched, but wildfires on the moors were another story altogether. In dry spells in late spring and summer, wildfires were always possible, ignited by a lighting strike, a carelessly discarded cigarette butt, sunlight focused by a piece of broken glass, or deliberately lit by arsonists.

During my second year at Ardverikie, the spring of 2003 was the driest for many years and eight weeks of glorious sunshine without a drop of rain left the hillside tinder dry. The once soggy ground crackled underfoot, the burns dried up and our water supply started to dwindle. In those conditions wildfires were inevitable. The first fire broke out on Creag Meagaidh nature reserve, right next door to us on the northwestern side of the estate. I was really anxious and annoyed as it was very close to the lecking sight of the black grouse I'd been working so hard to protect. Nearly a mile of heather, bracken and regenerated moorland was ablaze. All the staff from several nearby estates turned up to help, along with the fire brigade and a team of helpful locals. We battled the fire for three hours using besoms (heather beaters) to bat out the flames and eventually our efforts paid off and we managed to put the fire out.

One of the police officers then walked towards us, brandishing two large, fire-blackened jerry cans he had found among the ashes at the edge of the burned area, proof that someone had started the fire deliberately. As I walked down to the road to collect my water bottle from the car, a man in a Land Rover drove past. He was hanging out of the open window, screaming and laughing as he pointed to the burned ground, from which smoke was still rising. A few minutes later he returned on the opposite side of the road, wound down his window again and pulled a face at me, still screeching like a lunatic. If he wasn't the arsonist, he was certainly acting like one, but by the time I could tell the police about him, he was long gone.

The second fire broke out on the Glenshero estate. The shepherd had been burning molinia and nardus, long tough grasses which, though Highland cattle will eat them, are not generally palatable to sheep. The wind was quite strong that day and his small 'controlled burn' quickly became a raging inferno. A wall of flames 100 feet across was advancing rapidly towards the march of our estate. In its path lay a large Scots pine plantation which we were determined to save. Our estate team was quickly deployed to help the firefighters and, along with thirty other people, we formed a solid wall of beaters in front of the advancing flames.

The burning heather turned the fire different shades of purple and pink as it crept towards us; in other circumstances it would have been beautiful but now it was terrifying. The heat was fearful and dense smoke, smuts and glowing embers filled the air around us. The faces of every one of us were blackened by the smoke with white streaks where beads of sweat had washed it away. All around me, I could hear the spit and crackle of the burning heather, counterpointed by the rhythmic crash of our metal fire beaters as we thrashed the ground. We finally managed to stop the flames just thirty feet from the edge of our plantation. The rest of the estate hadn't fared so well, and by now Glensherow's own forest was well and truly alight. Water-bombing helicopters turned up and made valiant efforts to stop the flames, but the fire was now completely out of control.

As I listened on the estate radio I heard a heart-rending report: a group of sheep had been surrounded by flames and their fleeces had ignited, burning them alive. A keeper also saw a hen pheasant sitting on her nest as the flames crept towards her; she only abandoned her eggs and flew off when her tail-feathers were already ablaze. 'It was like a phoenix rising from the ashes', he said, shaking his head in disbelief at the memory.

We were sent home at eight o'clock that evening, as it was getting dark and nothing else could be done, so we were forced to leave 4,500 acres to burn uncontrollably. The next morning, led by the firefighters and with the help of every available volunteer, we finally managed to extinguish the flames, but by then, thousands of acres had been reduced to a blackened, smoking wasteland.

A few weeks later, a large group of ramblers turned up on the Ardverikie estate and, despite the drought, one of them decided that it would be a good idea to set fire to a toilet roll. The result of that moronic action was another 1,000 acres destroyed. After two days, just as we at last succeeded in putting that fire out, the Dalwhinnie estate caught fire. Although Dalwhinnie also marched with Ardverikie, we had to leave them to fight their own fire because after two days of non-stop firefighting on our own estate, we were simply too exhausted to do any more.

For the rest of that black spring of 2003, fires kept raging throughout Scotland, resulting in the destruction of thousands more acres of forest and moorland, and the deaths of more wildlife and livestock, and of one unfortunate old lady who had been out for a walk and became trapped by the flames.

During my time at Ardverikie I'd got to know *The Monarch of the Glen* film crew reasonably well and often watched the actors from a distance. Different film sets had sprung up all over the estate, giving us something to explore on our days off. One day as we were passing the film crew on our way to feed the deer, a woman appeared from their Portakabin and came running towards the Land Rover, waving her arms to flag us down. Dougie skidded to a halt and wound down the window.

'Good morning,' she said. 'Could we have a word with Portia?'

Puzzled, I looked at Dougie for approval. He shrugged. 'Sure, speak to the lady. I'll go and feed the deer and pick you up again afterwards.'

Slightly disappointed – feeding the deer was always my favourite job of the day because it was such a great chance to see them up close – I watched Dougie drive away and then followed the lady into the Portakabin, wondering what on earth she wanted with me. She made me a cup of tea and then said, 'The script writers are thinking of adding a new character to the series and as one of Scotland's only female gamekeepers, we feel the series could base some of our story-lines on your life. What do you think of that?'

I nearly choked on my tea. 'You want to base a character on me? I can't believe it, but yes, that would be amazing.'

'The new character's name is Jessica Mackenzie – Jess for short – and she's going to be the gamekeeper's daughter. She'll be the new estate ghillie and the storyline will be based around her attempts to assert herself in a male-dominated working environment. So we'd just like to ask you about your own experiences, so we can make it as real as possible.'

For the rest of the morning I answered a stream of questions about my life and my work as a gamekeeper, while the script writers made copious notes. By the time Dougie returned to pick me up, I was bubbling with excitement. A few weeks later, the actor, Rae Hendrie, who was to play Jessica, turned up on the film set. Sitting in the Land Rover, we craned our necks to get a better glimpse of her as she walked along the beach by the loch while the cameras rolled. Slightly to my disappointment, she didn't look like me at all.

When the new series of *Monarch of the Glen* aired later that year, we all crowded into my cottage to watch it together. Many of the local people had been hired as extras and every time we saw one of our friends in the background, the whole room erupted in cheers and shouting. Jessica's storyline involved her being given the cold shoulder by the men on the estate. However, slowly but surely, she showed them that she was just as capable as they were and as the series progressed, the men came to accept her and she became a strong and self-assured character.

It was great fun to watch – I never missed an episode – but Jessica's story was only very loosely based on mine. I'd had my share of sexist comments both at college and at work. Some keepers were sceptical about my ability to do the job and one or two were downright hostile, not always the older keepers who might have been expected to be the most conservative. However, they had been in the minority and most of the men I encountered had judged me not on my gender, but on the work I did, which was all I ever asked.

When I began working in that all-male environment, I pledged to myself that I would keep my personal life separate from my working life, and would try not to get into any relationships with any gamekeepers or ghillies working on the same estate. 'Office romances' are always a potential source of conflict and that would only be exacerbated in a job that involved long, often anti-social hours and sometimes required me to share accommodation with my fellow workers. So I made that decision and, though I was good friends with many male colleagues, if any of them began showing signs of wanting something more than friendship, I gently but firmly explained why that was not going to happen.

Almost all of them accepted it, but one particularly persistent and thick-skinned individual was so convinced of his own irresistible charm that he seemed to regard 'No' as just part of the courtship ritual. I soon got to know what the red deer must feel like because he was stalking me every bit as assiduously as we tracked them. Things finally came to a head when, after again refusing to take 'No' for an answer, he burst into my cottage and when I locked myself in my bedroom to get away from him, he broke down the door. That caveman approach might have worked with some women but I was definitely not one of them. I put any amorous activity right out of his mind with a well-placed kick, and then with the help of one of my less Neanderthal workmates, we hustled the intruder down the stairs and threw him out. He finally got the message and did not return.

The rest of the year flew by and before I knew it, I'd reached the end of my college course, though it finished with a huge anticlimax. I'd been looking forward to a grand finale, an enormous party where we'd all get very drunk, tell each we'd always keep in touch and then make our tear-drenched, hungover departures the next day. However, in the event there was no leaving 'do' at all because people left in ones and twos over the course of about six weeks, whenever they'd finished their coursework. Even my hopes of making the grand exit from Thurso I'd planned – gunning Brum's accelerator and roaring off in a blizzard of dust, music blaring, hood down, with the wind in my hair – were dashed. Disaster struck when my gear stick snapped off in my hand. As a result I had to make a rather less glorious exit, beginning a seven-hour journey back to Aberdeen on the bus while poor Brum was loaded on to a tow truck and carted away to be repaired. There was a graduation ceremony at the college later in the year, but by then I was too busy with work to attend.

However, it wasn't all bad news, because I passed my final exams with flying colours and although I wasn't the first woman to start the gamekeeping and wildlife management course, I was the first one ever to complete it. Once I'd qualified, my parents came to accept my choice of career, although I don't think they ever fully embraced it. They only ever wanted what was best for me and had been hoping I'd choose a much better-paid career, but of course they were happy that I was doing something I loved and were as supportive and loving as they've been throughout my life. They visited me a couple of times at Ardverikie, bringing much-needed supplies of food and clothing with them, and often slipped me some money when times were hard.

Sadly, the end of the course also meant the end of my work placement at Ardverikie. I knew I'd miss the estate and my workmates there, and there was also a more practical cause for regret: gamekeeping jobs were very thin on the ground at the time, so I was understandably worried about my future. However, while packing up my belongings, I took a call from a reporter for *The Field* magazine. They had heard that I was the first woman to pass the gamekeeping course and wanted to write an article about me. They also wanted to do a photoshoot and since it was an expensive glossy magazine, they didn't want me dressed in blood-stained, muddy and ripped tweeds. So I gave them my measurements and a week later a huge box from the Really Wild Clothing Company was delivered, containing long leather boots, tight moleskin trousers, a shirt and a leather waistcoat. Unwrapping it all, I figured I would be one sexy gamekeeper.

A few days later the photographer turned up at the cottage and together we toured the estate in search of good locations. He made me change clothes about six times and photographed me in a variety of different poses, standing with my rifle and my dog by my side, sitting on the rocks by the river and running along the hillside with Mint.

The magazine article took over a month to appear and, knowing that Dougie always got a copy of *The Field* delivered, I didn't bother to order one, reckoning I could simply read his instead. On publication day he turned up at the cottage early with a big smile on his face, said, 'Well, lassie, have you seen it then?' and thrust the magazine into my hands. I'd been expecting a couple of paragraphs and a small photo on an inside page, but there I was on the front cover, standing with one foot on a rock, my rifle slung over my shoulder and my dog at my feet. It was captioned 'Move over Mellors [the gamekeeper in *Lady Chatterley's Lover*]: the rise and rise of the girl gamekeeper', and there was a three-page spread inside. Now my parents really were proud of what I'd done and started telling everyone about it!

Every newspaper in Scotland now wanted to get in touch but after a few days of doing countless photoshoots and interviews, the media circus moved on and I turned my hand to something much more important: finding a job. I'd barely started on that when I got a phone call from the Countryside Alliance. They were planning a pro-hunting demonstration in Parliament Square in London, had seen the article in *The Field* and asked if I'd be willing to join the demonstration and take part in a photoshoot.

I was a supporter of fox hunting because, as anyone who has tried to keep animals without 'fox-proofing' their quarters will soon discover, foxes are relentless predators. They take lambs, chickens, grouse, pheasants, partridges, quail, ducks, geese and also family pets like rabbits and guinea pigs. Gamekeepers and farmers shoot a lot of foxes, but they never get as many as they would wish, and hunting was a useful additional control on fox numbers. Hunting them with hounds is a quick way of killing them because the hounds are trained to go for the fox's throat or the nape of its neck and a quick shake will then kill them. Animal-rights activists talk about the stress that foxes suffer when being hunted, but apart from shooting them the only other way to reduce their numbers is by snaring them, and to me that seems even more stressful for the animal, held helpless in a snare for several hours until the keeper comes along to put it out of its misery.

Twenty-four hours later I flew down to London. Parliament Square was packed with hundreds of hunt supporters who had set up loads of tents and stalls, and after the photoshoot, I wandered around the crowd, looking for someone interesting to talk to. Noticing a very jolly-looking, dark-haired woman sitting alone in a deckchair, I decided to stop for a chat. I couldn't have chosen a more interesting person. Her name was Caroline Tisdall and as well as being a board member of the Countryside Alliance, she spoke several languages and was a much-travelled art historian, journalist, film-maker, writer, conservationist and philanthropist who, with her long-term partner, Dutch billionaire Paul van Vlissingen, also ran two sporting estates, one at Letterewe in Scotland and the other at Conholt Park in Hampshire.

After chatting for twenty minutes or so, Caroline asked me if I'd like to share a bottle of wine with her. She filled two plastic cups and then said, 'If you're looking for a job, although we pretty much have a full stack of stalkers and gamekeepers at our estates, I'll phone Paul and see if we need any extra help.'

While she chatted to him on the phone, I did my best to polish off the wine. 'I have some good news,' she said, when she'd hung up. 'We need a ghillie at Letterewe for three months from the beginning of September and if you do well in that job, you can come and work for us down in Conholt for a month or two after that to help with the pheasants. I'm only sorry we don't have a permanent job to offer you, but at least this will help you get a start. It'll be a bit more experience and something to add to your CV.'

I didn't have to think twice and accepted her offer on the spot. However, as it was still only May, I now found myself with three months to spare. A college friend, Mark, who had been on a placement at Creag Meagaidh, the neighbouring estate to Ardverikie, had also just finished his course, and since we both now had nowhere to live we decided to rent a house together until September. We took a short lease on a pretty, 'chocolate-box' cottage, with white-painted walls and a big open fireplace. It was about a mile down the road from Ardverikie and nestled into a steep, rocky hillside, surrounded by pine forest and heather moorland with the river running within a few yards of the front door. We decorated the cottage with deer antlers and hunting pictures and made it really homely.

At thirty-six, Mark was unusually old for a student gamekeeper but he'd run a game-dealing business for quite a few years before reaching the point where he was ready for a career change. Dark-haired and dark-skinned, he was only five foot five, an inch shorter than me, but he had a wiry strength that belied his small size and an offbeat sense of humour that made him great fun to work with.

Mark was a one-off and was constantly getting into trouble with his bosses and sometimes with the police, but he could charm anyone – he could have sold sand to the Arabs – so although he was often on his 'final warning' or 'last chance', somehow he always seemed to find a way to get another one.

He was an obsessive collector of stuffed birds, including a hawk and a tawny owl, and feathers, bird bones and skulls; his bedroom looked like a shrine to death. He was also a keen angler and although I'd gone sea- and river-fishing before, he was the person who really taught me how to do it and I'm forever in his debt for that. However, as we'd had our work placements on different estates, I had not spent that much time with him before we moved in together and didn't realise quite what I was taking on.

When Mark was still living and working in Creag Meagaidh, my new – and, as it turned out, very temporary – boyfriend, Skye, and I had decided to pay him a visit one night. With drunken logic, we figured that Mark would be overjoyed when we turned up at his house at midnight, uninvited. We knew he was there as his car was parked outside and when he didn't answer our knock on the door, my boyfriend threw a stone at his bedroom window, which ricocheted off with a loud crack. When this still failed to draw his attention we decided he must be in a very deep sleep; the possibility he was ignoring us, or lying low, hoping we'd go away, didn't occur to either of us. After all, who wouldn't want a midnight wake-up call from a pair of wandering drunks?

Mark had left a window open on the ground floor, so I climbed in and opened the front door to let my boyfriend in. We then decided to surprise Mark in his bedroom: imagine his joy at seeing his two college buddies turning up at his house unannounced in the middle of the night. The lights were off and we tiptoed upstairs, straining our eyes into the darkness and giggling as the stairs creaked loudly when we trod on them. I turned the handle of his bedroom door and flicked on the light to be greeted by the sight of Mark sitting up in bed, half-naked and half-asleep, pointing a shotgun at the pair of us.

'For fuck's sake,' he said. 'What do you think you're doing? I thought you were burglars, I could have blown your heads off.'

'Good job I put the light on then,' I said.

The modest wage that the estate had been paying me on my work placement had covered my basic living costs but nothing more, and without it I was now completely broke. Mark was in the same state, so when we moved in together, we lived hand to mouth, taking whatever odd jobs we could find to bring in a little cash, but surviving on £75 a week between us. However, at least £40 of that was going on Mark's partying. That left us with just £35 for utility bills and food. The trouble was that to get to the nearest shop involved a thirty-mile round trip and cost so much on petrol that it didn't leave us enough money for a week's supply of food. When we came home with the groceries the food would only last three days if we were lucky, and sometimes even less.

After countless arguments, since giving up partying was apparently never going to be an option, we decided that it wouldn't be unethical to augment our meagre diet by raiding nature's larder. We had to face facts, we were hungry and there just wasn't enough food. Even my poor dog, Mint, was being fed on cheap £1 bags of mixer biscuits and I didn't have anything to mix them with. Luckily there was a stream outside our house so every morning and night, when the fish always seemed to be more active, Mark and I went out to fish for trout and came back fully laden. At seven to eight inches long, the fish weren't huge, but if we caught about twelve of them it was enough for a meal for the three of us: Mark, me and Mint. We put them under the grill, selecting the biggest ones for ourselves and I deboned the remainder and mixed them in with the dog biscuits for Mint to eat.

After doing this for a week or so, we decided to supplement Mint's diet with some rabbits. Some of the local farmers had given us permission to shoot vermin like rabbits, foxes and pigeons on their land, so we shot a few rabbits and took them home for the dog to eat. However, I didn't want Mint becoming infested with parasites so as a precaution, I always skinned, deboned and cooked them first. I froze most of the meat for future use but Mint was a young, energetic dog who needed lots of food, so we very quickly ran out and had to go back for more.

One day Mark shot a rabbit but didn't bother to skin it, claiming that 'the fur will just fall off in the pot'. He put the dirty, mud-spattered rabbit into a pan full of boiling water, then told me to keep an eye on it, while he went to make a telephone call. It was slightly too big for the pan and despite giving it a good prod down with a wooden spoon, it kept bobbing back up to the surface with its ears poking out. As I stirred it around, I felt like Glenn Close's crazed character in *Fatal Attraction* boiling the pet rabbit on the hob. After fifteen minutes the rabbit finally sank lower in the water and I replaced the pan lid, though its ears were still trapped on the outside. A foul smell of wet rabbit fur filled the kitchen as it cooked, so I opened the door for some fresh air.

Half an hour later I took the pan off the boil and carried it outside to drain off the water. Removing the lid, I was surprised to see that the rabbit's fur was still completely intact and hadn't 'just fallen off' as Mark had claimed it would. The water was a horrible congealing brown colour and it stank to high heaven, and when I used my knife to cut the rabbit open, I realised that Mark hadn't even gutted it, so its stomach contents had now completely ruined the meat. Mint took one look at it and refused to eat it and I couldn't say I blamed her.

I dumped the pan outside the door and left it there for Mark to clean up since it had been his idea to cook it in its fur. Over the next two weeks it became a stinking, writhing mass of decay, and when he got sick of the smell, Mark gave the pan a kick and sent it spinning into the ditch. Unsurprisingly, neither of us volunteered to rescue it and it's probably still there today.

Mark had written off his previous car, a Subaru, by crashing it into a pond. Somehow he had managed to veer off a completely straight stretch of road, smash through a deer fence and come to rest in a pond. He then got his hands on an old banger, a rusting red Lada, to get to and from the shops and transport the booty from our poaching trips.

Although fish and a few rabbits were enough to sustain Mint, we decided we needed some venison to keep us going.

We justified this by telling ourselves, 'One for the pot never hurt anyone; it's the gangs of commercial poachers who cause the trouble.' So one morning we got up at 3 a.m., grabbed a cup of coffee, picked up a rifle and a freshly sharpened knife, threw a groundsheet and a camouflage net into the boot to cover the animal should we be lucky enough to shoot one, and then set off to bag ourselves a stag. The first rays of the summer sunshine were starting to break through as we drove into the forest and although we were dressed in full camo gear with hats pulled down as far as they would go so no one would recognise us, I couldn't help wishing Mark had chosen a quieter colour for his car, because the bright-red Lada stood out like a sore thumb.

We drove around for miles before chancing on a group of fifteen stags in a field. I wound the window down and Mark loaded his .243 rifle, laid the barrel on the wing mirror and, breathing in to steady himself, took the shot. The echoes thundered around the glen, tearing apart the early-morning silence. The deer leapt up, took a few steps and then dropped down dead as the rest of the herd scattered in fright. Mark and I whooped in delight, high-fived each other and then jumped out of the car. Unsheathing the knife, I began speed-gralloching the stag but Mark didn't even wait for me to finish before he began dragging it to the car. The stag slithered and bumped over the grassy knolls as I walked alongside, still disembowelling it as we went along, so we left a steaming trail of entrails behind us but made it back to the car in super-quick time. We chucked it into the boot, slung the camouflage netting over it and then sped away in a cloud of dust. The whole process had only taken a couple of minutes and I couldn't believe how easy it had been.

We hung the deer up in the trees about a hundred yards into the forest from the cottage, just in case the police showed up, and then butchered it, first skinning, jointing and boning it, and finally mincing the offcuts. Mark had learned butchery while running his game business down south and he taught me how to do it. I learned quickly and after the first week, Mark left me to do most of the butchery while he did the cooking. It was a fair deal because I couldn't cook to save my life – when I tried, it invariably ended in disaster – whereas Mark was a trained chef and produced delicious venison stews, burgers, sausages and roasts.

When we ran out of meat, we went poaching again and, since we couldn't live on meat alone, we began selling the spare venison to a couple of local butchers and restaurants who didn't ask questions about the source of the meat. We used the money to buy other food and booze. As the weather grew hotter, we had to stop hanging the deer carcasses in the forest, and hung them in the bathroom instead, suspended from the shower rail and dripping blood into the bottom of the tub. That came to an abrupt end when the rail gave way under the weight of a carcass and came crashing down. Looking back now, I'm horrified at the way I closed my mind to the immorality and illegality of what I was doing, not to mention the potential consequences for my career and my future life, but somehow I was always able to convince myself that it was just a harmless bit of 'food for free'.

When we went out poaching, the deer soon started

recognising the Lada as the source of previous gunfire, so it became harder and harder to shoot them in easy locations and sometimes we had to try new areas, which was always a risky plan. One day, after a particularly unproductive poaching trip, we were heading back along the main road towards the cottage and as we rounded a corner, we saw a stag standing in the middle of the road. After ten seconds of indecision we decided to risk it and shot the stag. We left the car in the middle of the road while we retrieved the carcass, taking a chance that at six in the morning, even though it was fully light, no one else would come driving by in the time it took us to gralloch the stag. We were lucky and managed to stay under the radar that day, though we left a huge bloodstain in the middle of the road. It didn't rain for a few weeks afterwards and the bloodstain stubbornly refused to fade; every time we passed it in the car we exchanged guilty looks.

One morning Mark realised he'd run out of rolling tobacco. Hamish, the owner of the cottage we rented, had gone out for the day and had absent-mindedly locked the barrier, a long metal pole spanning the width of the drive-way, just off the main road. The solid metal pole could not be pushed aside, we were on the wrong side of it and the gap between the end of the barrier and the wall wasn't big enough to fit a car through ... or so I thought, but such was Mark's need for tobacco that nothing was going to stop him from reaching the shop. 'Jump out,' he said, then revved up the engine and drove towards the gap. It was clearly too small and unsurprisingly, the car got wedged between the gatepost and the barrier but that didn't deter Mark at all. With the engine screaming and smoke pouring from the burning clutch, he kept slowly edging forward, while with a sickening, grinding crunch of metal, the end of the barrier pole gouged a slit right along the bodywork, opening it up like a tin of Spam.

As I looked on in disbelief, the car exited the gap. Mark jumped out to survey the damage but then merely shrugged and said, 'Hop in.' Completely unfazed both by the damage and the wind howling through the gap in the car's doors and bodywork, he drove us to Kingussie to get his tobacco. Everything was going well until we got pulled over by a policeman who then marched us into the police station and it turned out that it was not the state of the Lada they wanted to talk about. 'We know you've been poaching deer,' the stern-looking station sergeant said. 'Stop doing it or you will be arrested and prosecuted.'

Mark spluttered a few feeble denials but I stayed quiet, knowing that nothing we said was going to convince the police that we were innocent. The sergeant then fixed me with his gaze. 'And it would be a real shame if you lost your firearms licence after training for two years to earn it.'

We still didn't admit anything, but despite our bravado in the police station, I was horror-struck at how close my stupidity had come to costing me the career I'd dreamed of. Had I been arrested and charged with poaching, I would never have been employed on an estate again. I did not need to be told twice; I never did it again. During our brief poaching career we had sold a lot of the meat to buy other kinds of food and had feasted on bacon and eggs, ciabatta bread, ice cream, olives and smoked salmon. Now we were back to living hand to mouth and we ended up arguing almost every day, mostly over money.

Not long afterwards, Hamish turned up with a friend I hadn't seen before. He had blond straggly hair and a rough, weathered face but there was no obvious reason for the bad feeling I at once had about him. They were sitting around drinking and in a quiet moment I asked Hamish who the new guy was. 'Just a friend of mine,' he said. 'He's just been released from jail.'

I left it there for the moment but later that evening I cornered Mark and asked him why the new guy had been in jail. 'Oh, he did ten years for murder,' he said, as matter-of-fact as if the guy had been given a speeding ticket. Our poverty and the trouble with the police had been hard enough to deal with, but a convicted murderer as a house guest was taking things to a whole new level. That was it; I knew I had to get out of there. Fortunately it was almost time to go to Letterewe. I had thought that would be a completely fresh start for me, but when I mentioned my job to Mark, he immediately applied to work as a ghillie at Letterewe as well. I had mixed feelings when I discovered that he'd been accepted and would be working on the same team as me, but I crossed my fingers and hoped for the best.

Just before I started work at Letterewe, Caroline phoned and asked me to go down to their other estate, Conholt Park in Hampshire, for a couple of weeks, to take a friend's sixteen- and eighteen-year-old sons out stalking. When I got there, the head keeper, Chris, showed me around the estate and then introduced me to the rest of the staff. Conholt House was a beautiful Regency building, its high-ceilinged rooms filled with antique furnishings, tapestries and paintings. It had a walk-in gun room lined with top-of-the-range rifles and shotguns, and a trophy room where the evidence of successful hunting trips on the Conholt and Letterewe estates – hundreds of sets of antlers – covered every inch of the walls.

The house was surrounded by beautiful parkland, studded with massive ancient yew and cedar trees, and the gardens included a maze shaped like a giant foot, winter and secret gardens, a fern dell, a walled garden with a flower cartwheel, a berry wall and an orchard. The estate was only 2,500 acres – tiny by Highland standards – but it had a very high-quality pheasant and partridge shoot. Thousands of pheasants, reared for the shoot, wandered the woods, fields and hills, and there were abundant roe, fallow and muntjac deer in the surrounding woodland.

I'd thought my Scots accent might be a problem when I went there – you can't put subtitles under real-life conversations – but in fact most of the staff had also worked on Paul and Caroline's Scottish estate, Letterewe, at one time or another, so they were quite used to Scots accents and quite accepting of them, though I did have to tone down a few words so they could understand them. However, I did have one or two surprises in store for some of them. I took the chef stalking one day, shot a deer and gralloched it, and then took it in the larder and cut it up. The chef watched all this, open-mouthed and wide-eyed, and then said, 'Portia, you should come with a government health warning!'

My living accommodation had once been the village post office but was now a cosy, single-roomed cottage with wood-panelled walls, and I soon settled in and got to work. However, although I managed to find the two boys some roe and muntjac deer to shoot, I never seemed to chance across any fallow deer, and in the end I enlisted the help of Dave, a seasoned stalker who had spent many years at Conholt Park. He gave a sympathetic smile when I told him about my struggle to find fallow deer. 'They prefer very dense cover and only emerge when they feel completely safe,' he said. 'And the vast majority only appear about fifteen minutes before nightfall, so with such a small window of opportunity, you have to know exactly where to go in order to find them.'

Luckily Dave knew all the hotspots and was happy to share his knowledge with me, so before taking the boys out, I went stalking with him. About an hour before sundown we made our way across the parkland towards a thicket of yew and hazel coppice. As we walked along, a pitiful squeak alerted me to a little ball of fur lying in the short grass. The poor thing cried out as we surrounded it. 'What is it?' I said.

'A baby polecat.'

There were no polecats in Scotland – they'd been hunted to extinction by gamekeepers in the nineteenth century – so as I'd lived in Scotland all my life, I'd never seen one before, let alone one as young as this. Its mother must have been moving it between nest sites and had dropped it, no doubt because a predator had appeared and frightened her into abandoning her youngster. Not wanting to alarm it and assuming the mother would come back for it, we moved off to find some fallow deer.

Dave's local knowledge paid off because exactly fifteen minutes before dark, a herd of fallow deer emerged from the dense undergrowth, warily scenting the air for danger. The first deer jumped out onto the grass and leapt in the air, kicking its legs out hard behind it. It ran around in circles for a few moments and was then joined by another two. Dave, who'd already set up his rifle for the shot, scanned the group for a suitable target. With lightning precision, he took aim and fired twice, knocking down two of the deer. The rest of the herd scattered, crashing through the undergrowth into the safety of the forest.

As it had only taken five minutes, there was still just enough time to find some more. Slinging his rifle on his back, Dave told me to follow him quickly around the side of the hill. He took such huge strides that I had to start jogging to keep pace with them, while the bipod attachment of my rifle banged into my spine, but the sun was going down fast and Dave was a man on a mission.

Minutes later we reached a small clearing in the woods and got down on all fours, crawling through the long grass towards a yew tree. Together we slithered along the ground and stopped at the base of the tree. 'There's usually fallow here,' Dave whispered as he peered through his binoculars at the empty clearing. We waited a few minutes and just as I was giving up hope, a fallow buck appeared.

'Shoot that one,' Dave said after studying it for a moment. Steadying myself, I breathed out, paused and then took the shot. The fallow buck jumped, ran in a circle and then dropped down dead. The light was fading fast and I rushed to gralloch the buck in the half-light, while Dave retrieved the vehicle. Pulling the carcass down to the dirt track, we loaded it onto the back of the pick-up then drove back to get the other two that Dave had shot. After gralloching and loading everything into the vehicle, Dave drove back while I made my way back to my cottage across the fields.

A few hours had passed since we'd seen the young pole-cat and I was surprised to find it still sitting on the grass in exactly the same place. The only difference was that now it was freezing cold and starting to go stiff. I realised it was too late now for its mother to retrieve it. Feeling sorry for the little creature, I picked her up and placed her in my pocket. Back at the house I christened her 'Bandit' and warmed her gently with a hot-water bottle. When she had thawed out a little, I tried to pick her up, but that resulted in a screaming fit. She screeched in anger and sank her tiny needle-like fangs into my index finger, causing me to start screaming as well. Although tiny and unable to walk, her teeth clearly worked perfectly well and now she'd established her boundaries, I decided to respect her personal space.

As she flapped her pudgy little limbs at me I used a spoon to feed her Bounce meaty chunks, keeping my fingers well clear of those fangs. Once fed, she fell into a deep sleep and I managed to pick her up using two half-used kitchen rolls like a set of chopsticks; there was no way on earth I was chancing those teeth again. I gently placed her inside an old birdcage, covered her with scraps of torn-up toilet roll to keep her warm and slipped a hot-water bottle under the cage to help maintain her body heat. She was a wild creature and I knew that when she had grown big enough to fend for herself, I would have to teach her to hunt for her food and then release her back into the wild, but for now it was enough to keep her alive and give her a temporary home.

However, my time at Conholt was nearing an end and I already had my flight booked to go back to the Highlands; the only problem was that British Airways did not welcome polecats on board their planes, not even as hand luggage, though for the life of me I couldn't think why. They were willing to take her in the hold in a suitable container, but they wanted to charge me over £200 for the privilege, which I just couldn't afford. Luckily for me, a student gamekeeper, Tony, was due to drive up to Letterewe a couple of weeks later and he kindly offered to look after Bandit and then take her up there for me. Although he was due to work on a different beat, it would be easy enough to meet up in town to hand her over. So having cleaned out Bandit and left Tony with plenty of food for her, I thanked him profusely and flew north, ready to start work at Letterewe.

5

THE LAST GREAT WILDERNESS

The Letterewe estate, among the white sand beaches, lochs and spectacular mountain ranges of Wester Ross in Scotland's far north-west, just 'over the sea from Skye', was described by the doyen of fell-walkers, Alfred Wainwright, as 'the last great wilderness of Scotland'. The estate contains what is officially the most remote place in Britain, reckoned by its distance – almost seven miles – from the nearest road, and as a cautionary note to hikers, Wainwright added, only half-jokingly, 'Weaklings and novices must expect to perish. Once committed, there is no easy escape.'

The sprawling, 90,000-acre estate included beautiful lochs, pine, oak and birch forests, open moorlands and steep mountains rising to the majestic summit of Slioch, domi-nating its surroundings like the stone keep of some giant's castle. Letterewe was home to golden eagles, merlins and peregrine falcons, red grouse and ptarmigan, badgers, pine martens, otters, wild goats and large herds of red deer. The main house – the Lodge – on the eastern shore of Loch Maree, was accessible only by boat. There were no paved roads anywhere on the estate and the outlying lodges were very remote: Carnmore was eight miles away from the main house on the other side of the mountain and Larachantivore was seventeen miles away.

Mark hitched a lift to the Lodge with Hamish, while I drove to Letterewe along the 'Destitution Road' – a road built as a make-work scheme in the 1840s, after blight destroyed the potato crop and brought famine to the Highlands, just as it did in Ireland. To prevent a massive death toll from starvation, labourers were employed to build the road in return for a daily ration of twenty-four ounces of oatmeal for men – soon reduced to sixteen ounces – twelve for women and eight for children. People could barely survive on such rations and malnutrition and destitution saw one third of the population eventually disappear from the Highlands, never to return.

The bright sunshine helped to dispel those black thoughts as I turned off the Destitution Road towards the jetty on the south shore of Loch Maree, where I met up with Mark. Leaving my car by the jetty, we piled our luggage into the estate launch, piloted by one of the gardeners, for the fifteen-minute voyage across the loch. The whitewashed Lodge was clearly visible on the far shore and though it was turreted, it seemed much less grandiose and far more welcoming than many Scottish estate houses.

We disembarked at the long pier next to the boathouse.

'You can stand on the pier and fish for trout if you're brave enough to face the midges,' the gardener said.

There are said to be two main reasons why people choose not to visit Scotland for a holiday: one is the weather and the other the midges ... not necessarily in that order. There are thirty varieties of midge, half of which don't bite people, and nor do the males of any species, but the female midges, or *Culicoides impunctatus* to give them their proper name, more than make up for the rest. They are only a millimetre long and live just a few weeks, but in that time they carry out an estimated 90 per cent of all biting attacks on humans.

They're less active during high winds and heavy rain, and they only appear between April and October, so winter visitors may wonder what all the fuss is about, but in spring and summer, watch out! You encounter them all over the Highlands and Islands, but they were particularly fearsome at Letterewe. Jungle Formula insect repellent offers some protection but the only thing that really keeps them at bay is wearing a veil like a beekeeper's helmet; it looks ridiculous, but those driven demented by midges are usually past caring about that. However, Mark and I had brought our rods and tackle so, midges or no midges, we planned to spend many of our evenings fishing for trout from the pier.

Before showing us where we'd be living, the gardener gave us a guided tour of the Lodge. No expense had been spared in furnishing the rooms with antiques and thick-pile tartan carpets. There were stags' heads mounted on the walls and blazing open fires in every room when guests were staying. Our own accommodation, discreetly screened from the main house by trees, was more modest – a low, whitewashed cottage – but we were overjoyed to find that it had an almost unimaginable luxury for this wild and remote area: satellite TV. Highland cattle and hill ponies grazed peacefully in the adjacent fields, flicking their manes and tails to ward off the plagues of midges.

The Gulf Stream washes this coast, giving it a more gentle climate than might be expected this far north and as proof of that, there was a large cherry tree in our garden, laden with ripe fruit. I spent the next half an hour or so gorging myself on black cherries while the juice ran down my chin. By the time I had finished, my hands and face were stained black from the juice and as it proved almost impossible to wash off, the evidence of my greed was written all over my face.

We then discovered that the Lodge had a large orchard of apple, plum and pear trees. Everything seemed to be ripe there as well, so Mark and I stuffed ourselves with yet more fruit while clouds of butterflies filled the air around us, feeding on the rotting plums which covered the ground. I laughed as a peacock butterfly landed on the end of Mark's nose, closed its wings and settled there, while Mark went cross-eyed trying to see round it.

Behind the Lodge there was an open-air swimming pool and as we hadn't brought swimming costumes, we swam in our underwear. Drawn by the fresh meat on display, clouds of midges hung around the edges of the pool, eyeing us hungrily as they waited for an opportunity to bite our exposed flesh, and we became very good at diving under the water to escape their unwelcome attentions.

We had a few days to settle in before starting work and I used the time to explore the shores of the loch and take a few walks up into the surrounding hills, getting my bearings. I fought my way through beds of waist-high bracken, sweat pouring from me in the fierce heat of the sun. Triggered by that heat, gorse seeds were exploding from their pods like gunfire. The purple-flowered heather was just beginning to come into bloom, and on the boggier ground the bright, star-shaped flowers of bog asphodels had mellowed from their spring yellow to a golden orange colour that gilded the moorland, while the white tufts of cotton grass were swaying rhythmically in the breeze. As I climbed higher, I heard the drum beat of a snipe's wings and grouse clacking their warning calls, while others burst from the heather in an explosion of wings. Far ahead of me I caught glimpses of the herds of red deer browsing among the tough moor grasses on the highest hillsides.

Small hill lochs and tarns dotted the moors, the still waters perfectly mirroring the sky overhead, while their black, peaty margins were marked with the footprints of scores of moorland birds. The one-note piping of golden plovers on their nests echoed eerily over the moor while overhead the liquid, bubbling call of the curlew was counterpointed by the 'oowoo-whoop-whoop' of lapwings in their ragged, tumbling flight. I sat down on a rock and just drank it all in; this was what I had dreamed of as I gazed at those distant mountains when I was a child. Now I was living my dream.

If I needed further proof of that, as I strolled around the edge of the loch early the next morning, my eye was caught by a movement in the sky and, looking up, I saw an osprey in a near-vertical dive, barely seeming to slow as it hit the water in a flurry of spray. A moment later it rose and flapped slowly away, struggling under the weight of the fish impaled on its talons.

If I was living the dream, the midges at Letterewe continued to try and make it more of a nightmare. They were like some kind of biblical plague; everywhere you went clouds of them followed you, trying to get a bite. We'd packed some Deet, the most potent insect repellent money can buy, and applied a liberal coating to our faces, but hordes of midges got stuck to it and our eyes, nostrils and mouths filled up with the pesky little critters, who simply would not leave us alone. We upgraded to the midge nets like beekeeper's helmets, which seemed to do the job, but of course the midges still found holes in our clothing to squeeze through. For some reason they seemed to particularly like me and each night when I took off my clothes, I would find my skin peppered with bites.

Even inside the house we were not completely safe as there was a half-inch gap under the door and a small air vent in the kitchen. Tracking the carbon dioxide in our exhaled breath, the midges crawled through the gaps and then hunted us down. There was very little we could do to defend ourselves except cover up as much as possible, and since midges have a fairly short lifespan very soon a half-inch thick layer of dead midges built up on all the windowsills, ledges and floors within our home. As fast as we cleaned them off, they piled up again.

The estate factor told us that it was a particularly bad year for midges. They had a midge trap on the go 24/7, attracting them by pumping out carbon dioxide. They crawled in, got stuck in the midge bag and couldn't get back out again, but though the trap caught hundreds of thousands of midges, it didn't seem to make the slightest difference to the numbers that were still preying on us.

Midges are very attracted to lights and fly towards the bulb, incinerating themselves in the process. One night Mark and I carelessly left the light on in the living room and he left his dinner plate on the couch below the light. When I came through for breakfast the next morning I was about to curse him for leaving a plate of food on the couch when I realised that it was actually a plate of burnt midge corpses that had fallen on to the plate, piling it high. Hardly believing my eyes, I picked up the plate and dumped the mound of dead midges into the bin.

We started work on the Monday morning when the stalker, David, a tall, ginger-haired man with a lined and weather-beaten face that spoke of a life spent out of doors, gave us our first job: to go and find the herd of hill ponies which, as had been the custom for centuries, were turned out at the end of the previous hunting season and left to run wild on the 10,000 acres of hills and mountainsides above us, until the new season began.

Armed with a map, a packed lunch and a flask of tea, we set off up the long mountain path. It was a warm, sunny day and the insects were out in force. Horseflies and midges buzzed around our ears, tormenting us relentlessly as we crossed and recrossed the hillsides without seeing a trace of the ponies, but in late afternoon we at last spotted them through our binoculars, grazing on a hillside above us. We breathed a sigh of relief as David had given us strict instructions not to come back without them and neither of us wanted to risk his wrath. He was very friendly and very good with the guests, but he was also extremely quick-tempered – a typical red-head, in fact – and if things weren't done exactly the way he wanted them, there would be trouble. He liked his dram as well which was a bit of an asset for a keeper or stalker, because all the guests were on holiday and wanted to drink whisky – that's what you do in Scotland – and they would almost get upset if you wouldn't have a dram with them, not that it ever happened to me, because I never needed to be asked twice.

The herd consisted of twelve ponies, all of different colours and sizes, but David had told us to grab a black pony, Archie, the dominant male. We put a head collar on him and one of the other ponies and began leading them down the hill towards Letterewe. The others followed reluctantly, dragging their heels and snorting angrily; after six months of doing nothing they were clearly not happy at the prospect of having to start work again. Finally arriving back around dinnertime, we turned the ponies loose in the field near the Lodge and got the tack ready for the following day.

The next morning, after saddling up two of the ponies, we followed David and the estate's first paying guests of the new stalking season up the hill. The Letterewe estate was split into four different beats, each managed by a different stalker and two ghillies during the season. Our beat, Letterewe itself, covered 10,000 acres, but that was relatively small compared to the other three beats. David had a cull target of thirty stags, all to be shot by paying guests before the end of the season.

Each morning, David and the guests left three-quarters of an hour ahead of us, while Mark and I tacked up the ponies and then followed them up the hillside. This worked well for the first few weeks while we got our bearings, learning the best ways to navigate around the hillsides, but when we felt ready, David split us up, with one person carrying the rifle for him, while the other led the two ponies up the hill. Carrying the rifle was a much better job as you were involved in all the action of the stalk, so we alternated the arrangement week and week about.

Two weeks after I'd started work at Letterewe, Tony arrived with Bandit, who seemed to have doubled in size and was now about as big as a stoat. Her musky smell also seemed to have doubled in strength and Tony complained bitterly about having to endure it on the 600-mile journey north. I sheepishly apologised to him as he handed over the birdcage containing her. She had now well and truly outgrown it and become a feisty youngster who needed lots of room to play, so I started looking for a better cage for her at once.

After turning the place upside down, I found a heavy-duty plastic water tank in one of the old barns; it wasn't perfect, but would have to do for now. I filled the bottom with fresh hay, creating a sleeping area for her, added food and water bowls and then introduced Bandit to her new quarters. She seemed pleased and frolicked in the hay while I searched for a lid. Although she was still too small to climb out, polecats are prodigious climbers and I knew it wouldn't be long before she'd be large enough to shin up and out of the tank like, well, a polecat up a drainpipe. I eventually found a large white Perspex sheet and placed it over the tank and, having ensured that she had an air gap, I secured the lid with a rock.

It wasn't long before Bandit had the run of the house as well. The old water tank she used during the day was safe and secure but didn't leave her much room to run around, whereas the house, which mostly had linoleum flooring, was a perfect space for her to stretch her legs and play. Every night after work, I let her into the living room for a few hours. At first she just explored every corner of the living room, leaping, twisting and turning as she ran, but it wasn't long before someone left the living-room door open and she discovered the rest of the house. For some reason, she loved my bedroom the most and spent the vast majority of her time hiding under the bed and nipping my toes every time she popped her head out.

As much as I loved her, I could never love her smell. Polecats smell very similar to ferrets: a strong musky scent that is definitely an acquired taste. As if that wasn't bad enough, she always pooped in the corner of my bedroom, ignoring my cries of distress every time she did it. I soon became an expert carpet cleaner and no matter how many times I shut the bedroom door, she always managed to get in somehow.

If I was asleep on the bed, she would brace herself between the wall and the side of the divan and shimmy her way up, grunting with exertion. I would always hear her coming because her claws scratched against the bed linen and the wall, announcing her arrival. A few seconds later she hauled herself onto the bed, climbed across my pillow and parked her backside right on my head. The smell was truly awful, particularly as she also left a scent trail on my bed sheets which was so offensive I could barely sleep for it. Although Bandit wanted attention, she didn't much like affection, so stroking was definitely not on the cards. She preferred to show her love for me by sitting on top of my head, though why she enjoyed it so much was completely beyond me; perhaps my body heat reminded her of the hot-water bottle I'd used to keep her alive when I'd first found her.

Obviously having a scratchy, stinking polecat on top of your head wasn't the best look and definitely not the best smell, so I always pulled her off and put her back on the floor, but this only seemed to make her enjoy the whole experience even more and no matter how many times I lifted her off, she always ended up back on my pillow within a few minutes. I often had to remove her twenty or thirty times before I finally dragged myself out of bed to take her back to her hutch.

Bandit lived purely to cause as much trouble and emotional upset as she could and although climbing on my head was great fun for her, it seemed that nothing quite compared to the pleasure she took from beating up the dog, which she did almost every day. Bandit would hide under the living-room sofa, quietly biding her time until Mint lay down on the rug, put her head on her paws and fell into a deep sleep. That was the moment the sneaky polecat had been waiting for. She popped her head out, checking for danger, then stealthily emerged and crept up on Mint. The poor dog's paws were usually the easiest target and Bandit would sink her sharp teeth into the soft pads of the feet. Mint would leap up with a yelp of pain while the polecat performed a quick victory dance before disappearing back under the sofa, emitting a high-pitched chattering noise which I could only assume was her having a good laugh at Mint's expense.

Of course Mint did not take it lying down and, barking and snarling, she would try to push her nose underneath the sofa to catch Bandit, but the wily polecat knew she was safe because the gap beneath the sofa was only two inches high. This didn't put Mint off and she would circle the sofa for the next fifteen minutes, hoping that Bandit would make a dash for it, but the polecat stayed put and if Mint was really unlucky she'd receive a few extra bites to the tip of her nose which made her yelp and howl even more. After a while, Mint would give up and lie down again and before long the whole process restarted; Bandit just never got tired of the game.

However, within a few weeks Mint was barely flinching as the mischievous polecat nipped her feet and since Bandit thrived on negative reactions and drama, she abandoned Mint's paws and turned her attention to my toes instead. After a long day's work, I liked to kick off my shoes, put my feet up and relax on the sofa but relaxing was never on Bandit's agenda; she much preferred anarchy and mayhem. My screams could be heard throughout the house as her needle-like teeth sank into my soft flesh. High on adrenaline, the polecat shrieked in delight and chattered loudly as I danced about the room, cursing and swearing. I learned very quickly always to wear my shoes in the house when the polecat was on the loose.

The brief vivid blooming of the heather was now over and the oaks were ablaze with autumn colours reflecting from the still waters of the loch. The yellow leaves of the birches shimmered in the pale sunlight, while high in the sky, wildfowl passed in V-formations, beginning their migrations.

The estate owners, Paul and Caroline, had now arrived and often went stalking with their two deerhounds, Tuesday and Wednesday. Writing in the *Independent* some years later, Duff Hart-Davis remarked that when Paul and Caroline began to crawl through the heather stalking a deer, the huge dogs knew to crouch down and crawl as well. It was a comment that drew a wry smile from those of us who'd worked on Paul's estates and the thought that Mr Hart-Davis must have been there on a truly blessed day, because the two hounds were the most badly behaved and disobedient creatures any of us had ever seen. Far from crawling through the heather, they were far more likely to be bounding through it, barking and baying, and scaring off every stag for miles around.

After the deer cull on Letterewe had been completed, Caroline told me that they were planning to go stalking on the Carnmore beat, the most remote beat on the estate. Since they'd need extra ghillies to help with the cull, Bill the gardener and I would be going over there with them for a week. That put me in a bit of a fix because I wouldn't be able to take Bandit with me. As the crow flies, it was only about eight miles across the mountains to the Carnmore lodge, but to get to it, we would normally have had to cross Loch Maree, drive twenty-five miles by road and then take another boat ten miles up Fionn Loch. However, Paul found this all a bit too time-consuming and had hired a helicopter instead.

Since Bandit's water-tank hutch was far too large to fit in the luggage compartment, even assuming that Paul and Caroline would have allowed me to take her with me, my poor polecat had to be left behind. I asked Mark if he'd mind looking after her for me and before leaving, I cleaned out her cage, filled it with fresh hay and placed a large pan of drinking water at the bottom. Not wanting her to starve, I also put a whole cooked chicken in there along with a plate of dog food; even a fully grown polecat would have struggled to eat all that in one week.

It was the first time I'd ever been in a helicopter and Caroline let me sit in the front to enjoy the view. As we rose into the air, there was the spectacular sight of the jagged peaks of the Torridon range of mountains to the south, and passing over Letterewe I could see the cliffs dropping sheer to the loch 500 feet below. 'That's a popular place for climbers,' the pilot said, pointing at the cliff face. 'Someone fell into a crevice a few years ago, but rescuers couldn't get his body out and it's still there to this day.' I shuddered, imagining myself and Archie the pony tumbling from the top of that dark rock face.

The helicopter touched down at Carnmore below the steep

mountains framing Fionn Loch. It was the largest beat on the estate, spanning 100,000 acres of the most rugged, mountainous ground I had ever seen, including two of Britain's most remote mountains: Ruadh Stac Mor and A'Mhaighdean. Walking into the lodge, nestled into the hillside at the foot of the sheer wall of Carnmore Crag, was like taking a step back in time. The floors, walls and ceilings were all panelled with wood cut from the surrounding forests a century before and blackened by age and peat smoke. It had obviously never been updated and looking around, I could see why: it was perfect. There was no telephone, no mobile signal and no electricity, just paraffin lamps and candles, but in the kitchen a Rayburn stove, which one of the ghillies had lit a few hours previously, was chugging away merrily, keeping the room warm.

The only problem was not having electricity for my hair straighteners; even in one of the most remote parts of the Highlands, I couldn't possibly go deer-stalking without having straightened my hair first! Luckily I'd planned ahead and bought a set of gas-powered straightening irons, which did the job reasonably well. Even the paying guests had to manage without modern conveniences, though there were compensations. Paul was a wine connoisseur and the 'few bottles under the stairs' that he kept for guests, to be drunk with a candlelit dinner or standing outside under the stars, included vintage Château Palmer worth hundreds of pounds a bottle.

There were four ponies at Carnmore, one of which, Glyn, was the most foul-tempered creature I had ever encountered. Each morning as we saddled up the ponies, Glyn would viciously bite and kick all the others. Trying to load a stag on his back was also an epic task, taking up to five people, because as soon as he caught sight of the stag, he knew what was coming and fought us with all his might. Once loaded, Glyn would vent his fury by charging down the hill, barging and trampling anyone who didn't get out of his way quickly enough. Every day we had to climb up to 2,000 feet with the ponies trailing behind us, but once we'd completed the climb, we always stopped to rest our worn-out ponies and take in the breathtaking views over the Highlands and out across the sea to Skye. We shared a cup of tea from our flask, feeling like we were on top of the world.

I arrived back at Letterewe from Carnmore a week later and went straight to check on Bandit but the lid of her hutch was off and she was nowhere to be seen. Dragging my suitcase into the house, I called out to Mark. 'Where's Bandit?'

'Oh, I let her go,' he said, deadpan. 'I felt sorry for her. She didn't have any food, so I just let her out.'

'What do you mean she didn't have any food? She had a whole chicken and a bowl of dog meal to go at.'

It turned out that Bandit had thrown her hay around, covering the chicken and making it look like there was nothing for her to eat, but evidently it hadn't even crossed Mark's mind to give her some dog food or something from the fridge. To say I was heartbroken was an understatement. Bandit was a wild animal and I knew that I'd have to release her when she was fully grown, but Letterewe was completely the wrong place to do so. There were no polecats at all in that part of Britain and even if she survived in the wild, there would be no other animals to breed with.

I'd always planned to release her back near Conholt where I'd found her and meanwhile I'd been trying to teach her to hunt her natural prey. A few weeks previously I'd found a mouse's nest near the compost heap. Bandit had killed the mice and very quickly devoured them so at least she knew how to hunt, but I really worried for her safety in the wild at Letterewe, because the gamekeepers all had dogs, many of which were trained to kill. I tried to get her back but it was too late. She had reverted to nature and although I saw her out and about a few times, try as I might, I just could not get hold of her and eventually I had to give up. Six months later I heard through the grapevine that a gamekeeper's dog had killed her. At least she'd had those few months of freedom before her death but I was still terribly upset when I heard about it.

When the end of the stag season arrived – 20 October for red deer in Scotland – it meant the end of the paying guests for the year, but while Caroline and Paul took their private plane back to London, I stayed on to help with the hind cull. The target was thirty-eight hinds and we wanted to get them shot quickly before the heavy snows started to fall.

Unlike the much bigger stags, we could fit two hinds at a time on each of the ponies, lying top to tail across their backs and tied on with strong leather straps. After a hard day's work on the hill, we came home and dressed the deer, removing the parts not fit for human consumption, like the head, legs and 'pluck' (heart, lungs and liver). Strangely, I really enjoyed doing it. There was a knack to doing it well and it had taken me quite a while to learn it, but now I would race the others, including the most experienced stalkers, to see who could do it fastest.

We buried the head, legs and pluck in a hole on the side of the hill and sometimes at night we went out with the lamp to look for foxes, which were attracted by the scent. One night, while creeping about with the lamp, we noticed hundreds of trout in the river that had come in to spawn. The large pools of brown, peaty water were filled to bursting with fish, so we put a fishing net in the water downstream, slowly and stealthily slipped it up underneath them and then jerked it upwards, scooping out a netful. Within a few minutes we had enough trout to feed ourselves for days, which was quite handy as our food stocks were running low and the nearest shop was over twenty miles away.

For the next couple of days we ate trout for breakfast, lunch and dinner, but you can only eat so much of a thing before you start to get bored with it. On the third day I decided to get up early and avoid the fish by eating cereal instead. Imagine my horror when I opened the kitchen door to find someone already happily frying some breaded trout. Plonking the plate of fish down in front of me, he gave me a warm smile. 'Oh no!' I thought, but thanked him so as not to hurt his feelings. He left the kitchen as I eyed the fish, wondering how I could get rid of it without anyone noticing. A few minutes later one of the other ghillies walked into the kitchen, bleary eyed with sleep.

'What's for breakfast?' he said.

'Trout!' I said, thrusting my plate into his hands and running away.

Two weeks later I received a telephone call from Caroline, asking me to come back to Conholt Park. The pheasant-shooting season had now started there and they needed me to help. I felt quite disappointed to be leaving Letterewe just as the first snows had fallen, making the hills look even more spectacular, and sad to say my goodbyes to the friends I'd made while working there. They waved me off as I crossed the loch in the Letterewe launch and then drove off, heading south.

During my first week back at Conholt, Caroline hosted a celebrity pheasant shoot and I was recruited as one of the loaders for the day, though my excitement evaporated a little when I discovered that my 'celebrity' was so low profile that I'd never even heard of her. Loading guns was one of my favourite jobs, but you had to be quick. As the name suggests, double-barrelled shotguns only fire two shots at a time and when the birds were coming over thick and fast, I sometimes found myself loading continuously at full speed for up to ten minutes. If you weren't quick enough, the shooters could accidentally close the gun too fast, trapping your fingers in the breech. Having had it happen to me once before, it was not an experience I was keen to repeat. Usually I stood beside the guests and used my sharp eyes to spot birds flying towards us from far away. That ensured the guests had plenty of time to shoot, helping us get our quota of pheasants and partridges for the game dealers. Most of the birds ended up in high-class restaurants in London and New York.

Conholt Park was also home to a large collection of unusual animals including wild boar, bison, llamas and Soay sheep. They were held in large, open pens, like a small safari park, and it was my job to help feed and clean them out, which I loved because it gave me a chance to observe the animals at close quarters. There were also thirty chickens in the barn and each day I would go searching for the fresh eggs they laid.

The main part of my job was to help control the deer numbers on the estate. During the rut, I accompanied shooting guests to cull the bucks, but mostly I went out alone to stalk. This was a great opportunity for me to learn how to stalk in a woodland setting. However, pheasant-shooting days were always my favourite as so many people were involved. Thirty or forty pheasant beaters lined up with flags to drive the birds towards the guns, while trained gun dogs bounded around the stubble in the crop fields trying to sniff out any birds that were hiding. A team of 'picker-uppers' waited behind the guns with their eager dogs, ready to search for shot birds, which were put into the game carriers that the picker-uppers wore slung around their necks.

All the beaters were transported around the estate in a purpose-built wagon pulled by a large tractor. Chris, the tractor driver, was very keen on shooting foxes, which were a big problem on the estate, regularly killing the pheasants and free-range chickens. As the beaters pushed forward, Chris would hide in the bushes at the edge of the drive, waiting patiently with his loaded shotgun before jumping out at the last moment to shoot any foxes flushed out by the beaters.

Such was his success that all the local farmers used to hire him to cull the foxes on their land. With over 10,000 acres to patrol, Chris was always kept busy and turned his pick-up truck into a 'foxmobile' with a powerful lamp on its roof for searching the fields after dark. He also built a strong, two-seater shooting platform with attached rifle-rests, so that someone sitting in the back could take an accurate shot at a fox as soon as it was illuminated by the lamp. Many of the fields were quite flat and you normally had to be very careful where you took a shot, as without a safe backdrop, the bullet could travel a long distance and possibly hit a house, car or person, but having a height advantage from the back of the pick-up meant that we were always shooting down at the foxes, creating a safe backdrop in even the flattest of fields.

Since foxes generally hunt at night, we would set off at about eight in the evening and spend hours driving around the fields, scanning the corn stubble with the lamp. With so many different animals emerging at night, including deer, badgers, cats and farm livestock, we had to be very careful to shoot the right ones. Foxes eyes showed up a reddish-orange colour in the lamp and the powerful light made it easy to identify the animal from a distance, especially as we always kept a set of binoculars handy. Chris often shot up to three foxes a night but no matter how many he killed, more always showed up in their place a few days later, so it was a never-ending job.

At the end of the pheasant season, Paul and Caroline always hosted a 'Keeper's Day' when the gamekeepers and beaters stood at the shooting pegs with our shotguns, while volunteers drove the pheasants towards us. A lot less formal than normal shoot days, it was the one time in the year when we got to experience 'how the other half lives'. Lunch was a grand affair in the dining room of the house. We sat around the huge table, and the chef brought through steaming cauldrons of game stew and rice. Paul and Caroline had chosen vintage bottles of wine from their cellar downstairs for us all to try, and the usual bottles of sloe gin – my favourite drink – were also passed around.

I had now been working for Paul and Caroline for seven months, a lot longer than I had been expecting, but there was still no full-time position available, so at the end of the shooting season it was time to leave. The sadness I felt at that was lessened a little because, after a few months in southern England, I was dying to return to the hills of Scotland. The estate manager gave me a glowing reference to take with me and I felt quite confident that I would soon pick up some work.

6

THE TRUSTAFARIAN

Soon after I arrived back in Aberdeen, a local gamekeeper I knew told me that an estate owner needed some temporary help building pheasant pens. It would tide me over while I looked for something more permanent, so I called the estate and arranged an interview with the owner, Ian. His estate spanned about 4,000 acres of gently rolling hills. There was heather moorland and peat bog on 'the tops', mature woodlands on the lower slopes and a broad salmon river cutting through the rich farmland of the valley floor. As I turned into the estate entrance and drove over an old stone arched bridge, I could see a fisherman casting his line. With a flick of his wrist, the line sailed through the air and the bright orange fly he was casting drifted down onto the surface of the fast-flowing river.

I drove along a rough, potholed dirt track, past a block of

kennels where the dogs were barking furiously and hurling themselves at the galvanised steel doors. An immaculate silver Toyota Hilux, looking as if it had just emerged from the showroom, but fitted with a rooftop lamp for night-time fox hunts, was parked on the drive in front of the house.

As I knocked on the door, I hurriedly straightened my shirt and ran my fingers through my hair, hoping to make a good impression. I needn't have bothered because when Ian eventually opened the door, he was half-dressed and looked like he had just dragged himself out of bed. 'We'll do the interview in my bedroom,' he said. 'The house is full of people and it's the only place where we'll get enough privacy to talk.'

I felt a little uneasy about that but I was confident that I could cool any unwanted advances with a well-placed kick, so I followed him upstairs and as it turned out, the conversation was strictly businesslike. He read my CV, asked me a few questions about myself and then told me I could start the following Monday. He gave me a briefing about the estate, the duties I would be undertaking and the modest wages I would be earning.

He also told me a bit about himself. Both his parents had died many years before, when he was quite young, and he had been a 'Trustafarian': a trust-fund child with a very alternative lifestyle. However, the previous year, having reached the ripe old age of twenty-seven, he had decided to embark on a proper grown-up career and had invested in the sporting estate. It wasn't clear whether he knew much about his new business before that point, but most rich people tend to have at least some acquaintance with sporting estates, if only as a guest shooting, stalking or fishing, and at the same time as he had acquired the estate, he had hired a full-time keeper called Alan to help him manage it. They were in the process of building eight huge pheasant pens to house the thousands of young birds that would be arriving at the end of September, so they only had four months to get everything set up for that, and needed extra help.

I went back home to collect my gear and the following weekend I arrived back at the estate. Ian showed me to my room inside the main house and then introduced me to the head keeper, Alan, who turned out to be tall, dark and very handsome. Both of us had our own rooms but we shared the kitchen and bathroom. The whole house looked as if it had just been recently and very expensively refurbished from top to bottom. All the furniture, carpets and curtains were brand new and an equally new widescreen television dominated the living room.

Alan also doubled as the house chef, cooking mouth-watering game stews, pasta bakes, chunky soups, fry-ups and a whole host of other culinary masterpieces. He was a good bit bigger than Ian but I felt reassured by that; as the old saying goes, 'never trust a thin chef'. Alan told me that he'd been working as a pub chef when he met Ian. They got chatting one night at the bar, struck up a firm friendship and when Ian bought his sporting estate, he offered Alan the job of gamekeeper. He had no formal qualifications but he'd spent a lot of time hunting, shooting and fishing, and jumped at the opportunity. He packed his bags the same day Ian offered him the job and left to start a new life. Whether he'd known what he was doing when he'd started or had simply learned on the job, by the time I arrived there he was very knowledgable ... or certainly seemed so to a newly qualified novice keeper like me.

After I'd unpacked and settled in, Ian gave me a tour. Jumping into the Hilux, we bombed around the uneven dirt tracks that ran the length of the estate. We drove up the hillside, with the trees giving way to heather moorland, which Ian was planning to manage for grouse. He had also just let the deer-stalking to some locals who had promised to sort out his deer problem for him. He certainly had one. I had never seen so many roe deer in one area before; it seemed like every time we turned a corner, yet more of them appeared.

After showing me the estate, we got down to work on the pheasant pens. At each corner of the pen we first had to install a large strainer post. That involved digging a hole about three foot square and three foot deep and placing the strainer post in the middle of it. One person then held the post upright while the other piled stones around the base and tamped them down, securing it in position. Finally the earth was piled back into the hole and compacted down.

In between the strainer posts, to help secure the wire, we placed fencing stobs (round posts) about every ten feet. We had a large metal 'post basher' with a handle on either side, designed to be used by two people. We slotted it over the top of each post, lifted it up and brought it down hard, driving the stob deep into the ground. After that, we strung the wire around the outside of the pen and tensioned it with 'monkey strainers'. My job was then to go around the fence with a hand-held ringer, a tool that looked like a nut-cracker and was used to close the open ends of the wire rings connecting adjoining sections of fence wire. It took a strong pull on the handles each time and by the time I'd finished, the pheasant pen was as secure as Fort Knox, but my hand felt like it was ready to drop off.

At the end of our hard first week's work, Ian's girlfriend, Laura, arrived, looking like a million dollars. Her shoulder-length blonde hair was newly styled, her long nails were manicured, she had a stunning size-eight figure and was dressed in designer clothes, with jewellery and handbag to match. When she walked across the room, she left a trail of Armani perfume in her wake.

Although we were very different people, she was warm and friendly with a very open personality. She'd had a difficult upbringing but meeting Ian had transformed her life. She truly loved him; in her eyes, he had saved her from a life of poverty and deprivation, and at every opportunity she would declare her love for him.

To give Ian and Laura some privacy, Alan suggested we took the dogs for a walk, so we rounded them up and went for a stroll along the river. Summer had arrived and the trees and flowers had burst into bloom. Out on the river, I could see fish rising, creating overlapping circles on the water as they took flies from the surface. There was a splash as one leapt up to snap up a fly hovering just above the water. The dogs were bounding and leaping along the river bank, playfully jumping on each other, barking and running in circles.

Further along the bank, a buzzard, frightened by the noise of the dogs, took flight from its perch on a dead oak tree. The gnarled, leafless branches served as an ideal lookout post and hunting platform, giving the buzzard a perfect view over the nearby field, where there were hundreds of rabbit burrows, the sandy soil providing an easy place to excavate a warren. As the dogs ran around, flushing the rabbits from their cover, they shot out of the long grass and, white tails bobbing, zig-zagged their way towards the safety of the burrows with the dogs in hot pursuit.

As we approached the old stone bridge, I could see a stoat running along the drystone dyke (wall) looking for mice and birds' nests among the cracks in the stonework. The black tip of its tail flicked back and forth as it explored every nook and cranny, trying to sniff out its prey. It disappeared into a hole and emerged a few moments later with a bird's egg in its mouth. It jumped and bounded along the grassy bank, its jerky movements making it look like someone was pulling it on a string, and then it disappeared under a log pile, either disturbed by our presence or just using it as a safe place to devour its trophy.

When we got back to the house I noticed a plastic carrier bag lying on the front doorstep. When I opened it, I found a large salmon staring back at me. 'It's probably been left there by Jake. He's the local poacher,' Alan said, pointing at a beaten-up-looking car parked in the driveway. 'That'll be a thank-you present for Ian and most likely he'll be inside talking to him.'

'Why is he giving him a thank-you present?'

'Ian has been having a problem with poachers on the estate for quite a while now. They've been hare-coursing with dogs and netting the river to catch the salmon.'

'Why does he let them get away with it?'

He gave me a smile as if to say, 'Seriously? Are you kidding me?' 'Because they tend to be big rough lads,' he said. 'They can be very aggressive, they have vicious dogs and they usually carry weapons of some sort, so the sight of Ian isn't going to strike fear into their hearts. If he tried to confront them, he'd probably end up in hospital. So he came up with a cunning plan to see them all off. He allows one poacher, Jake, to have free run of the grounds and hunt and fish to his heart's content. In return, Jake sees off any other poachers who dare to venture onto his patch. Jake catches a few salmon, shoots the odd deer and helps himself to a bit of other game, but however he's done it – and we don't ask, because we don't want to know – he's got rid of the other poachers who were plaguing the place. Even allowing for what Jake takes, Ian is now losing an awful lot less game than he was before.'

Although I'd done a bit of poaching myself until the police warning shocked me to my senses, I'd never met a 'proper' poacher before and I was intrigued. Kicking off my boots, I left Alan to put the dogs back in the kennels while I went inside to meet Jake. There was only one way to describe him and that was 'as rough as a badger's arsehole' and if you've ever suffered the misfortune of seeing one close up, you'll know that's pretty rough. Jake's hair hung in rat's tails around his neck, framing a weather-beaten face that was the colour of dark wood, though I wasn't quite sure whether that was caused by the sun or dirt. He was powerfully built, with ripped and mud-stained jeans and a thick red and black checked shirt that had obviously seen better days. His accent was so strong that even a Scot like me sometimes had diffi-culty in understanding him and he had a 'don't argue' look in his eye whenever he was making a point about something, but despite his intimidating appearance, he proved to be a warm and friendly character. He greeted me with a wide grin, revealing several missing teeth; the few that were left were all chipped and tobacco-stained.

His gingery-red lurcher dog, Ruby, sat next to him. She came up to his waist and was a powerfully built, classic poacher's dog but, sitting in Ian's living room, she just looked sleepy and bored as Jake regaled us with a few poaching sto-ries. Poachers could be a real problem on sporting estates, decimating the salmon stocks, killing and wounding deer, coursing hares, and sometimes badger baiting, while also intimidating the estate workers and any of the local pop-ulation unfortunate enough to come across them, but Jake seemed more of an old-school kind of guy. As I got to know him better over the subsequent weeks, I got the impression that a lot of what he caught was simply handed back to Ian and his keepers as a gift. We certainly had a steady flow of venison, salmon and wood pigeon delivered to our door.

Jake had bagged a roe deer as well as the salmon, so Ian decided to throw an impromptu barbecue party. While I was taking a shower, the men wheeled out Ian's new state-of-the-art, £2,000 barbecue, a gleaming, stainless-steel monster with three different grilling shelves. An hour or so later, after a shower, blow-dry and a lengthy hair-straightening session, I was ready to join the party. If I wasn't hungry before, the smell of charcoal-grilled venison in the air as I stepped out onto the terrace certainly made sure I was now. The table was covered with plates of sausages, venison steaks, salmon, salad and bread, a bottle of vodka, beers, cokes and bottles of wine. Laura and the guys had had an hour's start on me and were already pretty merry, but I did my best to catch up.

After twenty minutes or so the guys were starting to act quite lairy. Whether under the influence of alcohol or just because that was what he did at parties, Jake suddenly jumped on the table, ripped off his shirt to show off his torso and then began screaming at the top of his voice while laughing maniacally at the same time. I was glad Jake was on our side; if that was how he acted when he was relaxed and happy, I would have hated to be one of the poachers who got on the wrong side of him when he was not.

Jake peaked too soon and left the party early to walk home with his dog, Ruby, leaving the four of us, Laura, Ian, Alan and me, alone together. My previous relationship with Skye had ended not long after it started and I'd fancied Alan since I'd first set eyes on him. The way he looked at me sometimes suggested that the feeling was mutual, but he had never made any moves at all and I'd decided that either I'd been mistaken – my old inability to read the signals again – or he was so incredibly shy that it was never going to happen. However, Laura now leaned across the table and whispered in my ear, 'Alan really likes you and he wants to know if you'd go out with him.'

I did wonder why he hadn't simply asked me himself, but he was a very good-looking bloke and, even better, a good cook as well, so I decided to give it a whirl. I'd always steered clear of work relationships before as I knew they could get very messy, but this time I threw caution to the wind and we were soon a loved-up couple sharing a room, and in the early stages of our relationship I was very happy with him.

Laura usually turned up at the house on a Friday and left on the following Tuesday. Sometimes, if Ian was in a good mood, he would give her a couple of hundred pounds and tell her, 'Go enjoy yourself in Aberdeen.' She already had an extensive wardrobe of clothes and shoes but she loved shopping and needed no urging to buy a few more outfits, though she always managed to overspend, leaving her in Ian's bad books for a day or two.

If he was feeling particularly generous, Ian sometimes gave me the day off work to keep Laura company and carry her shopping bags for her. Walking around town with her was much more fun than building pheasant pens and I was never jealous of the amount of money she was spending. I was happy in my own skin and anyway I was far more comfortable in camouflage clothing and hill boots, though I could scrub up quite well when I was out on the town.

Ian was determined to be a hands-on estate owner and checked the trap lines himself every morning. He had installed a long line of snares, Fenn traps and live-catch cage traps. The estate contained some capercaillie, large birds that were members of the grouse family but so rare that they were on the RSPB's 'Red List' of endangered species, and Ian had been given a £5,000 grant to trap the birds' predators over the course of the next five years. He had also been given another few thousand pounds to attach orange plastic flags to the deer fences because capercaillie – we called them capers for short – were clumsy flyers and had a habit of flying into the fences and killing themselves. By tying the flags to the wire we ensured that the birds could see the fences and avoid them.

Capers are ground-nesting birds so their eggs and young are vulnerable to most predators. Weighing up to seven kilos, they look more like big black turkeys than their much smaller cousins, the red and black grouse. Very cumbersome and slow, they looked as if they had been purpose-designed for extinction but I had a real soft spot for them and was delighted that I could help with their preservation. The females are relatively drab with a reddish-brown chest and brown wings, but the males, which are twice the size of their mates, are beautiful birds with a dark-purple neck, an emerald-green chest, brown wings and black, fan-like tail feathers, and, like the other grouse, a distinctive red half-moon above the eyes. When displaying in the mating season, the males stand with their heads back and their beaks pointing at the sky. They raise and fan out their tail feathers and spread their wings, and then make their distinctive mating call, a sort of dry clicking sound, followed by a popping noise like a cork being pulled from a bottle, and finally a rattling, scraping sound.

Our efforts to preserve the capers were helped by the fact that poachers tended to avoid them because, unlike other game, they apparently taste awful. My uncle Angus once gave me what he said was a fantastic recipe for cooking caper. 'Stick a brick up its arse,' he said. 'Cook it for three days, then remove it from the oven, throw the bird away and eat the brick.' When he'd finished laughing at his own joke, he told me that back in the days when capers were plentiful, he had once had the misfortune to eat one. 'It tasted like bloody pine needles,' he said, and, even if they had not now been endangered and therefore off the menu anyway, I would have been willing to take his word for it, rather than trying one myself.

American mink, escaped from fur farms in the 1960s, roamed the river bank in force. To deal with these, Ian had laid out tunnels with Fenn traps inside them. They also served as stoat and weasel traps, although we didn't catch as many of those. Ian set snares to catch foxes too, although sometimes he caught other animals instead by accident. One day he watched a badger wandering into the snare but by the time he had got out of the car and walked over to release it, the badger had already bitten clean through the wire and was off, running up the hill.

He also installed a line of snares on the north side of the estate, where the majority of the capercaillie lived in the pine woods that are their preferred habitat, so he placed the snares along natural animal runs where he thought foxes might appear, but unfortunately the first thing he caught was a plump male capercaillie. Opening the snare, he let the caper slope off, feathers slightly ruffled. It was unhurt but the snare had done nothing for its dignity and it let its displeasure be known as it stomped off. After that, Ian moved the snares further away and successfully caught a few foxes.

Sometimes when he was away, he left me to check the trap line. There were so many traps that I had to remember carefully where they all were because if I forgot any, I would have to trudge all the way back again to find them, just in case they had caught something. Checking traps was always one of my favourite jobs, although it wasn't often that I actually got to do it as Ian had so many other tasks lined up for me.

One Monday morning, Ian had a particularly nasty job in store, although to give him his due, he did help us with it. A load of old blue plastic barrels that had been used to store mangos had just been delivered. We were going to use them as pheasant feeders and had been under the impression that the barrels would be empty and clean when they arrived, but when we removed the lids, we found that each barrel still contained putrefying pieces of mango flesh and pulp which had fermented in the summer heat and were now stinking to high heaven. When we turned them upside down, the stubborn mango refused to budge, so we had to get out the pressure-washer.

After a couple of hours of hard slog, the barrels were clean but we were all soaking wet and covered in slimy, rotten mango fragments. We tipped up the barrels and left them to drip dry, then attached legs to the bases so the feeders stood upright. We drilled a hole in the bottom of each one and attached a long spring to it, allowing the grain to dribble out slowly and steadily as the birds pecked at it, rather than dropping all at once.

A couple of months after I'd started working for him, Ian transferred the estate rifles onto my firearms licence, making me legally responsible for them. Alan was waiting for his licence to be renewed and so couldn't do it, but I was happy to keep them on mine while I was working there. The wall in Ian's gun room was not strong enough to bolt the gun cabinet to it so Ian had improvised by laying it flat on the floor and securing it there instead, which was a bit of a strange arrangement but seemed to keep the Firearms Officer happy when he made his inspection.

In order to get the pheasant pens built quicker, we decided to team up with the keepers from another estate. The old saying 'many hands make light work' was certainly true, and in return we then helped them out on their estate, where they were also building some pens. One of my main jobs there was operating the chainsaw, since my forestry work had given me years of experience in tree cutting. Normally I would have cleaned and maintained my own chainsaw, painstakingly sharpening it to ensure maximum efficiency, but this time the gamekeeper handed me a very blunt old saw that would have struggled to cut my toast in half, never mind a tree. There were no files or guides for sharpening it, the rakers were clearly far too long and to make matters worse, the timing was well out. As a result of all this, the chain span continuously even when my finger was off the throttle. That was extremely dangerous but the only way to stop it was always to put the chain brake on. Unfortunately when the brake was applied, the engine continued to rev, making a high-pitched whining noise which drove me mad. If I'd had the correct tools, I could have sorted it myself but as it was, I just had to use it in that state.

My job was to chop down some small trees and cut the stumps close to the ground, allowing the fence wire to be run over the top. Predictably, the saw performed poorly and to compensate I had to use force on the blade to make it cut the wood; in fact, I wasn't so much cutting through it as using friction to burn my way through it. The very last tree stump to be cut turned out to be the hardest of them all. By now the chainsaw had just about had enough and refused to cut through the awkward stump. Slipping the saw blade out of the ragged cut I'd made, I placed it on the ground and took a closer look at the stump.

The chain was continuing to spin slowly so I leaned over to apply the brake, but somehow my hand slipped over the top of the brake and the saw cut a deep, inch-long gash down my palm. Blood gushed from the wound and ran down my hand as I stared at it in disbelief. This was the first time in six years working with chainsaws that I'd ever cut myself, and all because of a poorly maintained saw. However, as the blood continued to pour, I picked up the saw again, determined to finish the job. The stump was not going to get the better of me and I didn't want anyone thinking that I was a useless woman, unable to get the job done. However, the game-keeper had other ideas and demanded that I stop immediately. Of course he was quite right but my pride had been hurt and I felt very disgruntled as I left the site and went to his house to get the first-aid kit.

After I'd been working on Ian's estate for a few months, he began to worry about the arrival of the young pheasants. The pens were still not completely finished and there had been several reports of foxes around the area. A fox that manages to get into a pheasant pen can do untold damage, so keepers work very hard to stop this from happening. A few months previously, Ian had set up some 'high seats' – metal shooting platforms, usually positioned about fifteen feet up a tree and accessible via a rickety ladder at the base. He decided that the four of us – Ian, Alan, me and another temporary keeper he'd hired – should go out one early evening and sit on the high seats to see if we could shoot a fox or two. He had sited them at the four corners of the estate, so we had all our bases covered. As we set off, he handed me a 'fox squeaker', which made a noise like the cry of a distressed hare when you blew through it, and said, 'Make plenty of noise.'

I had been given the furthest high seat, set on a lonely hill-side, and although it would have made a good place to shoot deer, I couldn't really see a fox turning up there. However, climbing up the wobbly ladder, I dragged myself and my .243 rifle on to the small plastic seat at the top. It didn't take long before my backside was starting to go numb. Shuffling about uncomfortably, I positioned my rifle on the foam rest and peered through my binoculars as I began to blow through the squeaker. The sun was starting to go down, casting long shadows across the moorland. I could see a couple of roe deer grazing on the heather further up the hillside, while at the foot of the hill there were large clumps of gorse and broom, the yellow flowers filling the air with their sweet fragrance.

After an hour of squeaking, I was starting to lose hope. The weather had been completely calm and sound travels a long way when there is no wind, so either my impression of a dying hare was no good or there were no foxes for miles around. However, I had no choice but to sit there and keep squeaking until I was picked up by Ian. Nothing at all had shown up in response to the squeaker, not even a stoat, which I found quite unusual given the amount of noise I was making, but suddenly a kestrel flew into view in front of me and started circling the tree where I was sitting. I was decked out in full camouflage and with my hood up I was hoping to pass for a clump of moss or an old tree branch. It certainly seemed as if the kestrel was fooled by my cunning disguise as it kept flying in closer and closer, searching for the source of the noise.

Keeping as still as possible, I continued to squeak until curiosity got the better of the kestrel and it landed on the branch above me. Unbelievably it then hopped down and tried to perch on the barrel of my rifle. Just as it was an inch away from landing with its claws outstretched, I jerked my rifle aside. As much as I would have liked to have seen the kestrel at such close range, I had only just bought my rifle and I didn't want scratch marks from its claws on the barrel. The look of shock on the bird's face was comical as it twisted sharply in mid-air, desperately trying to turn around, before flying away. I knew my camouflage was quite good, but I had not realised just how good and it left me feeling quite pleased.

Within the hour the three others turned up in the pick-up truck. Ian had managed to shoot a fox but, like me, the other two had blanked. When I told them what had happened with the kestrel, Ian laughed at me. 'Don't talk crap, Portia,' he said, 'that wouldn't happen in a million years.'

I fought down the urge to make him eat his words; after all, he was the boss and I didn't want to get the sack just yet.

A few weeks later, after a long, hard day's work, Alan and I were rudely awoken at two in the morning when Ian and Laura, who had been partying hard in town, decided to bring the party back to the house. Crashing through the front door, they cranked the music up to top volume. The floor and ceiling started to vibrate and the walls shook. Ian then burst into our room and told us, 'You've got to come and join us in the living room, we need a bit of extra company.'

With the music blaring, there wasn't much point in trying to go back to sleep anyway. I was feeling really tired, but figured that the party couldn't go on much longer, so we staggered into the living room. By four o'clock my eyelids were drooping but the music was still thumping away and Ian kept pouring us more drinks and insisting that we stay up with them, though all I really wanted was the soft, warm comfort of my duvet. Dawn broke and still the party continued until finally Ian killed the music and said, 'Right, I'm off to bed. You two, it's eight o'clock, time you were off to work.'

At first I thought he was joking but it turned out that he was deadly serious, so after a night's compulsory partying, we stumbled out of the door to go and do our day's work, somewhat the worse for wear and more than a little tired and irritated.

One day, very hungover, Ian asked me to deliver a box to another sporting estate about a forty-five-minute drive away. I relished the thought of getting away for the day but I wasn't exactly sure of how to get there and didn't have a map of the area, so I asked Ian for the route. He gave me very precise directions: 'Go right, then left, then left, then left again, then right, then right, then left and you're there.'

We stared at each other in silence, while I tried to work out whether he was being serious. It turned out he was, so I tried again. 'I'm not sure if that's enough to get me there, Ian, I think I need a bit more information. Do you know any road names or numbers, or landmarks, or anything else that would help?'

After arguing for about three-quarters of an hour, I finally managed to get him to produce a map which I marked in pencil. Ian sulkily pointed out the place on the map, still claiming that his first set of directions had been perfectly adequate. When I set off, it was no surprise to discover that in his bleary state, he had forgotten about several turnings; had I followed his original directions I would have ended up in the river.

I found the place with relative ease but on my way back I got lost and, finding myself passing Jake the poacher's cottage, which stood in total isolation on a hillside a few miles away, I thought I'd drop in and ask for directions. The place looked in serious need of some TLC. The grey-brown render on the walls was chipped, cracked and damp-stained, and the garden was unkempt and overgrown. I had to step over a few broken toys lying abandoned in the long grass to reach the front door.

Jake was in the kitchen, a can of lager in one hand and the daily newspaper in the other, while his wife, a good-looking blonde woman with a warm smile, bustled between the stove and the sink. Jake's lurcher, Ruby, slipped in from the back garden to inspect me, sniffing me cautiously before turning around and nuzzling Jake. She didn't dislike strangers, but nor did she have much interest in them.

'So it's directions ye want, is it?' Jake said, taking a long swig from his lager. Belching loudly, he wiped his mouth on his sleeve and then pointed his arm to the right. 'Ye ging doon the hill until ye reach a field full o' stinking coos, then ye ging right, nay left mind, or ye'll end up on the farm. Dinny ging tae the farm, the farmer's a richt cunt. Bastard threw me off his land the other day so ah went to his hoose and there was a bucket ootside at the ootdoor tap and ah pished all over the handle o' his bucket!' He laughed so hard at the thought that he had to wipe his eyes before he could go on. 'Anyway, where was I? Och aye, well ging past the coos and keep going till ye get tae some trees and turn left, no, sorry richt, then carry on till ye get to a crossroads . . .'

At this point, his wife, who had been listening with mounting impatience to Jake's rambling monologue, interrupted him. 'Can ye no get to the point a bit quicker than that, Jake?' she said. 'The poor lassie'll be here for the night at this rate.'

Had a man interrupted him like that I suspect Jake would have flattened him, but his wife was clearly not to be tangled with because he meekly fell silent and she took over. She drew me a rough map and gave me some less colourful directions, but somehow I still got lost, though I made it back to the estate eventually. Despite the detours, it had been a good day out, a lot better than cleaning out mango barrels.

*

Alan and I had now been dating for four months but a relationship that had begun so well was now heading for the rocks. We had lived together, worked together, eaten together and slept together, and what I had not really counted on was how difficult it was to be with someone 24/7, particularly when they were as jealous as Alan turned out to be. He had been fine when we first started going out, but pretty soon the arguments began. If I so much as spoke to another man, Alan would accuse me of fancying him or having an affair with him. One day I went to the shop for a pint of milk and because the shop was short-staffed that day, the queue was a mile long. By the time I got back half an hour later, Alan accused me of meeting up with another man and cheating on him behind his back.

Things came to a head at Scone Game Fair. It was one of the big events of the local year, drawing gamekeepers, stalkers, ghillies, hunters and anglers from all over the Highlands, but Alan told me not to speak to any of the former gamekeepers I knew from Thurso College. That really upset me, because I'd been looking forward to seeing everyone again, but in the hope of avoiding yet another argument, I promised him that I wouldn't.

I felt very on edge, though my mood lifted a little when we got to the fair. It was a fine, sunny morning and Laura and I walked around the shops together, ate venison burgers, viewed the shows and, of course, ended up in the beer tent. Luckily they served Bacardi Breezers, one of my favourite drinks and, since I was not driving, I decided to make the most of them.

Alan spent most of the time ignoring me, except when shooting dirty looks in my direction. Luckily I had not bumped into any of my friends from college or things might have turned really ugly, but as we sat on the bus back to the estate, I came to a decision. Alan was jealous, aggressive and prey to the most terrible bad moods and I felt I had no option but to finish things before they got any worse. The sad thing is that I had really cared about him and it had never even crossed my mind to cheat on him. I had never done that to any man and it really hurt me to be constantly accused of being unfaithful. Fortunately my contract only had a few more weeks to run, so to avoid the atmosphere becoming even more tense, I decided to keep my head down, focus on my work and avoid any more social activities until the estate, Ian and Alan were all safely in my rear-view mirror.

Things were also going rapidly downhill at the estate. Ian had become very erratic about paying his workers, including me. He was a spendthrift and his parents had placed his inheritance in trust for him, giving him an income but preventing him from blowing his fortune. The family lawyer was responsible for doling out cash to him each week, including the money for our wages, but Ian had taken to keeping most of our money and spending it on hard partying and luxuries for himself. Trying to get our wages was now like getting a hind away from a rutting stag, but just as the squeaky wheel gets the oil, I stood up for myself and complained long and loud until he finally handed over the money he owed. It created a poisonous atmosphere between us and I was counting down the days until I could leave.

Finally my last week came around. I was due to finish on the Friday night, but Ian said to me, 'You can leave on the Thursday if you like, because the pheasants are being delivered on Friday morning and you won't be strong enough to lift the crates, so you won't be any use to me.'

I wanted to see the job through to its conclusion anyway, but his patronising comments infuriated me. 'Actually, Ian,' I said, 'I can manage perfectly well. In fact I'm stronger than you are, so I'll work Friday and then I'll leave.'

We had already filled all the feeders and water-drinkers in the pens, so all that was now needed were the birds. The pheasants were due to be delivered at six o'clock sharp on Friday morning but predictably enough, the lorry driver turned up very late, by which time we'd already been standing around the pens for two hours. We unloaded the crates, stacked them in a pile on the ground and then began carrying them into the pens and releasing the young pheasants. I watched them stumbling around in bewilderment before making a beeline for the feeders. It took all day and into the evening to complete the job, so it was Saturday morning before I could pack my belongings and clear my room.

All I had to do now was collect my last month's wages. Ian was still in bed when I knocked on his bedroom door and asked for my pay. 'I'll send you a cheque in the post,' he said. 'Oh, and take the estate rifles back to the gun-shop on your way home, will you? Alan'll have his licence back in a couple of weeks and he can collect them when it comes through.'

I wasn't convinced that the cheque would actually arrive, so I decided to keep the rifles as an insurance policy until my wages had been paid. By law they could only be kept by someone holding a rifle licence and until Alan got his back, I was the only qualified person. Even better, the guns were registered in my name. I mustered the most sickeningly sweet smile I could manage and said, 'All right Ian. Well, this is goodbye then,' and walked out. As I went to retrieve the two rifles from the gun cabinet, I couldn't stop myself from whistling. I loaded them into my car, set off down the drive in a cloud of dust and took the rifles back to Aberdeen with me.

A week went by, during which I did not hear anything from Ian or Alan, and nor did the promised cheque arrive. At the end of the week I sent a text to Alan, assuring him that I would hand the rifles over as soon as I received my wages. I could imagine the explosion as Alan relayed the message to Ian but once he calmed down again, I knew he would realise that I had him over a gun-barrel. The rifles were worth three times what he owed me and as he had transferred them into my name, in the eyes of the law they belonged to me. Within a week the money I was owed was paid in cash, delivered right to my door; now that's what I call service! I handed over the rifles and then heaved a sigh of relief that I would never have to see Alan or Ian again.

Working for Ian had been fun at times but it was a huge relief to be out of it and back to relative normality. I'd always known that it was only a short contract and that I'd be moving on at the end of it, so I was mentally prepared for that. Now, having left there, I knew I'd have to move quickly because if not, all the ghillie jobs on Highland estates would be taken and I'd have to wait until the following year. So there really wasn't much time to pause and reflect on what had happened; I just had to pick myself up, put it behind me and get on with my life. However, I was very sad and upset about the way my relationship with Alan had turned out, but not because I loved and missed him. It was more that I was angry: with him for treating me that way, and with myself for allowing that to happen. It did affect me quite badly, so much so that I didn't date anyone for two years after that, though as it turned out, where I was heading next, there weren't that many potential dates anyway.

I was now twenty-five years old and ready to make a fresh start. Back in Aberdeen, when I looked through the Scottish Natural Heritage website, a job advert at once caught my eye: 'Ghillies wanted for the Isle of Rum'. With Eigg, Muck and Canna, Rum was one of the 'Small Isles', a group of four islands in the Inner Hebrides, a few miles south of Skye. The largest of the four, Rum was only about eight miles wide and eight and a half miles long, and the whole of the island was a National Nature Reserve run by Scottish Natural Heritage.

The closing date for the job was the next day so in great haste I printed off my CV and faxed it to the SNH office on Rum. Two days later, the manager rang me up and carried out a telephone interview. We talked for over an hour and by the end of it I felt sure I'd got the job, because he'd asked me so many questions. A message on my answering machine later that week confirmed it, asking if I could be on the island within three days. I made it over to Mallaig two days later and took the early-morning Caledonian MacBrayne – always shortened to 'CalMac' – ferry to the island.

I was travelling alone because I had given Mint to Mark. It was a real wrench to say goodbye to her but I had no choice. I was now going to be a full-time red deer-stalker and they are the only game animals that you don't need a gun dog to stalk. Roe deer lie up in heavy cover, so you need a dog to drive them out, and of course you need a dog for grouse and pheasant, both to flush them from cover and to retrieve the shot birds. However, in the Highlands and Islands of Scotland, wild red deer live on open hillsides and a dog is of no use there and may even be a handicap, one more thing for the deer to spot and be spooked by.

Although I was very sad to part from Mint, I was glad that Mark was taking her, because with him she'd continue to do the job for which she'd been trained, rather than just being a pet. I'd spent so many hours training her to be a gun dog and she was a strong, hardy creature; throw a stick and she would come back with a tree. She needed to work, it was what she'd been bred and trained to do, and I knew she would not be happy sitting in some suburban living room and only going for a walk twice a day. It was a decision I never regretted, because she had a great life with Mark. She was a well-loved and well-cared-for working dog to the end; she died recently, just two months short of her fourteenth birthday, a very good age for a Labrador.

7

THE ISLE OF RUM

The crossing to the Isle of Rum took over two hours and seemed even longer in the swell and rough seas, but when I went out on the deck to get some fresh air, I had a great view of the sea-cliffs and rock-stacks of the coast and, rising above them, shrouded in mist and low-lying clouds, the dark, foreboding Rum Cuillin, the precipitous, scree-strewn mountains at the island's core. The island was formed from a huge extinct volcano and its rugged, ice-shattered peaks all rose over two thousand feet above sea level. Their names: Ruinsival, Ainshval, Askival, Trollaval, Hallival and Barkeval, the last two flanking the beautifully named Bealach an Oir – Pass of Gold – hark back to the early Norse naviga-tors who named them and used them as landmarks.

As the ferry docked, I could see several Land Rovers and a tractor waiting by the pier. Rum's weekly food and drink order had arrived on the ferry and was being carried off in huge crates. An eccentric-looking sandstone building, Kinloch Castle, stood in the centre of the tiny village, overlooking Loch Scresort, the sea loch that was the island's only anchorage. Surrounded by a long, arched colonnade and flanked by beech trees and wych elms, the castle looked like a grandiose Victorian station left high and dry by the closure of its railway line. The only other buildings were ten houses, three bothies, a community hall, a small shop and an old red telephone box.

Back in its heyday, the castle had been the home of Sir George Bullough, the heir to a Lancashire textile dynasty, who owned the whole island and ran it as a hunting estate, entertaining aristocrats and nouveau-riche industrialists on a lavish scale. Bullough spared no expense when building and furnishing the house, spending the equivalent of £15 million on the house and grounds. The red sandstone for the buildings was transported to Rum from Dumfriesshire, 250,000 tons of topsoil for the gardens came from Ayrshire, and his contractors also built a walled garden, water features, a Japanese garden with an arched bridge over the burn, heated greenhouses where his gardeners grew peaches, grapes, figs and other exotic fruits, and a palm house where humming birds flitted among the trees. One of the water features housed turtles and, for a while, small alligators. When some of them escaped, Bullough had them shot to avoid them 'interfering with the comfort of the guests'.

Transferred the short distance from the ferry to the house in a chauffeur-driven limousine, guests who avoided falling prey to the alligators could entertain themselves on a squash court, a bowling green or a nine-hole golf course. To further amuse his guests, Bullough paid all his estate workers an extra shilling a day to wear tweed kilts, which he felt made them look 'more picturesque' for his visitors.

Sadly the palm house had blown down during a storm and no trace of it remained when I arrived on Rum, but on the far side of the island, near the long-abandoned crofting hamlet of Harris, Bullough had created another lavish and even more permanent residence: the mausoleum, styled like a Greek temple, in which he was buried, alongside his father. He had originally created a beautifully tiled mausoleum, but when one of his guests sniffily remarked that its tiling made it look 'more like a public lavatory than a mausoleum', the furious Bullough had it dynamited and only a few fragments of the tiles marked the place where it had once stood.

I'd been allocated a room in the castle and, as I explored, I came to a galleried Grand Hall, with hand-embroidered silk wallpaper and a beautiful parquet floor half-hidden by a garish and very worn pink carpet. There was a vast inglenook fireplace, stained-glass windows, rows of mounted stags' heads on the walls and a grand piano surrounded by lion-skin and leopard-skin rugs that were souvenirs of Sir George Bullough's hunting trips abroad.

Sir George had sailed around the world in his yacht in the 1890s and had befriended the emperor while in Japan. The fruits of that friendship in the form of gifts from the emperor stood around the walls, including a bronze sculpture of an eagle eating a monkey and two huge and very ornate bronze incense burners, decorated with eagles fighting dragons. There were also two huge porcelain vases on the galleried landing. Under the main staircase, there was an orchestrion, an electrically driven barrel organ with an array of gleaming pipes. Like a player piano, it was operated by a punched card roll and I had to fight the urge to set it going.

I wandered on around the deserted building, passing through the drawing room, library, dining room and the Golden Ballroom which had a sprung floor, a minstrels' gallery and a vast crystal chandelier. There were oak-panelled smoking and billiard rooms, the latter complete with a full-size snooker table, and a red and gold 'Empire Room', named by Bullough's wife, Lady Monica, in honour of Napoleon, from whom she claimed to descend. Upstairs were several lavishly furnished bedrooms with four-poster beds. Although spectacular, the interior had an air of neglect and faded grandeur and there was a damp, slightly musty smell.

During Bullough's time, uninvited visitors to the island were discouraged, giving Rum its nickname of 'The Forbidden Island'. As one writer remarked in the 1930s, 'Unless you are a deer, you are not welcome', and the castle gates were always kept shut to keep out the 'riffraff': the estate workers. However, it had never recovered its former glories after the Great War and went into a long decline, with the castle and its contents remaining virtually unaltered from its Edwardian heyday. Sir George Bullough died in 1939 and his widow eventually sold the island to Scottish Natural Heritage in 1957, reportedly for £1 an acre – £26,400 in all – whereupon Rum was declared a National Nature Reserve. As time went on, more and more people came to Rum for recreation as well as research, and a hostel opened in Kinloch Castle, providing a place to stay for longer visits.

In contrast to Bullough's era, my welcome was warm and there was one thing guaranteed to make me feel at home at once: the midges. One of the wettest places in Britain, Rum was a perfect breeding ground for them and I had been warned that they attacked any exposed flesh with a ferocity that put even their cousins on the mainland to shame, so I applied a liberal coating of midge repellent before setting off to explore my new surroundings.

I hadn't done any food shopping before boarding the boat as I'd been assured the shop on Rum was well stocked, but when I eventually found it, I discovered that it was only about ten foot square and sold mainly alcohol, cigarettes and pack-aged food. Fruit and veg had to be ordered separately a week in advance, and because I'd missed the order day, I'd have to wait a full week without any fresh veg. To make matters worse, they had run out of meat as well, so I had to stock up instead on noodles, spaghetti hoops and bags of crisps. If only my fellow ghillie from Ardverikie, Owen, had been there, he would have loved that diet . . .

As I wandered around the village, one of the first people I met was Derek, one of the island's two deer-stalkers. He wore the traditional gamekeeper's outfit of tweeds and a deerstalker hat, and was only about five foot four and of a very slim build, but as soon became apparent, he had a big personality and didn't take any crap from anybody. As I got to know him better, I realised that he lived to debate and would argue with anyone, about anything, at any time. If there was no one else present to argue with, he was perfectly capable of picking a fight with himself.

Most of his arguments were with Scottish Natural Heritage, who he hated with a passion and a loathing, and at least twenty times a day I'd hear him muttering 'fucking SNH' under his breath. His disagreements with them were usually about what he saw as their excessive culling of the island's red deer herds to allow more trees to grow. On that tiny, windswept island there were few places where trees would thrive anyway, and he saw no point in erecting fences to keep the deer out, as SNH had done, and then killing the deer anyway.

However, if he was argumentative, he was also as warm-hearted and generous with his time as he was with his opinions, and would always help anyone out without any thought of reward. He was also a very patient guy – with everyone except the SNH – and since I tended to be very impatient, he was a real calming influence on me and we soon became good friends. He also had a degree in politics and an encyclopaedic knowledge of history; his room was lined with books and he'd read every single one of them. That made him an eagerly sought team member at pub quizzes because if you were on Derek's team, you always won.

Having stashed my shopping back at the castle, I set off into the hills to get a feel for the island, walking along the Northside Trail past Kinloch Glen. There were fine views of Hallival and Askival and the waterfalls of Primrose

Burn – when I saw it in spring with the wildflowers in bloom, it was obvious why it had got its name. I also found a hide overlooking an otter holt and, up on the moors, an ancient deer trap, used in the days before firearms. The deer were driven off the moor towards a long dry-stone wall that gradually funnelled them towards a stone-walled enclosure. Once trapped in there, the deer could be cornered and killed for food.

Rum's isolation from the mainland had ensured that there were no stoats, mink, foxes or badgers on the island, no snakes, frogs or toads, and no hedgehogs, rabbits, voles or squirrels. In common with almost every island in the world, there were brown rats, but a combination of the harsh climate, the lack of crops and a shortage of prey in winter when most of the bird population of the island migrated, coupled with the very small human population, had kept rat numbers low.

With only the rats as ground predators, burrowing shear-waters – small black and white birds which, as the name suggests, nest in burrows underground – had thrived and Rum had one of the world's largest populations of them. They spent the days feeding at sea – their scythe-shaped wings slicing through the waves earned them the name shearwaters – so to see them I had to climb the mountainside and wait for them to fly in at night, when their eerie 'eewa-eewa' calls filled the air. When the shearwater chicks fledged, they flew straight out to sea, following the light of the moon which guided them to safety, though inevitably some got it a bit wrong and ended up flying towards the lights of the village instead.

There were golden eagles on the island too and Scottish Natural Heritage had also reintroduced white-tailed sea eagles. They had been hunted to extinction in Britain, the last one being killed in 1918, but in 1975 SNH began releasing sea eagles that had been reared in Norway, where they were not endangered. Although a few of the locals told me that most of the Norwegian imports had taken one look at Rum and then flown off to the neighbouring islands, enough had remained to establish a breeding population. They also now bred on Mull, Skye and in the Western Isles.

If the island was full of wildlife, humans were in short supply. The ruins of Iron Age forts, beehive dwellings, crofts, blackhouses and sheilings – small, remote huts occupied by women during the summer when livestock was kept away from the settlements to prevent damage to the crops the men were cultivating – showed that Rum had once been relatively well populated. But in more modern times, its story was a familiar Highlands and Islands one: forced clearances and emigration. One abandoned hamlet on the coast was known as the 'Port of the Turnings' because no one had stayed there long.

The old blackhouses were built by crofters. As I explored one, I could still see the blackened hearth of the fire pit in the centre of the building. Most blackhouses had no chimneys, just a hole in the thatched, heather stem roof, and they were called blackhouses because smoke and soot from the fire pits stained the stone walls; I suspected that the inhabitants must have been as smoke-stained as their houses. There had once been three separate communities at Kinloch, Kilmory and

Harris, but during the Highland Clearances of the 1820s, the 350 crofters living on Rum were permanently removed in a forced emigration to Port Hawkesbury in Nova Scotia, leaving only one family to tend the 8,000 sheep that were then brought in. The roofs of the abandoned houses had caved in and the walls crumbled, leaving only derelict remains.

I felt sad thinking about the people who had once lived in those ruins, especially as the population of Rum, once numbering over 400 people, had never recovered and was only about thirty when I arrived there, almost all working for Scottish Natural Heritage in one capacity or another. However, my sadness was soon dispelled by the beauty of the landscape and the dramatic views of the other Small Isles, Skye and the distant Outer Hebrides beyond. I had only been there a few hours, but already Rum felt like home.

The first Monday after arriving on Rum, I had to turn up at 8 a.m. sharp for the 'byre meeting', which, as the name suggests, was held in a byre (a cowshed-cum-haybarn). This was because, with the exception of the castle, it was the only covered space on the island large enough to accommodate all Rum's permanent population. The purpose of the meeting was to bring everyone up to date with Scottish Natural Heritage's plans for the year and any other developments affecting the island and its inhabitants. All SNH's workers were expected to attend, so I donned my tweeds and walked down the track towards the old byre.

The others were already there, sitting on hay bales with cups of tea in their hands, but looking around the barn, I couldn't see a kettle anywhere, so I gave up thoughts of a cup myself and perched on the end of a bale as the meeting began. I hadn't yet been introduced to many of the islanders, so I just had to guess who each person was. While I tried to understand what was going on, Ed, the Reserve Manager, who was short, stocky, dark-haired and had a strong Birmingham accent, started talking about island politics. True to form, within five minutes, Derek had started a furious argument with him about the deer cull.

After the meeting was over, I began work with Derek who, freed from the irritating presence and opinions of the Reserve Manager, was now showing his sunny side again. As I got to know him over the next few days, I learned that he had turned up on the island twenty years previously and started working on the Kilmory Deer Project, a very long-running research programme studying the behaviour patterns of the red deer, the effects of weather and density on the deer population, and, in more recent times, the consequences for them of climate change.

Derek met his wife on the neighbouring Isle of Eigg and after marrying they moved to Rum together and had a son. She managed to get a job with Scottish Natural Heritage, so she went out to work while Derek stayed at home to raise their son. However, after four years together, she left Derek. Taking their four-year-old son with her, she went off to start a new life with her new man on an even more remote island in the Outer Hebrides.

Derek had raised the boy, but now he was gone, and his wife's departure had produced another unfortunate consequence. Their house, Stalker's Bothy, was a tied house, which came with his wife's job, and as she had left, the SNH expected Derek to vacate the house as soon as possible. After losing his wife and child, Derek had no intention of giving up his home as well, so he asked his MP to help fight his case and meanwhile barricaded himself inside Stalker's Bothy. After months of fighting, he won the right to remain in the house.

The following day, Ed took me to meet the rest of the stalking team, including Karl, the ghillie with whom I'd be working for the next few months. A Welshman, Karl was four years older than me and a couple of inches taller, with brown hair falling in curls above his eyes and covering his ears. With his big brown eyes and prominent front teeth he looked a little like the pet hamster I used to have.

As at Ardverikie and Letterewe, we would be using ponies to bring the shot deer down off the hills. In my previous jobs as a ghillie I'd been expected to lead two unwilling ponies up the hill but Karl told me that working for Scottish Natural Heritage was going to be a little less strenuous because on Rum we were only expected to lead one pony each, and would work together rather than splitting up. Karl often led the pony at the front while I followed behind with one of the mares, Betsy, with whom I'd struck up a friendship. To keep out the cold, Karl always wore a furry black and grey trapper's hat which covered a large part of his face. The two flaps were permanently pulled down over his ears and I was surprised that he could hear at all. He wore a green Buffalo jacket with an expensive set of binoculars that he used for birdwatching slung around his neck, not that the ponies gave him much time to look for birds because they always seemed to misbehave the moment he took his hand off the lead rope.

A sea eagle would suddenly appear, soaring on the stiff sea breeze as it scanned the hillside for food. Immediately Karl would lift his binoculars for a closer inspection, only to have his efforts thwarted by his bad-tempered pony nudging him hard in the back, so that Karl would fall forward, cursing and swearing in his thick Welsh accent. If he let go of the rope to study the eagles, the pony would immediately turn around and start back down the hill towards home. The reaction from Karl always left me in hysterics, as he ran after the escaped pony with his arms and legs flailing, shouting abuse at the mischievous animal.

As the island did not have a pub, the local shop, the only one on the island, was the hub of social life and the villagers often met up there for a drink after work. Weather permitting, milk, bread and vegetables came in on the Monday boat and we would all rush down to the shop to get our weekly supplies. More and more people turned up, crowding into the tiny space, and more and more drink appeared as the locals swapped gossip and talked about island politics. It was not unusual to see the entire population of the village at the shop on a Monday night. It was definitely the place to catch up on all the local gossip – and I have to admit that before long I was probably the biggest gossip in the whole village, with one of the local characters, Norman, coming in a close second. The locals called us '*The Times* and the *Telegraph*' because if anyone ever wanted to know anything specific, they could count on one or other of us to know and spill the beans.

Norman, 'a proper Yorkshire comedian', as one of his mates described him, worked hard and played even harder. He had been a chef in the Navy most of his life and had originally come to Rum on a short-term contract to feed the builders who were erecting a new pier. The old Rum pier had been more like a small jetty for mooring fishing boats and day cruisers, and was too small for the ferry, which had to anchor in the bay, buffeted by waves and bad weather, while all the passengers and supplies were transferred to a small tender boat, the *Rhouma,* that shuttled between the ferry and the old pier. Eventually a new pier was built, long enough to dock the large CalMac ferry the *Loch Nevis.* When it was finished in 2004, Norman's contract to feed the workers was at an end, but by then he had fallen in love with the island and simply refused to leave, ending up staying permanently. At first he worked as a volunteer for SNH, but after a hip-replacement operation, he had to spend a year in recovery and, no longer able to do hard physical work, he eventually took over the village store.

The shop wasn't my only source of supplies because my mum used to send food parcels to the island as well, care packages for her poor daughter trapped on that lonely, benighted rock poking out of the Atlantic! She worried about me not getting enough fresh fruit and vegetables, and would send packages of fruit, though they rarely survived the journey through the post intact. Often I'd open the package to find either fruit puree or, if the post had been delayed, grey fur growing over the over-ripe fruit, and sometimes juice dripping from the package like blood from a stag's carcass would tell me I was probably wasting my time before I'd even opened it. Derek, who as well as a deer-stalker doubled as the island's postman, was always complaining about packages of raspberries, strawberries or figs that had turned to mush before they'd even reached the island, leaving the mail bag full of sticky, syrupy gloop, courtesy of my mother, though it was all done with love, of course.

When I first arrived on Rum, the shop was jointly owned by the Community Association and was worked on a shift rotation, with everyone on the island expected to cover at least one shift a week, manning the counter, cleaning up, re-stocking the shelves or bringing the week's new supplies up from the pier after the ferry dropped them off. The shifts were usually from 4 p.m. to 7 p.m., although the times could vary. The rule was that if you wanted to stay on after 7 p.m., you had to man the till. If we needed something from the shop when it wasn't open, we simply went to retrieve the key from the secret hiding place behind the recycling bins – we'd have left it under the doormat if there'd been one – and opened the shop ourselves. We then did our shopping, rang the items through the till and wrote down the amount on our tab. Once anybody's tab got to £100 they were expected to clear it with a cheque made out to the Community Association.

Unfortunately, although this system had worked perfectly well for years, it was wound up after four islanders ran up huge tabs, one in excess of £1,000. Unable to pay their bills, they then simply left the island on the CalMac ferry one day, leaving the shop and the Community Association – that is, the rest of us – well out of pocket. That was when it was decided to put the shop into private ownership and Norman duly became the Rum shopkeeper.

He was in his element and at first kept the shop open all day. This was much more convenient and saved me a lot of time in the mornings, because I always seemed to run out of something I needed for breakfast or my packed lunch, and under the old system, I would have had to try and open the shop to get the supplies I needed without being seen by the many tourists who visited the island. Somehow I always seemed to be spotted and the unbreakable rule was that if you let them in, then you had to serve them.

Having tried to sneak in for a bag of crisps, I would end up having to serve half a dozen tourists who wanted to do their weekly shop. At least one of them would inevitably want something from outside in the barn and I would then have to go rummaging through the many freezers looking for sausages or pies or whatever it was. Often it was easier to get my own supplies at night, when no one was around to see me, although that made me feel a bit like a robber as I stumbled around in the dark with my head torch on, trying to find toilet rolls and food.

Norman, also known as Normski, was quite eccentric and had many unusual outfits, as if he'd been let loose in the costumes department of a theatre at pantomime time, so you never knew quite what to expect when you called at the shop. In his travels around the world, he had picked up lots of strange clothing and his different outfits included Arab sheik, English country gentleman, Wild West cowboy and a slightly camp hippie clad in tight leather. However, my favourite was probably his 'Desert Rat' look, when Norman would appear in full desert camouflage, complete with army boots, but with a woman's black French beret with a cloth daffodil stuck in it on his head.

Norman also owned a small wheaten terrier, named after his idol, Frank Zappa. It was a very cute dog with soft blonde fur and a long curly tail, and everywhere Norman went, Zappa was never far behind, because the two of them were inseparable. Shortly after taking on the shop, Norman had bought a Jaguar car in British racing green. He took off the number plates and replaced them with personalised plates reading 'Zappa', and the dog would sit alongside him in the front passenger seat of the Jag, with Norman's favourite heavy-metal music blaring out of the car stereo, as the pair of them cruised along the island's handful of dirt roads like a Hebridean Bonnie and Clyde. The tyres had been brand new but a few months' driving over the rough roads of the island left them in shreds. Norman had to pump them up every time he wanted to go for a drive, and in the end he simply gave up, bought a more practical Shogun 4x4, and committed the Jag to the great Rum car graveyard behind the old squash court at Kinloch Castle.

Karl and I would usually go to the shop for a drink after work and, sitting at the counter on the rickety old wooden stools, he would drink his nightly three cans of Caffrey's stout. His girlfriend in Wales, Sarah, phoned him every night at seven and woe betide him if he didn't make it back for her call. Any more than three cans and he wouldn't get home in time; cue a very angry girlfriend.

Moaning was one of Karl's favourite activities but somehow he always did it in a funny kind of way, like Karl Pilkington in *The Moaning of Life*. When he wasn't moaning, he would be joking around, telling funny tales and making us all laugh. He also loved to be rude and would say the most outrageous things just to get a reaction.

Since Karl and I were new to the island, we were given the task of writing poems for the Burns Night dinner. I had to write the 'ode to the laddies' and Karl did the 'ode to the lassies'. Karl was very popular with the ladies; he was such an open and friendly character that he drew them all to him. He never really encouraged them as he had his long-term girlfriend, Sarah, back in Wales, but women just seemed to fancy him. Although we were good friends, I never really saw him in that way because to me he was just a workmate. Sometimes I felt like we were joined at the hip; we worked together all day, spent the evenings drinking together and sometimes we even had dinner together or went out walking during our time off.

When I went back to Aberdeen for a family party, I showed my mother a group photograph of the stalking team on the castle steps, and she took a particular liking to him. 'Who's he?' she said. 'He's so handsome!'

Given Karl's enthusiasm for older women, I made a mental note never to introduce them.

*

Karl and I were soon hard at work with the rest of the stalking team. We were scheduled to complete some very large deer culls over the next two years, aimed at reducing the deer population on Rum to between 1,000 and 1,200 animals. Red deer numbers in Scotland as a whole had doubled in fifty years and culling was necessary to keep the numbers in check. However, far more than the normal level of culling was planned on Rum because, as Derek had already told me, SNH aimed to restore the ancient woodlands by planting large areas with hardy native trees: predominantly Scots pine and birch, with some oak, rowan, holly, hazel, willow, alder, aspen and juniper. In order for that to be successful, red deer numbers had to be greatly reduced or their grazing would destroy the saplings and young trees before they could grow. At least that was Scottish Natural Heritage's theory. Derek's opinion, and one that was shared by me and almost everyone on the island, was that culling the deer to allow the ancient woodlands to regrow would largely be a waste of time. The prevailing winds were so strong – and with climate change, they were only going to get stronger – and storms so frequent that, except on the more sheltered eastern side of the island, trees would either not grow at all or would be so wind-blasted and stunted that they would barely justify the effort of cultivating them. However, SNH were calling the tune and, as paid employees, our job was to dance to it. So despite our reservations, we went ahead with the cull.

Although we had to reduce overall red deer numbers, it was essential to maintain a healthy breeding population, because Rum was an important refuge, helping to preserve the pure red deer strain from hybridisation. Sika deer had been introduced to the Highlands from Japan 150 years ago, and have proved to be an ongoing threat to native species, since they readily crossbreed with red deer. That led some conservationists to fear that the pure native strain might cease to exist altogether and made the red deer herds on Rum vital to the breed's survival, so stringent rules had been imposed to prevent Sika and other non-native deer breeds being imported to the island.

The influence of the Gulf Stream gave Rum a mild climate, despite the high winds. We had warm, sunny summers and mild winters, and although it did snow on a couple of occasions, it quickly melted. It was so warm that cabbage palm trees grew next to the rubbish dump, grown from seeds washed up on the shore after floating all the way from New Zealand. However, its exposed west coast position also led to very high levels of rainfall – over 100 inches a year – so keeping dry in that waterlogged climate was difficult, even for hardy Rum ponies. When I collected them in the morning, there were often water droplets hanging from their long eyelashes and their thick winter coats were soaked through.

The rain in winter could be relentless, sometimes lasting for weeks on end, but to meet our cull target we had to go out every day, no matter how bad the weather. The only thing that would stop us was the low-lying fog that rolled in from the sea at least once every few weeks. It was as thick as porridge, reducing visibility to a few metres, and all shooting activities had to be cancelled until the wind picked up and blew the fog away.

Rain was another matter altogether; we just had to grin and bear that. Often we would have to put the soaking-wet saddles back on to the damp, muddy ponies, because nothing ever seemed to dry out quickly enough, even when we resorted to using a dehumidifier. As we walked up the hill, dragging the unwilling ponies behind us, the rain came down in sheets. The incessant west wind lashed the raindrops into our faces, leaving us feeling like we'd been pricked by hundreds of tiny needles. The rain fell so hard it hit the ground and bounced back up, soaking us from every direction at once. The path turned into a river, tumbling down the mountainside, stripping the sand and loose rocks from the surface. Slowly the path started to resemble a rocky riverbed which we had to scramble over towards the top of the hill. To either side, the bogs were overflowing with rainwater and if we missed our footing, we could end up in the muddy, slimy bog up to our knees.

That never bothered me because I loved to get covered in mud and do blokey kinds of jobs. I really put my back into it, got clarted with mud and blood and didn't give a shit about it, but I had very yin and yang sides; I was still a woman and I also enjoyed looking good. Derek once said to me, 'With most people, what you see is what you get, but with you, what you see isn't what you get at all. You look more like a hairdresser or a beautician than you do a gamekeeper, but when you get to work, the contrast is shocking.' He was generally very complimentary about my capacity for hard work, though sometimes when I was on the hills and it got a bit misty, I'd be moaning that my morning hair-straightening session had been wasted because the damp air had made my ponytail go frizzy and Derek would just roll his eyes and shake his head in disgust.

During the times of heavy rainfall, the burns were in spate, swollen and highly dangerous to cross. One slip and you could end up getting swept over a waterfall and into the sea. A few hillwalkers had succumbed to that fate over the years and we were always cautious. We tried to use alternative stalking areas when heavy rain was due, but we were often caught out by it and there were then two choices: risk crossing the swollen burns or stay out the whole night in the pouring rain. Of course it helped having half a ton of pony to hold on to should you slip, always provided you managed to hang onto the lead rope.

Derek was an absolute hero in such conditions. Whenever he approached a burn that was in spate, he would always wade into the middle and stand there up to his waist in the torrent, while the rest of us made our way across. Bracing himself against the wall of water he would hold onto us until we managed to find a firm footing on the slippery riverbed and drag the pony across. There was no way of crossing quickly – or dry – you just had to accept it was going to be another 'wet pants day'.

The moorland on Rum was very boggy and walking the ponies across it could be perilous; if you weren't careful you could end up sinking into peat bogs that were as treacherous as quicksand. Getting ponies stuck was a regular occurrence and it took a lot of effort to free them. Although we never had any really serious accidents on Rum, I still remembered the tragic story that Dougie had told me at Ardverikie. When he was a young lad, he and his friend were working as ghillies and leading two ponies across some boggy moorland when one of them became trapped in a peat bog, unable to free itself. The stalker and the ghillies spent hours trying to get the pony out, but the unfortunate animal just sank deeper and deeper into the cloying, thick black peat. Eventually all that was visible was the pony's nose and ears and the stalker took the decision to put it down. Sending Dougie and the other lad away, he pushed a bullet into the chamber of his rifle and took aim. As the two ghillies walked away, they heard the bang echoing around the hillside and knew the pony was dead, but they took some solace from the fact that the poor animal had not been left to drown in cold, wet peat.

The story was forever burned into my memory and ensured that I took great care whenever I was leading the ponies. Any time we did have a 'bogging' – and despite all our precautions they did sometimes happen, because the boggy ground wasn't always obvious until you were already crossing it – we all rushed to free the pony as soon as possible. Luckily, although we had a couple of narrow escapes, we never lost a pony in all the time I was working there.

8

THE EAGLE WITH THE SUNLIT EYE

As ever, the 2004 hind season began in late October and, right on cue, the hinds disappeared from the hillside, leaving the corries empty. Derek had a ready explanation for this phenomenon. 'It's quite simple, Portia,' he said. 'On the first day of every shooting season, the hinds open a secret trapdoor in the side of the hill. They hide inside the hills all winter, laughing at us as we walk past with our rifles, and as soon as the close season comes around again, they all pile out through the trapdoor and go back to their hillside pastures.'

In reality, if not quite as clever as that, at the first hint of gunfire many of the deer certainly knew enough to go and hide on the rocky ledges of the steep sea-cliffs where no human would dare to go, or not without a rope anyway. There was no way to extract deer from the cliffs because it was inaccessible to ponies and humans alike. Any deer shot on the cliffs would simply crash down into the sea below and by the time they were retrieved would be condemned as unfit to eat by the game dealers. So the hinds were safe as long as they stayed on the cliffs and they certainly seemed to know it.

They weren't the only animals that knew what to expect when they saw us. A herd of Highland cattle also had free range over in Harris, on the other side of the island, where their long shaggy coats made them perfectly suited to the harsh environment. Every day I, or one of the other members of the Scottish Natural Heritage staff, would be sent bouncing and jolting in a Land Rover over the rough track to Harris with two bags of food. As soon as they caught sight of us, the Highland cattle stampeded towards the vehicle, jostling for a better position and kicking each other out of the way. We always tipped the bag of food out in a long line across the grass to ensure all the cattle were fed, but the biggest cattle would take up the prime positions and if the smaller ones came too close, they would get a large set of horns stabbed into their rump; it really was survival of the fittest.

The first sleety snow showers and heavy gales had now arrived, heralding the start of my first winter on the island. The few trees had long since lost their leaves and their stunted, wizened trunks were bent over in the wind. Storms whipped the hillsides as huge waves crashed against the sea-cliffs, sending clouds of salt spray high into the air. Waterlogged lichen formed dense mats spreading across the ground and trailing from trees and rocky outcrops.

The winkle pickers who worked the shoreline in summer

returned to the island as Christmas was approaching and the price of shellfish was rocketing. They were picking for days and had filled several net bags, each one containing about a hundredweight of winkles, piled in a heap, ready for a swift exit from the island. As I watched the pickers one morning, bent over the rocks as they gathered yet more winkles, I saw an otter bounding across the shore towards them. Unseen by the pickers, the otter crept towards the bags, sniffing them inquisitively as it looked for an easy meal. Unable to open the bags, it leapt and bounced around the outside of them instead, playfully nudging them with its nose as it looked for a way in. Then one of the pickers spotted it and let out a shout, and the otter turned and bounded back the way it had come.

Overhead the harsh cry of the hooded crows filled the air. They gathered on the beach in force each morning and evening at the turning of the tide, waiting for the water to recede. Mussels exposed as the tide went out were plucked from the rocks and greedily consumed by the hungry crows. Having picked up a mussel in its beak, the crow would fly up about twenty feet in the air and then drop it onto the rocks below, smashing open the shell and exposing the succulent flesh inside. Young hooded crows could take a while to perfect this art and I watched a succession of them dropping mussels on to the soft sand of the beach instead of the rocks and growing increasingly frustrated at their inability to open them and get their meal.

I had kept in close touch with my family – I used to phone my mother every week – and this year, as every year, I went home for Christmas. My parents had come to see me at Ardverikie a couple of times but they never visited me on Rum; having travelled a lot earlier in life, they now needed a powerful reason to persuade them to stray far from hearth and home.

My brother lived in London, a much longer haul, and never came to Rum either, but we got on well and I did stay with him in the capital a few times. Strangely enough, although going into a shopping mall in Aberdeen after the quiet and isolation of Rum could be almost enough to induce a near panic attack in me, I actually loved London, maybe because my brother took me to places like Kew Gardens, the London Aquarium and the Wetlands – all sorts of 'naturey' things – so even though I was in the heart of the city, I felt at home there.

Having gone home for Christmas, I was back on the island in time for Hogmanay, a habit I kept up all the time I lived on Rum. The winter population of the island had dwindled to the thirty or so permanent residents and, when I wasn't hanging out at Norman's shop, I used my time off to explore Rum's wild landscapes and watch the abundant wildlife. Oystercatchers and eider ducks lined the shores of the bay around Kinloch, and I could have happily sat for hours listening to the oystercatchers' plaintive piping and the 'woo-oo' call of the eiders, sounding like 'surprised pantomime dames', according to one naturalist. Guillemots, kittiwakes and shags bred on the steep rocky cliffs, and red-throated divers nested around the hill lochs inland.

The sight of a soaring golden eagle, its wingtips flexing as it effortlessly rode the updraft, with the crest that gives the bird its name gleaming in the sunlight, always left me breathless no matter how many times I saw it – and there were several breeding pairs on the island. In autumn there was the silvery flash of leaping sea trout and the ferocious clash of antlers as red deer stags locked horns during the rut, their breath steaming in the cold, crisp air. As well as the herds of red deer, there were the Highland cattle and the wild goats picking their way among the rocks of even the steepest crags.

There were a dozen different raptors and a score of species of ducks and geese; shearwaters, fulmars, grebes, petrels, cormorants, gannets, terns, gulls and skuas; plovers, curlews, turnstones, lapwings and sandpipers; ptarmigans, quail, pheasants, woodcocks, snipe and red grouse. There were grey and common seals around the rocks on the coast; otters hunting among the kelp forests; basking sharks in the bays and sheltered inlets around the coast; dolphins, minke whales, and sometimes humpbacks and killer whales too, blowing jets of spray as they sounded out in the bay; as well as the vast flocks of sea and shore birds filling the skies. It felt like – it was – a paradise.

Most wonderful of all was to watch the courtship ritual of pairs of sea eagles over the rocky coast of Rum. The largest British bird of prey, the sea eagle has a wingspan of nearly two and a half metres – half a metre broader than the golden eagle. It has a distinctive white tail, with grey-brown feathers on its body and a paler head. The beak and talons are yellow, as are its eyes, giving rise to its beautiful Gaelic name '*Iolairesuilnagreine*': 'Eagle with the sunlit eye'. When it is in flight, but for its white tail, you could easily mistake it for a big vulture, circling with its wings flattened and the feathers at its wingtips spread like outstretched fingers.

The sea eagles' courtship display was absolutely breath-taking. Often starting in early winter, it built to a crescendo in spring, when pairs of eagles performed eye-popping mid-air routines, grappling their talons and spinning each other around in an airborne Highland fling, as one plummeted from the heavens and the other soared upwards. The eyrie, an untidy heap of large sticks and small branches, was usually perched on a rocky ledge high on a sea-cliff. They laid two or three eggs and two chicks would often survive, unlike the ruthless young of golden eagles, whose dominant chick would often devour all the food its parents brought to the eyrie, leaving the smaller one to starve.

Although sea eagles primarily fed on fish, they also took rabbits, hares and birds like eiders and shags, and as well as catching their own prey, they were happy to steal from other predators like otters. In winter, when other food was harder to find, they also scavenged for carrion. While ospreys took fish after a breakneck dive from height, sea eagles often flew much closer to the water, and more than once I saw one glid-ing a few metres above the waves before swooping down to sink its talons into a fish with barely a splash.

When the stalking season finished on 14 February, that left Karl and me without a job until the next deer-culling season came around. However, that prospect never bothered me at all, in fact I always looked forward to finding other work out-side the deer season. Those jobs were wonderful, some of the best things I ever did, and I'd never have had those fantastic experiences if I'd taken a full-time position on an estate.

Among the jobs advertised on the SNH website in 2005, we found what looked like an ideal stopgap, working in the Western Isles. The Wader Project on the Hebridean islands of North Uist and Benbecula was looking for twelve hedgehog trappers and Karl and I immediately applied. Hedgehogs were not native to the island but a few had been released into a garden in 1974 by a crofter who had brought them to the island with the very best of intentions, to help control the slugs and snails. Unfortunately, he had no idea of the devastation that introducing an alien species could bring.

Like most Scottish islands, North Uist has very few ground predators apart from a few otters, rats and house cats. On the mainland, hedgehog numbers are in decline, thanks to predation by badgers, the huge numbers run over on our roads every year and the effects of pesticides and the slug pellets that poison the hedgehogs' principal food source: slugs and snails. However, on North Uist, there was very little traffic, no badgers and few poisons and the imported hedgehogs thrived and bred like there was no tomorrow. Within twenty years the hedgehog population had reached an estimated 5,000. By then they'd also colonised the adjoining islands of South Uist and Eriskay, which are joined to North Uist by causeways.

The east coasts of the islands are rocky and mountainous, but all along the west coast there is a low-lying and very fertile coastal plain known as 'machair', flanked by broad sandy beaches that extend the full length of the islands. The sandy soils are covered in spring and summer with a carpet of wildflowers. Kelp forests offshore protect the beaches from erosion and the piles of kelp washed up by the tides and left to rot on the beaches are the perfect habitat for sandflies. They in turn provide food for one of the world's largest breeding populations of wading birds like oystercatchers, dunlin, redshank and ringed plover, as well as other rare birds like the corncrake.

As the hedgehog population soared, the numbers of wading birds plummeted and it didn't take a David Attenborough to decide that the two things were linked. The eggs of the ground-nesting waders were a tasty, protein-packed treat for the hedgehogs and they devoured them with relish. Whether that was the sole or even the principal cause of the declining numbers of wading birds is still in some dispute, but the Uist Wader Project was set up to reduce or eliminate the hedgehog population. At first the trapped hedgehogs were simply killed but that provoked an outcry from hedgehog lovers. Eventually the trapped animals were all carefully transported to the mainland and then released there in areas where they would be a welcome addition to the declining hedgehog population.

Karl and I were both offered short-term jobs with the project, so we packed our bags and made our way to Benbecula, the small island between North and South Uist. I crossed to Skye on the ferry, headed up to Uig on the north-west point of the island and made the two-and-a-half-hour ferry crossing from there to Lochmaddy on North Uist, before driving south across the causeway to Benbecula. The causeway connecting the islands was formed from tons of huge boulders that had been dumped into the sea – and given the ferocity of the storms that sweep in from the Atlantic they had to be huge – and then a tarmac road was laid along the top.

The Western Isles landscape was different from anything I'd ever come across on mainland Britain, with gentle rolling hills, great expanses of exposed rock and spectacular white sand beaches on the west coast. The road was raised a few feet from the boggy moorland and was narrow and twisting, with passing spaces every couple of hundred yards. The weather was dry and calm, uncharacteristically so for the time of year as I was soon to discover. Red deer stags and sheep stood at the side of the road and sometimes on the road, casually eating grass and watching the world go by.

Croft houses dotted the landscape, looking like they'd been built directly onto the moor with no surrounding fence or wall, but what surprised me most about the landscape was the number of abandoned stone buildings. If they had been over on mainland Britain, property developers would have snapped them up but in the Western Isles the crofters just left them alone and allowed them to slowly go back to nature. Each crumbling building provided a home for at least two families of starlings, which nested in the holes between the stones. Sheep also huddled inside the ruins, the walls making a welcome barrier against the wind and rain.

The place where we were staying was at the northern end of Benbecula, and Karl and I shared a house with a young man with a degree in ecology. Another group of trappers lived in the centre of the island and the rest were in the southern part. Our place was an old-fashioned granite house used as a holiday let, with a garden tended by four bad-tempered geese. The angry geese kept a watchful eye over us every time we got in and out of our cars and one of them always followed me around the driveway, hissing and pecking me. They did a very good job of keeping the grass short but left us lots of little gifts all over the pathway and the front doorstep.

Outside the house, a large salt marsh stretched into the bay and flocks of wading birds criss-crossed the muddy flats, looking for small insects and crustaceans. I decided to go for a walk along the mudflats on my first afternoon in Benbecula and promptly wished I hadn't. As I sank up to my knees in wet sticky mud, I realised it was actually quite dangerous. The mud could get very deep in places and since I didn't know the ground well, I thought it safer to avoid those areas in future.

Sunday was a day of rest in the Western Isles and everything stopped for the Sabbath. All the shops closed, the ferry did not run and the whole place seemed eerily quiet. However, the churches were packed out and it seemed religion was a very big deal over there. As I drove along the island roads, I noticed several play parks with the swings tied up. I presumed this was to stop them from squeaking in the wind but later discovered that the religious types tied up the swings to prevent children from playing on them on the Sabbath. It seemed they didn't want to insult the Lord by letting children enjoy themselves on Sundays. We christened those people 'the swing tie-ers' and they were a great source of hilarity.

On Monday morning all the trappers congregated in the village hall to meet each other. Amazingly there were an equal number of men and women and I loved being able to work with other women for once. We had plenty in common, all being lovers of wildlife and the great outdoors. The team members had mixed backgrounds: there were a few game-keepers, a pest controller and a couple of older individuals who had been on the project for a few years, but the majority were university graduates doing their first job since gaining their degree.

The project was run by Mick and Gwen. Mick had pre-viously been one of the SNH reserve staff on the Isle of Rum, so we had plenty to talk about. Gwen told us that on Benbecula it was the local custom to wave to everyone you passed in the car, but in keeping with the stern religion of the island, there were no effusive greetings, you just lifted one finger off the steering wheel to acknowledge the other driver's presence. Anyone who failed to do so was either – heaven forbid – a mainlander or just plain rude. The whole team adopted this local custom and it quickly became second nature, though Gwen told us that one day she had passed the local vicar and accidentally forgot to wave. The vicar was so disturbed by this apparently hostile act that he turned up at her house later that day and said, 'You didn't wave at me. What's wrong?'

After a brief 'getting to know you' session, we were sent out into the field in small groups, led by a more experienced person who taught us how to trap hedgehogs. We used rec-tangular live catchment traps. The door was held open by a long metal pin and at the other end of the cage was a foot-plate. We used fresh mackerel as bait, placed just beyond the footplate, and when a hedgehog lured by the fishy smell stood on the plate as it tried to reach the fish, it sprang the trap. The hedgehog would then have to wait inside the trap until one of us arrived to remove it.

We usually placed the traps about 200 yards apart around the edges of fields and along the dry stone dykes (walls) where hedgehogs were likely to roam, and we dug the traps into the ground and covered them with large clods of earth, which not only camouflaged the trap but kept the animal warm and dry during its incarceration.

Although I got on really well with nearly all of the team, there was one guy who put me on edge from the start. He had a bit of an attitude, and kept boasting about his days as a professional egg thief, stealing the eggs and young of rare and endangered birds like golden eagles, sea eagles and ospreys. He would sell the eggs to collectors and sell the chicks to rich Arabs who used them for falconry. He told some of the other trappers that he could get up to £20,000 for an eagle chick, though I don't know if that was true. I had to wonder why on earth anyone who did stuff like that would choose to work for a wildlife conservation agency and why he would be stupid enough to actually admit to it.

No one told Mick or Gwen because we didn't want to be labelled as snitches but I remained wary and kept him at arm's length. I even wondered if he was using this job purely as cover while he looked for potential nest sites to raid, but he swore that he'd turned over a new leaf and put his egg-thieving days behind him and, as dodgy as he looked, he turned out to be a very good trapper, catching more hedgehogs than anyone else.

We split into three groups and for two weeks we'd do daytime trapping and on the third week we'd go 'lamping' at night. Everyone loved the daytime trapping but the night lamping was really hard, tedious work, trudging across the wet, boggy fields in all weather conditions. Occasionally we were 'stormed off' when really bad weather blew in, but mostly we just had to accept a good soaking as we walked around the fields for eight hours, carrying a heavy car battery in our backpacks, attached to a hand-held lamp. We walked in formation, slowly covering the ground. Finding hedgehogs was always the highlight of our night, but if we found nothing, the hours dragged by. For some reason there were plenty of footballs lying around that the crofters' children had abandoned in the grass. The coloured coating had been weathered away by the wind and rain, but the dirty grey leather footballs provided us with an endless source of amusement. I would point to an abandoned football and shout, 'I've found a hedgehog,' then run towards it and give the ball an almighty kick, sending it flying into the air. The 'hedgehog' would then land with a huge thump as we all fell about laughing. When we did find a real hedgehog, we placed it carefully inside a pillowcase in our rucksacks and once we got back to the car, we transferred our catch to a large wire cage filled with shredded paper from the office.

Although hedgehogs were our main quarry, we frequently caught other animals such as rats, starlings and rabbits. The beauty of a live catch trap is that you can simply release non-target animals back into the wild. We usually killed the rats, however, which pleased the croft owners greatly. Some of the things the other trappers caught made me giggle. Tourists or locals would sometimes find one of the traps and put beer cans or other objects inside it. One team member even caught a banana which I strongly suspect was placed there by a member of the night-time lamping team.

One day I found one of my traps had been dug up and was sitting on the ground next to the hole it had come out of. Even more strange, it was full of little cubes of diced carrot. I was still scratching my head about this, wondering how on earth they had got there, when a crofter came up to me. 'You're probably wondering what's been going on,' he said. 'Well, you'd caught a rabbit in your trap yesterday and my daughter – she's eight – found it, decided she wanted it as a pet and was feeding it carrots from our fridge. We worked out how to open the trap and put the rabbit into a hutch we had left over from the last pet rabbit. I did explain to her that wild animals shouldn't be kept as pets but I let her keep it for one night. As soon as she went to school today, I released it back into the wild, but I forgot to replace your trap. Sorry.'

'Mystery solved,' I said. 'No problem. I'll reset the trap and rebury it and with luck, it'll have a hedgehog in it next time. Your daughter won't want one of those as a pet, will she?'

He laughed. 'I hope not – too many fleas!'

After two weeks trapping, we moved to a holiday-let cottage in Torlum which was fairly central on the island and, much more important, was within walking distance of the pub – the Dark Island Hotel – that the whole team frequented regularly, except on the Sabbath, of course, when all the pubs on the island had to stay closed. It became a regular thing to have a few drinks after work and was a great way of finding out how the others were getting on. As we all worked independently of each other during trapping weeks, it could get quite lonely, but luckily our whole team was a friendly bunch and we got along very well.

One of the other groups had rented a house owned by a woman who was desperate to sell it. Since a potential buyer could come for a viewing at any time, she told them that the house had to be kept spotless. The rooms were very small and sparsely furnished and as each team member had a mountain of personal possessions and work equipment, this became a bone of contention with the house owner, who complained bitterly at the piles of stuff in each room, claiming it looked untidy and might put off potential buyers.

I had some sympathy for her because she did have a very good reason for wanting to sell the place. There had been a particularly savage storm a few months previously. Storms were not unusual on Benbecula, but this had been no ordinary one and the strong winds, coupled with an unusually high spring tide, had caused a huge storm surge to sweep in, submerging the surrounding land. The houses were only a few metres above sea level and the storm surge posed a very real danger to them, but most of the house owners just battened down the hatches and sat tight, hoping that the floodwaters would quickly recede.

However, the woman's next-door neighbours took fright when the waves started to lap around their front doorstep and, not wanting to stick around and see how much worse it was going to get, they took the decision to evacuate the whole family. They quickly packed some belongings into their car and headed out along the causeway linking Benbecula to South Uist, but just as they did so, a huge wave crashed over the top of them and swept the car into the sea. The car was trapped upside down underwater, pinned against the stone causeway and, very sadly, three generations of the family all drowned together.

A few days later, when the storm had subsided, their neighbour opened her door to discover that the body of one of the poor souls had washed up on her front lawn. She was so traumatised by this experience that she immediately put her house on the market, but it had not sold as fast as she had hoped. She blamed the mess in the bedrooms for putting off potential buyers, but I suspected it was more the stigma attached to the house since the tragedy that made people wary. News travels fast in the islands and everyone knew what had happened. Superstitious or not, no one wanted to live in a house associated with such a tragedy. I strongly suspected that her only hope of a sale would have been if a mainlander took a liking to the house.

Since most of Benbecula is low-lying, it is extremely wet and boggy and I first became acquainted with the special perils of blanket bog when I was out trapping one day. Blanket bog forms when a pond becomes covered with sphagnum moss, forming an extremely unstable crust on top of the water, which can be very deep. Many hillwalkers have fallen foul of a blanket bog, sinking up to their necks in cold dark bog water and some have even drowned. If you did fall through a hole in the crust and slipped beneath the water, there would be no certainty that you would surface again in the same place and you could quite easily find yourself trapped underwater.

Given that, to start jumping up and down on the crust of the first one I encountered, watching the ground rise and fall and the little waves running across the surface of the moss, was a singularly stupid thing to do. I was having great fun until one of my legs broke through the surface and I became trapped up to my hip. To make matters worse, I couldn't feel the bottom of the pond with my feet, just the freezing cold water seeping through my trousers and pants. An angry crofter appeared while I was making unsuccessful attempts to retrieve my leg, and gave me a fully deserved bollocking and a lurid warning about the dangers of the terrain.

Eventually I lay down on my back and with a loud sucking, squelching noise, I managed to drag my leg out of the bog. Needless to say, it was the last time I ever jumped up and down on one. I felt more than a bit silly, though I wasn't the only one who got stuck. Sheep also frequently got trapped and I rescued several during my time on the island. Once stuck, the sheep's fleece rapidly became heavy and water-logged and if they were unable to free themselves, they either died of hypothermia or had their eyes pecked out by ravens while still alive.

There is a very good reason that corvids (members of the crow family) like ravens take an animal's eyes. Sheep are far too big for a corvid to kill, but no animal can survive in the wild without being able to see. If the raven pecks the eyes out, the animal will be dead within the week and the crafty raven will then have a feast for weeks on end, dining on its carcass. It is a clever but cruel survival trick.

All around the coast of Benbecula, the sea created shallow inlets that filled up with seaweed. As the seaweed broke away, it ended in great decaying piles along the shore, which stank to high heaven and in calm weather attracted clouds of flies. One of the local bays, about a mile from the Dark Island Hotel, had been named Stinky Bay for a very good reason, because the smell just about knocked you out, but as well as stinky inlets, the island had beautiful beaches with golden sands stretching as far as the eye could see. In some places the beaches almost looked tropical, though they were definitely lacking tropical weather, unless you counted tropical storms.

The weather on Benbecula was some of the most extreme I've ever faced. The winds swept in off the Atlantic Ocean with nothing at all to act as a barrier. One morning I went out in a force twelve gale and it was so windy that it blew my eyelids inside out. Every step into the wind took a huge effort, leaning forward like a ski-jumper. As an experiment I even tried to let myself fall forward into the wind, but I barely moved an inch because the force of the gale held me upright. That day I practically crawled around my traps as the wind screamed around me and the rain lashed my face. By the end of the day I was soaked to the skin and emotionally traumatised for life.

Crawling through the front door, my wet hair plastered

to my face, I was greeted by the sight of my completely dry housemates. It turned out that the boss had sent a text message to everyone telling us to stay at home as the weather conditions were too dangerous, but since we were in a poor reception area, my mobile phone hadn't picked up the text. An hour after I got in, it at last beeped with the delayed text, helpfully telling me to remain at home. My housemates had put the day to good use, drinking, eating and watching TV, and to top it off I hadn't even caught a thing.

For some reason our team never found many hedgehogs while out lamping, mainly because we were Team 3 and therefore the third lot to lamp in that particular area. Team 1 usually got their hands on the new territory first, cleaning out the majority of hedgehogs. Team 2 took over in the second week, getting a good number, although not as many as Team 1. Finally it was our turn and we usually only got a few stragglers. It was a bit depressing, especially when Gwen tried to tell us that some groups were just better at lamping than others. I strongly disagreed with that theory because hedgehogs were very easy to spot in a flat grass field in the powerful beam of the lamp; you would have to be blind to miss them. It was just a simple case of the first team into an area catching the most and the last team catching the least.

When we 'lamped' the airport, Team 1 caught about twenty hedgehogs. A week later Team 2 caught twelve, and a week after that it was our turn. Greatly encouraged by the results of the others, we were sure we would come home laden with hedgehogs. Needless to say, we didn't catch a single one. We promptly renamed ourselves 'Team Crap' and, side-lit by the rising sun, we lined up for a team photo, spelling out the word 'CRAP' with our bodies, Village People's 'YMCA'-style.

After three months of trapping we were now winding down. We weren't allowed to trap during the months hedgehogs were nursing young as it would be cruel to separate mothers from their babies, and since hedgehogs hibernate for six months, wake up and forage for three months, and then give birth, there were only those three months in the year in which we were able to trap them. That time was now over, but before we left, the whole team decided to do a bit of sightseeing. Five of us climbed the tallest hill on South Uist, which gave us an amazing view over Benbecula. There were so many small lochs it actually looked like there was more water than land. We also took a look at the monument to Flora MacDonald. After the Jacobite defeat at Culloden, Bonnie Prince Charlie fled to Uist. Disguising him as her Irish maid, complete with dress, Flora sailed with him from Benbecula 'over the sea to Skye', in the words of the 'Skye Boat Song'. From there he fled to France, never to return.

As well as hill-climbing and monument-bagging, we also took a boat trip to the Monach Isles, known as Heisgeir in Gaelic, a small group of islands off the west coast of North Uist. The islands had been uninhabited for seventy years although there was a ruined church and an old schoolhouse, now used as accommodation by visiting conservationists. The isles were home to thousands of grey seals which lined the beaches, undisturbed by humans and dogs. They basked in the sun, occasionally waving their flippers at annoying flies.

We had reached the end of the project. It had been a great

experience with a fantastic bunch of people and I was sad to be leaving. Since most of the trappers had come from the mainland, we all had our cars booked on the Saturday-morning ferry and queued up in lanes at the terminal, waiting for the ramp to be lowered. However, the weather had different ideas and a fierce gale blew in. After waiting in line for an hour it was announced that the sailing would be delayed until the storm had died down and meanwhile CalMac offered all the passengers a free breakfast at the café next door.

The tables rapidly filled with passengers and the other trappers found seats wherever they could. That left a trapper called Charles and me as the last in the queue, by which time the only place left was a small table for two. That made me smile from ear to ear, since I quite fancied him and was pleased to have his undivided attention for once. We were both served with a huge fry-up of bacon and eggs, tomato, black pudding and beans on toast, all washed down with a large pot of tea and I spent the next half an hour trying to charm Charles with my witty banter.

As I recounted a tale from Rum I became ever more animated, flinging my arms round to accentuate my point. However, I was still holding my knife and fork and a large lump of fried egg flew off my fork and hit one of the other diners in the face. I failed to notice this and carried on with my story while Charles, who had seen the airborne egg take off, cracked up laughing. I assumed he was laughing at my funny story and it wasn't until I saw the furious diner glaring at me as he wiped egg from his face, that I realised what had happened.

Charles was a fair bit older than me, but he was a Christian and a real good guy, who never swore, minded his manners and had great respect for women. In fact he was perfect, everything I'd been looking for in a man, but since he was married, that clearly wasn't going anywhere. When I was younger I'd had a tendency to fancy older men, perhaps wanting someone who would take care of me emotionally. However, as I got older myself, I realised that you've got to do that for yourself and you can't rely on others to do it for you. I had also become so very independent and capable of looking after myself that I found myself thinking, 'I don't really want someone else to be in charge of me, trying to make my decisions for me. It's my life, I want to live it my way.' Coincidentally or not, I then started dating men who were my own age or even slightly younger.

The storm that had delayed the ferry petered out that afternoon and I made the journey back to Rum. Never the height of elegance at the best of times, my clothes had taken a real battering, first on Rum and then on Benbecula, and my wardrobe was now a disgrace. Rum really was the place where clothes came to die. No matter how hard you tried to look after them, somehow they always ended up torn or damaged. Having an outdoor job meant my clothing never lasted long anyway, so the longer I stayed on the island, the emptier my wardrobe became. Every so often I would have to leave on a much-needed shopping trip and return with new jeans, jackets and boots, but before long they would also be falling apart.

By now I looked a complete state, like I'd been dragged through a hedge backwards. I always kept up my skin care, my make-up and my hair straightening, even if an Atlantic gale sometimes left my hair looking like an abandoned sheep's fleece ten seconds after I stepped out of the door, but my clothes were in shreds, and my boots and trainers were falling apart. In those days before internet shopping, I had two choices: I could either order stuff from mail-order catalogues that might look hideous and/or not fit me when it finally arrived, or just load up with clothes when I went back to the mainland and hope they would last me until the next time. Yet even when I did go back, there were always other things to do, like catching up with my family and friends, going to the dentist for a check-up, etc., that all ate into the time. As a result, I rarely managed to have more than an afternoon here or a morning there to get everything I needed, including medical supplies, toothpaste, deodorants and, of course, restocking with make-up.

I was sitting in the little shop in Rum one day, quietly enjoying a Bacardi Breezer. I was long overdue a trip to the mainland; the worn and faded combats I was wearing had seen much better days and my poor trainers were on their last legs. Even my seven-year-old Realtree jacket no longer zipped up and half the buttons had fallen off. Two workmen over from the mainland on a job came in. They were scarcely a picture of sartorial elegance themselves, dressed in paint-splattered trousers, worn boots and old sweatshirts, but when they clocked me sitting on the bar-stool, I heard one of them say, 'That's what I love about this place: no one gives a shit about their appearance. It makes me feel right at home.'

I laughed at the time – he was right because I did look terrible – but as the time ticked by, I started to feel more and more embarrassed and uncomfortable about how bad I actually looked. It was a real wake-up call for me. I'd always prided myself on being quite well turned-out, so for them to say that I didn't give a shit about my appearance was quite a shock, even though it was probably true at the time. A lot of the other women on Rum were the same. It wasn't necessarily a good thing, but it was a hard life in a tough environment, so clothes were bought for warmth, durability, and wind and weather resistance, not for glamour.

The remark by those workmen triggered a decision; later that week I boarded the boat back to the mainland for a shopping trip. I wasn't exactly looking forward to it because leaving Rum and going to the mainland was always a complete sensory overload for me. On Rum I lived in a tiny village, in a very natural environment, surrounded by lochs, mountains and abundant wildlife, with few people and only a tiny handful of cars. The mainland was full of cities, dual carriageways, noise, bright lights, traffic and crowds of people, and it often left me feeling completely overwhelmed.

If the city streets were bad enough, the inside of the shopping malls with their pumping music, harsh lighting and huge advertising slogans made me feel even worse; I just wanted to turn and run. The longer I spent on Rum the harder I found this mainland experience, but it was a necessary evil. Women passed me wearing the latest fashions and I felt inferior in comparison but didn't know where to start. When I was inside the shops I felt anxious and panicky, and I could only relax when I had bought something and was able to leave. I longed to be back on Rum, where camo jackets were the height of fashion and combat trousers were cool.

Looking around me, I also felt saddened by how materialistic people had become. It seemed that everyone had lost their sense of community and become obsessed by the latest gadget or fashionable trend. Some people didn't even know their next-door neighbours, let alone talk to them. While I was back in Aberdeen, I read a story in the newspaper that seemed to sum up the way things were going: an old woman had died but had lain undiscovered in her home for several months and was only found after complaints to the council from neighbours plagued with flies.

Something like that would never have happened on Rum. Everyone mattered over there and if someone didn't appear for a few days, you would go and check on them. If they failed to answer the door, you would just walk in. Of course it wasn't all happy families and plain sailing, but people genuinely cared about each other. Loneliness was a big problem on the mainland, where some elderly people might not talk to anyone for weeks on end, but that would never happen on Rum because people there were valued regardless of their age. No one needed ever to be lonely because there was a constant stream of islanders coming in and out of the village shop.

For most of the time I lived on Rum, the population hovered between thirty and thirty-five. People often said to me, 'Gosh, it must be such a lonely life,' but the complete opposite was true. When I lived on the mainland, I was surrounded by thousands of people, yet I often felt quite lonely. They all led busy, independent lives and social life had to be planned well in advance. On Rum I rarely if ever felt lonely and if I wanted company, all it took was a quick trip to the shop. If the shop was shut, I just knocked on someone's door and shared a cup of tea and a chat.

My mother told me that was how things used to be on the mainland as well, until about the 1960s. Most people grew up surrounded by three generations of their family, and stayed in the same place all their lives. Your childhood friends all lived within a few streets and a short walk from your home, and loneliness was almost unheard of. Nowadays families and friends are spread all over the country, people have to move frequently for work, communities are fragmented and townships have grown into small cities, full of people who barely know each other.

Rum is unique in the way that it still maintains a really strong sense of community and is probably one of the last places in the UK to do so. Sometimes it felt like I was part of a real-life soap opera where everyone knew everyone's business. Before I lived on Rum, I never used to believe it when characters from soap operas would lie, cheat and treat each other terribly, and then be friends again a short while later. If people treated you like that on the mainland you would just go and get a new set of friends, but on Rum it was very similar to the soap operas. People had terrible falling-outs, but would end up friends again sooner or later. It was the only way to survive island life and to be honest, if people didn't forgive and forget, they would end up with a terrible social life. There were only a couple of places on the island where you could go to socialise so it was easier to just get over it and accept that people had different views and opinions. Although some folks still did hold the odd grudge – we were all human – after a while you tended to develop a thick skin and let things wash over you that might have provoked a very different reaction back on the mainland.

However, living and working in that environment did come with its own set of problems. Friction between islanders did occur and it could boil up into arguments and fights, usually in the shop after the consumption of too many alcoholic beverages. Everyone had an opinion on how things should be done and of course the dominant personalities always wanted it done their way. In my opinion it didn't really matter how a job was done, as long as the end result was the right one, but the right way for one person might be the wrong way for another.

At four o'clock every afternoon, everyone finished work and headed down to the shop for a drink. It was just about the only time that all the SNH workers could get together to chat and at first all would be well, with everyone buying drinks for one another, talking nicely and calmly, and putting their point of view forward like civilised human beings. However, before long the dominant characters would disagree about something or other and a heated debate would ensue. Sometimes it ended in one or the other stomping off in a huff, or in a shouting match, but too much drink could also cause tempers to flare even more, resulting in a punch-up that always involved a couple of the same small cast of characters.

As we were all squeezed into a tiny shop, the glass jars on the shelves were usually the first casualties. With fists flying, bottles of ketchup and jars of mayonnaise came crashing down and smashed on the floor, leaving a horrible sticky mess for Norman to clear up. People would jump in to try and stop the fight and the belligerent pair would then be thrown out to finish the fight outside where the only damage they could cause was to each other.

Once they had calmed down and sobered up, they were expected to pay for the damaged goods and apologise to Norman. On rare occasions if a fight had been really bad, someone would call the police, but since there was no policeman on the island and the ferries only ran every few days, that gave everyone the chance to reflect on the wisdom of involving the police and plenty of time to think about what they were going to say to them. The inevitable result was that when the police finally arrived and began trying to take statements from the islanders, no one had ever seen a thing because when the fights had taken place, we were all outside the shop gazing at the stars. If we knew the police were coming we also made ourselves scarce; many of us were conveniently not in when they called.

For years the police force had tried and failed to appoint a Special Constable on Rum, purely because no one wanted to take on the job. Since Rum had such a small population, everyone knew everyone extremely well. The other inhabitants were the people you relied on every day to sell you food and drink, meet the boat for you, fix your house, repair the roads, deliver the post, and so on, so you really didn't want to piss anyone off. Not only that, but the person taking on the job of Special Constable would have had to be a righteous and upstanding citizen who never did anything wrong. Of course there was no such person on Rum, so the position remained unfilled. Had anyone taken on the job, they might not have been chased away by an angry mob of pitchfork-wielding locals, but they would have been ostracised. So, unless things got really out of hand, most disputes and grievances did not lead to a call to the police but were quietly settled among ourselves.

9

DAVY CHAINSAW

I had lived in the castle for the whole of my first year on Rum, but at the start of my second year I moved out and began living at Rock Cottage, owned by Sandy, the village car-penter and legendary player of the bodhran – the traditional Celtic drum. Sandy was very friendly and a big character in the island community. He always had the same look, owning several pairs of boot-cut blue jeans and white T-shirts, with his long, brown hair tied up in a ponytail, a short stubby pencil behind his ear and his leather tool-belt dangling from his waist. He liked a dram, loved music and was always having parties and barbecues where the music and singing could go on all night. He also organised the ceilidhs at the village hall and set up the annual Rum music festival.

I was given his spare room downstairs, with an open fireplace and a large, south-facing window. Sandy had two daughters from his first marriage, who lived with their mother on the mainland but would often come and stay with him in the holidays. His girlfriend, Fliss, also had two girls and she had her own cottage, so she and Sandy divided their time between their houses and I often had Rock Cottage all to myself. It was decorated like a hippie commune, with brightly coloured paint, wind chimes and tie-dyed wall hangings. Outside, rows of coloured buoys recovered from the beach were laid along the path and round the garden. I was so happy there that I ended up staying for two years.

Next door to the cottage was a small caravan owned by a character known as Davy Chainsaw. He came from Edinburgh and had been a supervisor slinger – responsible for attaching and detaching loads on cranes – and then a tree surgeon, but after visiting the island several times, he had given up his life in Edinburgh and come to live on Rum permanently. He bought a caravan, parked it next to Rock Cottage and, with Sandy's permission, hooked up an electric supply from the house to his caravan. Although small, it was very homely and Davy announced he was on Rum to stay, saying that coming to the island was 'the best decision I ever made in my life. I've already spoken to the minister to get a burial place sorted out. It sounds a bit morbid but there's no way I'm going off the island now.'

He lived at Rock Cottage for a number of years before finally moving his caravan to a more permanent site and when I was renting a room in the cottage, Davy and I were sort of housemates. He was a really gregarious character who would talk to absolutely everyone; he chatted to every single person who came off the ferry as if they were his best friend, telling them his life story and getting to know theirs as well.

When he first arrived on the island, he had looked fairly normal with blond hair, blue eyes, jeans and a T-shirt, but the island somehow has a way of changing people and it was not long before his appearance altered dramatically. He grew his hair really long and took to leaving it completely wild and unbrushed, so that it grew into a blond mane which stuck out at all angles from his head. He walked everywhere in hill boots – I never saw him in anything else and he even wore them to his own wedding – and started donning a kilt and tartan blanket. His hill boots, crazy hair and tartan apparel made him look like a wild Highlander from the Rob Roy era. However, one day, disaster struck. Poor Davy noticed a tiny bald patch at the back of his head and was so traumatised that he immediately grabbed his razor and shaved off all his hair until he was as bald as a seagull's egg.

Davy was a seasoned veteran when it came to wielding a chainsaw and the carvings he did with it earned him his nickname, though somewhere along the line it was changed first to 'Chainsaw', and then shortened again to just plain 'Chain'. Not long after he first came to Rum, he had carved a wooden totem pole, capped by a large sea eagle with out-stretched wings, that stood in the courtyard outside the shop. It remained there for years and he also carved several other pieces for tourists and friends passing through. When he carved an owl for a friend, so many people admired it and wanted to buy one for themselves that he was carving owls for months afterwards. However, large chunks of seasoned wood were hard to come by on Rum – the harsh climate ensured that there were few trees and those that did grow were contorted by the ferocious winds – so he did his carvings only as and when logs became available, either washed up as driftwood on the beaches or from trees uprooted by winter storms.

For the first few years Davy earned his living from chainsaw carving and working in the tea shop, but eventually he managed to get full-time employment as the Rum Pier Master, meeting and greeting the ferry. At that point, Davy decided he was living too far from the pier, so he moved his caravan from Rock Cottage over to the Old Boathouse next to the pier.

Davy had earned himself a bit of a reputation as a ladies' man and had his fair share of women while on Rum, but he had broken off a long engagement when he left Edinburgh, so he probably felt he was making up for lost time. Four years later, he still hadn't settled down and I was beginning to despair of him ever escaping his 'confirmed bachelor' status, but in May every year, a group of conservation students came over to the island to gain some practical experience within the nature reserve, and among them that year was a young woman called Sylvia. I first saw her when she walked into the Rum shop with a group of her fellow students. She was striking looking with long, dark, corkscrew curls and piercing blue eyes and somehow I just had the feeling that she was Davy's type. Making a mental note to try and introduce them later, I sloped off in search of my friends.

Later that evening, I decided to pop out for a drink.

Opening the door, I could see a large group of students chatting to a few of the islanders and, standing in the middle of the group, there was Davy Chainsaw talking animatedly to Sylvia. I smiled to myself; obviously my match-making services would not be required on this particular occasion.

Within the year, I was attending their wedding and by that time Sylvia was already four months pregnant. The service took place in the village hall and was attended by almost all of the islanders, plus family and friends. It was a very laid-back affair with no formal dress code and plenty of whisky, and the party went on well into the early hours of the following morning.

Five months later their son was born and they all moved into a large static caravan together. However, shortly after the birth, in a truly horrific coincidence, both Davy and Sylvia were diagnosed with serious medical conditions and had to leave Rum to seek treatment on the mainland. Their story had a happy ending though, because after several operations and some gruelling treatment, both of them were given the all-clear and they moved back to the island. Last year Davy and his family finally got a proper roof over their heads when they moved into a three-bedroomed house on Rum.

Summers were short on the Isle of Rum and my friends and I packed in as much as we could while the days were long and the weather was kind. We were all conservationists, so what might have seemed like childish activities to an outsider – peering into rock pools, picking up caterpillars or probing lochs and ponds – were entirely normal to us. There was nothing more enjoyable for me than digging up a really big worm, chasing after butterflies trying to identify them or poking about in a rock pool to see what I could find. It also brought back happy memories of my childhood, roaming the shoreline at Stonehaven with my long-suffering dad.

Beachcombing at Harris, on the far side of the island, where the tideline was always full of flotsam and jetsam, was another big thing among the islanders and we would often make crafts or decorate our houses with the objects we found. The kind of activities you could do on Rum were pretty limited anyway so if you weren't interested in walking, climbing, sea-swimming or nature, there really wasn't much else going on beyond a very occasional ceilidh and an odd drunken fist-fight outside the shop.

There was very little between Harris and the east coast of America and the Atlantic gales whipped up the sea into huge, white-crested waves that came crashing onto the rocky shoreline, depositing all manner of exciting treasures there. The stiff breeze on even the gentlest summer day also helped to keep the flies and biting insects at bay. As I gazed into the rock pools I could see anemones waving their delicate fronds in the water, trying to catch a meal. Winkles slowly made their way across the bottom of the pool, eating the slimy green algae on the stones. Hermit crabs crawled around the pebbles and battles were won and lost over empty winkle shells. Occasionally a small fish, crab or prawn would catch our attention and we would rush to try and catch it. We rarely succeeded. Even after we'd removed every large stone in the pool, the poor creature usually found a crevice to hide in and escaped our unwanted attentions.

The sand was littered with large boulders from the corries above, and all along the beach lay broken crab pots, torn nets and frayed ropes, washed up from the Minch. The storms had also laid waste to all manner of fishing equipment which now lay ruined on the sand. I loved collecting the brightly coloured fishing floats, but I wasn't alone in that; most houses on Rum had a colourful array of buoys and floats hanging outside their houses and arranged along their driveways.

One day the office took a phone call from a group of walkers who had seen a dead body washed up on the beach at Harris, so we jumped into the Land Rover and drove over there at breakneck speed. When we arrived, we could see a body lying face up on the shingle, but when we sprinted over to it, we did a double take and burst out laughing. The 'body' turned out to be a dummy, dressed in fishermen's waterproofs, that must have been lost during a search and rescue training exercise, but we removed him from the beach anyway to prevent further upset to visitors and fresh false alarms for us.

The Isle of Rum had two mountain bothies, one at Dibidil in the south and another at Guirdil on the north-west coast. The easiest way to get to Guirdil was to scrounge a lift to Harris and then walk up the coastline over Bloodstone Hill before dropping down towards the bothy. One beautiful summer weekend I decided to spend a night there, so I packed my sleeping bag and rucksack, got a lift from a friend, and then shouldered my pack and set off along the coastal path.

Leaning heavily on my walking stick, I dragged myself up the long, winding path, climbing steadily higher until I could see all the way over to the Western Isles. A group of hinds were grazing peacefully above me. Their spotted calves had not long been born and lay motionless in the heather, hiding from predators, and from me. Soon they would be big enough to follow their mothers and take their place in the herd.

I reached Wreck Bay, where many years before a fishing vessel had met its end on the sharp rocks, though to my disappointment, there was very little left to be seen of the wreck apart from a heap of rusted metal. The steep sea cliffs dropped down to the beach a hundred feet below me. At intervals along the cliff face, feral goats were grazing on ledges so narrow they would have left me white-faced and clinging to the rock for dear life, but the goats took their precarious footholds and the perilous cliffs in their stride. They chewed the cud noisily as they watched me peering down at them. At the base of the cliff, on the rocky shoreline, guillemots, kittiwakes and shags stood preening themselves in the sunshine.

I shouldered my pack again and moved on towards Bloodstone Hill. It was one of the most imposing hills on the island with the sea-cliffs on its western face plunging hundreds of feet down to the shore below. The hill took its name from the mineral found there. Bloodstone is a form of agate, often a beautiful jade-green colour, though it has many shades from pale green through to very dark. It is often flecked with red traces of the iron ore haematite, which were thought to resemble spots of blood and so earned the stone its name. Mined on the hill from the earliest times, bloodstone could be worked like flint to make tools and axes, and was probably the reason why Stone Age dwellers on Rum formed one of the earliest recorded settlements in Scotland. In more modern times, Queen Victoria was presented with a table made from bloodstone, while twenty-first-century crystal healers claim it can be used to treat disorders of the blood.

A pair of golden eagles had been nesting for years on the precipitous north slopes of Bloodstone Hill and had already successfully raised many chicks. I could see their large eyrie through my binoculars and as I rounded the flank of the hill below it, I was stopped in my tracks by the spectacular sea views. A school of porpoises was leaping and diving in the sparkling water offshore and the small white houses and even the grazing livestock on the Isle of Canna were clearly visible a couple of miles away. Several miles beyond Canna, just visible in the haze, were the Outer Hebridean islands of Barra and South Uist, and to my left, the white tower of the unmanned Hyskeir (Oigh-sgeir in Gaelic) lighthouse stood on a large, black rock rising from the sea, sited there to warn off ships in the Sea of the Hebrides approaching the southern entrance to the Minch.

In the old days, the lighthouse was always manned by two people who would stay there for months at a time. Derek had once delighted in telling me what happened when one of the lighthouse keepers died soon after arriving there. 'There were no radios or telephones in those days,' he said. 'So calling for help was not an option, and since the lighthouse was perched on a solid rock, he was unable to bury the body. He kept it inside the lighthouse for a week but by then the smell was becoming overpowering. He didn't want to leave it on the rocks outside in case the sea-birds ate it or storm seas washed it away, so in the end he tied a rope to it, hung it out of the window and left it dangling down the wall of the lighthouse until the boat arrived with the relief lighthouse crew.'

I was now right above Guirdil Glen, where the bothy was sited, but the path continued in a different direction, towards the *bealach* (mountain pass) leading to the north coast and eventually back to Kinloch. In order to reach the bothy I had to leave the path and scramble down the rugged slopes of Bloodstone Hill. In between the screes were patches of grass, some descending all the way down into the glen. The grass had been cropped short by grazing deer and as walking down was difficult and time-consuming, even with a stick, I decided to slide down the grass on my backside instead. It turned out to be not the best idea I'd ever had. By the time I'd slid down the first hundred feet, I had given myself a complete 'wedgie'. My trouser bottoms were on my thighs, the waistband was up around my chest and my trousers had turned into shorts.

When I reached the bottom, having readjusted my trousers, I squelched to the Guirdil bothy across the marshy ground, mostly sphagnum moss studded with marsh orchids and bog cotton. There was no lock on the door, of course, and the bothy was clean and well kept with a fireplace and a stock of fuel to warm its small rooms, two on the ground floor and one up in the rafters. Hikers, climbers and Munro-baggers staying there had left pieces of bloodstone, shells and fishing floats lining the window ledge, and on the table there was an old blackened kettle and a few tealights. I lit a fire, filled the kettle from the burn and put it on to boil, then sat watching the sun sink towards the sea.

As darkness fell, I rolled out my sleeping bag and settled down beside the fire, with the flicker of a candle the only visible light in the whole vast sweep of sea and landscape. I fell asleep to the crashing of the surf on the shore. It was the most peaceful, untroubled night's rest I'd had in years. My working life up to then sometimes seemed to consist of nothing but a succession of moves to ever more remote areas, and in that context, the night at Guirdil was the logical endpoint. Short of pitching a tent on an empty beach in the Outer Hebrides or bivouacking on Rockall, the uninhabited rock in the middle of the Atlantic, it was hard to imagine anywhere further from 'civilisation'. However, the isolation at Guirdil was too extreme even for me. I loved the time I spent there, but I valued the company of my friends on the island too much to contemplate ever leading a hermit-like existence, remote from all human contact.

The start of the stag season on 1 July 2005 brought with it the arrival of the first stalking guests, most of them coming from Europe, in particular Norway, Sweden and Germany. The stalking was good that season and when we had obtained the week's quota of stags, we often took the guests off around the island for some sightseeing in Derek's white Toyota Hilux pick-up, or the 'Taliban Van' as the locals liked to call it. Battered and bent, the poor pick-up had taken severe punishment on Rum's unforgiving, rocky roads. There were only about a dozen miles of roads on the island and the speed limit was fifteen miles an hour, but they were all dirt roads and the surfaces were so pitted, pot-holed and rock-strewn that only four-wheel-drive vehicles could negotiate them safely, and only then at the probable cost of damage to tyres, exhausts, sumps, suspension and bodywork.

Derek's Taliban Van had taken such a pounding that it had almost been shaken to pieces and it was a miracle that it was still drivable at all, but somehow, if it wasn't exactly an armchair ride, it never broke down as we drove the guests down the bumpy road to Kilmory. The stretches of neat, close-cropped turf and gentle, rolling hills made Kilmory vaguely resemble a golf course gone wild and because of the research project, unlike the rest of the island, deer were never shot there and were extremely tame. Large groups of hinds carried on calmly grazing the short grass, even while people and vehicles were passing by with the tourists' cameras clicking and whirring.

Summer on Rum was always a brief affair and before long the heather was starting to lose its bloom and the grasses were withering in the cold autumn air. The long molinia grass stems bent before the strengthening winds sweeping across the hillside like a Mexican wave and we were soon picking the autumn harvest of chanterelle and porcini mushrooms that grew in abundance along the pathways through the pinewoods. The large bright-orange caps of the chanterelles provided a splash of colour on the forest floor and the porcini mushrooms, if less brightly coloured, were equally tasty. Many of the islanders had favourite places where the most succulent and exotic specimens grew and, guided by them, I often came home with a bagful to add to our casseroles and stews. Any excess we dried or froze to use at a later date.

When the deer rut began in September, Kilmory Glen was the best place on the island to view it at close quarters. The marshier areas between the 'greens' contained deer wallows: wet, boggy, peat-filled holes where the stags would thrash around, emerging with their antlers festooned in peat and vegetation. The stags would also urinate in a wallow and then roll in it, anointing themselves with their musky aroma. They apparently thought that the heavy scent would make them more alluring to the hinds, although I had my doubts. Covering themselves in the thick, black peat also served as an optical illusion, making them look larger and more imposing to rivals and potential mates among the hinds. The tactic didn't just work on deer. Many stalkers told of shooting an apparently huge black stag on the hillside, only to find that it was a modest-sized animal of less than 100 kilos. Distance could also make them seem larger, reflected in the old Gaelic saying: '*Is àrd ceann an fhèidh sa chreachann*': 'Lofty is the deer's head on the top of the mountain'.

The wild goat rut was also in full swing over on the west coast around Harris. The billy goats gathered in small herds as the dominant males fought for supremacy. After standing and pawing the ground, the big males hurled themselves at their opponents with the clash of horns echoing along the seashore like gunfire. At that time of year their pungent smell just about knocked me out and I wondered if they had stolen the stags' idea of anointing themselves with their own urine.

*

I had still been working as a ghillie in the early stages of the stag season, but not long after it began, Derek got in touch in something of a panic. He had recently set up his own business offering red deer-stalking to paying clients. After agreeing a deal with Scottish Natural Heritage, Derek paid a sum of money for a percentage of the deer cull, allowing him and some of the other islanders to work independently of SNH. He advertised through a company that attracted hunters from all over Europe, and he also booked private clients though his website. All was going well until he found that he was double-booked because the hunting company had taken a booking from an English couple at the last moment and Derek hadn't realised until it was too late.

The deposit had been taken, so the show had to go on and he asked if I would mind taking out one group of guests for the week. I readily agreed. It wasn't the first time I had taken paying guests out hunting, but I was still quite nervous as I wanted to do well. My fears were unfounded, however, as we shot four stags within four days. I was given a generous tip and Derek was so pleased that he offered me a permanent job, allowing me finally to graduate from ghillie to full-time deer-stalker.

It was quite unexpected because I'd almost given up hope of ever getting the chance to achieve my dream and become a fully fledged stalker. I was even beginning to think that I might have to revert to my first career and go back to wielding a chainsaw as a tree surgeon but, all of a sudden, I found myself moving up from ghillie to stalker in the space of a week. That wasn't at all what I was expecting. I'd originally thought that if it happened at all, it would be after taking up a full-time job on an estate, with a house and a car as part of the package, but realistically, those jobs were becoming more rare with every passing year. Like many other businesses, estates increasingly preferred to hire part-time, seasonal workers, avoiding all the additional expenses that came with employing full-time staff. So my dream was becoming less and less likely, and working as a part-time stalker on Rum was probably the best I could ever have hoped for.

However it had come about and however far from my original idea it was, I was absolutely ecstatic to have finally achieved my dream. I was a fully qualified gamekeeper and deer-stalker, and I was also a woman. I almost wished that every student, keeper and client who had ever made a sexist comment to me had been there so I could ram their words back down their throats. No job for a woman? Tell that to the stags!

It was so exhilarating to go out on my first day, no longer a ghillie following in the stalker's footsteps, but a stalker striding out ahead of my own clients and ghillies, choosing my stalking ground, leading the client to the point where he could take the shot and then summoning the ghillie to load the stag onto the pony. My first week of stalking was absolutely wonderful and at the end of it I remember thinking, 'This has been so exhilarating; it's everything I always dreamed it would be.'

From then on during the culling season, Derek and I worked as stalkers, while some of the other islanders took turns to ghillie for us. As it was a seasonal job, they couldn't afford to give up their full-time work, but they took a few weeks' holiday and came to work with us each time the stag season came around. The ponies we used belonged to Scottish Natural Heritage, but they were leased to us as part of Derek's deal with them. Each morning Derek and I would pick up the guests and leave the village in his battered white pick-up while the ghillies followed behind with the ponies. Stopping to spy the hillside for deer, Derek would make a plan of action for the day and then we'd set off in different directions with our respective clients and it was a matter of pride for us both that we did not return from a stalk empty-handed.

Although the bulk of the population of Rum were adults, there were also five children who attended the local primary school. The schoolhouse was near the pier on the far side of the village and the children, aged from six up to eleven, were all taught by the same teacher, Liz. There was a head teacher but he looked after all the primary schools of the Small Isles: Rum, Eigg, Muck and Canna, and made a regular circuit of them using the CalMac ferry, so he could check the progress of the students and give support to the teachers. Although such a low number of students probably meant a better education for the children, it also had its drawbacks. While pupils on the mainland schools had Christmas and Halloween parties, our island kids were somewhat limited, because five children did not make for much of a party. Liz was determined that they would not miss out and enlisted the help of the Reserve Manager, Ed. So when Liz organised a Halloween party, Ed simply told us during our Monday morning byre meeting, 'Find a costume to wear to the party and turn up at the schoolhouse at seven o'clock sharp on the evening of 31 October.'

Finding a costume wasn't easy. There were no costume shops, second-hand stores or joke shops on the island and our internet connection was intermittent at the best of times, making buying a costume online a risky business. We only had two weeks' notice anyway, which might not have been enough time for a parcel to reach the island if the ferries were cancelled because of autumn gales.

There was nothing for it, I would have to make myself a costume somehow, but I had no idea what I could use. My fellow ghillie, Karl, had decided to go as Jason, the machete-wielding, masked serial killer from the *Halloween* movies. His mother had posted him a mask and he had raided the mechanic's workshop for a blue boilersuit, made a machete out of cardboard, spray-painted it silver and then covered it with splashes and drips of red paint to make it look like blood splatters.

Everyone else on the island also seemed to know what they were going as, apart from me. I always had my best ideas while walking along the beach; it gave me a feeling of freedom with the wind in my hair and the soft sand underfoot. So I set off along the shoreline, picking my way through piles of driftwood and plastic fishing floats and all sorts of interesting objects that had been washed up and come to rest in a long, haphazard line, just above the high-water mark. Single shoes, plastic bottles, fishing buoys and old netting were the most common, although if you looked hard enough, you could sometimes find something really worth taking home. Fliss had a large shed which she had turned into a craft shop, and as well as hand-knitted hats and gloves, candles and soap, she sold all sorts of other items made from beachcombed material, including polished bloodstone and driftwood mirror frames.

As I headed around the bay towards the rocks, I noticed a flash of silver and went to investigate, picking my way between some large boulders. It turned out to be a metal buoy, something I'd never seen before. All the ones I'd found up to then were made of brightly coloured plastic so that the fishermen were able to spot them from a distance. This one was unique and resembled a ball and chain, or at least it would have done had there actually been a chain to go with it. It wouldn't have looked out of place in the Tower of London and it got me thinking that if I could find a chain, I could use it as part of a Halloween costume.

I picked up the metal fishing float and headed over to the mechanic's workshop. He very kindly dug me out a length of old iron chain. It was covered in oil and rust but I knew that it could be cleaned up and, best of all, it clipped onto the buoy, making a perfect ball and chain. Back at the house, I spent a couple of hours cleaning off the oil with detergent and getting rid of the rust with a wire brush. I then clipped the chain around my ankle and practised walking along the corridor, dragging the fishing float behind me, while the chain made a satisfying clanking noise. All I needed now was an outfit of some sort, but I wasn't quite sure what. Inspiration came to me while I was sorting out the washing later that night.

One of Sandy's double bedsheets was hanging on the clothes airer. It was crisp, white, fresh-smelling and absolutely perfect. That was it; I would go as a ghost, courtesy of Sandy's laundry pile.

The night of the Halloween party arrived and after a quick dinner and bath, I donned my outfit but when I slipped the bedsheet over my head, I realised I hadn't quite thought things through, as I couldn't see through it. The party started in an hour and I had no time to prepare another costume; it was the bedsheet or nothing so, grabbing a set of scissors, I cut two round eye holes in the centre of it and another hole for my mouth, so I'd be able to drink. Of course I knew it was wrong and I was probably going to go straight to hell for my thoughtless action, but it didn't stop me, I was a woman on a mission.

When I arrived at the schoolhouse, most of the islanders were already there. Everyone had turned up in fancy dress and there was even another bedsheet ghost like me. The ball and chain attracted a lot of comments, most of them positive, as I paraded around the room trailing it behind me. Two large tables at the side of the room were filled with party food and alcohol, and after tucking into the food, we started on the alcohol while Liz played games with the children. Whisky, vodka and wine were served to the adults in plastic cups with straws, just like a proper children's party. It continued long after the children had gone to bed and when we were evicted from the schoolhouse, we simply adjourned to the village shop and carried on partying there.

I'm ashamed to confess that I never admitted my

destruction of Sandy's bedsheet to anyone, least of all to Sandy himself. I sneakily covered my tracks by folding the sheet and placing it right at the bottom of his laundry cupboard. I then piled all his other sheets on top of it and tiptoed quietly away ... sorry Sandy.

Having moved around so many times over the previous few years, I was now really feeling settled on Rum, but my work on the island was still seasonal. We stalked deer between August and February but the months when the deer were raising their young were generally devoid of any work for me and, as usual, I was forced to leave Rum for three or four months to find work elsewhere. So in the spring of 2006 I was pleased when I was again offered work as a trapper on the Western Isles – the Outer Hebrides – though this time the prey was not hedgehogs but mink.

The mink we were trapping were native to America but back in the 1960s, when fur was more fashionable, a large mink farm had been set up on Lewis. Animal-rights activists had raided the farm and released the mink and these ferocious predators were now running riot all over the Western Isles, eating the eggs and fledglings of rare birds. The Western Isles had very few trees because of the force of the winds, and the birds laid their eggs directly onto the ground. Just as in Rum, there had been no ground predators and the birds had thrived until the mink arrived, when bird numbers rapidly declined. So Scottish Natural Heritage had set up an elimination programme to trap the mink and allow the bird population to recover.

Accommodation was not provided so I and two other mink trappers rented a whitewashed cottage nestling among the heather moorlands near the fishing village of Geocrab on the Isle of Harris. There were traditional peat stacks around the cottage that we used to fuel the open fireplaces in each room. Our garden was set in about half an acre of ground, surrounded by sheep-proof fencing and before renting us the cottage, the owner asked us to mow the lawns regularly. We assured her that we would and we genuinely meant it at the time, but after a hard day's work, gardening was the last thing on our minds. In any case, none of us actually owned a mower and we were reluctant to buy one with so many eco-friendly ewes running around, so we decided to open the gate and let the sheep in instead, and they did an excellent job of keeping the grass short.

I was enjoying my life and my work but life in the islands would never be complete for me without a pet. After having my pet crow, Tennis, when I was twelve, throughout my teenage years and twenties I had always kept an eye out for any more injured crows, but I had never found another one. Getting a budgie was out of the question; if I was going to get a pet bird, it had to be more exotic and challenging than that.

In my downtime on the Isle of Harris, I scrolled through a selection of unusual birds on the Birdmart website, including vultures, kookaburras and adult golden eagles. Providing that the birds or the eggs from which they've hatched have been legally obtained and not stolen from the wild, even golden eagles can be purchased ... at a price. Halfway down the page I noticed an advert for a five-week-old baby raven. I called the breeder who assured me it came with the correct documents, which was vital because taking ravens from the wild is a criminal offence.

The breeder said his three adult pairs of ravens had produced nine chicks that year but only one was left, which he had been hand-rearing in his home. 'Ravens are highly intelligent and skilled flyers,' he said. 'I must warn you though, they get bored easily, are constantly on the move, and are very destructive birds that will peck anything they can get their beaks on. The chick, which we've named Hagrid, quickly took over our house and is now demolishing it bit by bit.'

'Thanks for the warning,' I said, 'but I'm sure I'll be okay with it. After all, I've owned a pet crow before; how bad can a raven be?' If only I'd known ...

The breeder told me that he'd acquired his ravens back in the 1970s, in the days before taking wild birds became a criminal offence. His friend, a gamekeeper from the Western Isles, had regularly trapped and killed them because they were a serious threat to the crofters' livestock, pecking out the eyes of newborn lambs. However, the raven breeder had urged his friend to simply pass on the trapped birds to him, rather than killing them. They could live in his aviary and produce chicks which he could sell to the Tower of London and falconry centres. When the laws changed a few years later, prohibiting taking birds from the wild, he was one of the very few legal raven breeders.

'We live in Cornwall,' he said, 'but my wife and I have always wanted a holiday on the west coast of Scotland, so we'll kill two birds with one stone – not literally of course – and we'll bring Hagrid up there for you.'

I was overjoyed; not only was I getting a pet raven but I was saving a fortune too, because it would have cost me a packet to have gone all the way to Cornwall for it. A week later, armed with a mobile cat carrier, I met the breeder at the Uig Ferry Port on the north-west coast of Skye. In the back of his white Transit van there was a large birdcage. There were no windows in the back of the van, but peering into the gloom, I could just make out a pair of charcoal-black eyes staring back at me. Bits of tin foil and sparkly material littered the floor of the cage. 'Ravens love anything shiny,' the breeder said, following my gaze, and I made a mental note to hide my jewellery.

'I've put a pair of anklets on her feet for you,' he said, 'so you can take her outside on a glove. I'll just grab her for you and stick her in your cat carrier.'

The raven was reasonably docile as he took her out of the cage but when he put her in the cat carrier she squawked furiously and then began attacking the plastic box with her sharp beak, outraged at being so confined. However, CalMac had strict rules on the transportation of pets, so she would just have to put up with it as I said goodbye to the breeder and boarded the ferry for the voyage back to Harris.

She had cost me £400, which I thought was quite cheap for a bird of her rarity, but since my raven was a 'she' not a 'he', I decided that Hagrid was not really a suitable name and renamed her Babe instead. I sat in the upstairs observation lounge of the ferry, while the cat carrier next to me rocked back and forth furiously. Slowly but surely the other passengers began to notice the commotion and came over to have a look at what was causing it, taking it in turns to peek at my unusual companion.

It was late at night by the time Babe and I arrived back at the cottage and I could finally let her out of the carrier. Breathing a sigh of relief, she hopped out and began preening herself with great vigour. She looked tentatively around the room before hopping onto the bed for a closer inspection. I had not had time to build an aviary, so the house would have to do until something more suitable could be found. The mess she made meant that my bedsheets went through the washing machine every day for the first month and the drone of the spin cycle became a constant background noise.

In the wild, ravens hide surplus food for later consumption and Babe was a master of the art. Many times I picked up a favourite novel only to find the pages stuck together by a congealed ball of mince. However, even worse was the night when, half-asleep, I slid my hand under my pillow, only for my fingers to curl around a slimy lump of uncooked chicken. I recoiled in horror and glared at Babe, the picture of innocence, sleeping peacefully on top of the wardrobe.

It wasn't long before I discovered how inquisitive Babe could be and what the consequences were. Using her sharp beak, she inspected everything by the simple expedient of tearing it to pieces. Anything she was unable to break, she picked up and hid in one of her secret hiding places instead. Whenever anything went missing (which was frequently) I had to search the room, checking in all her usual hiding places. When I eventually found her secret stash, it would invariably be filled with pound coins, jewellery, hair clips and a myriad of other shiny objects. I soon realised that Babe was simply bored and needed some stimulation, so I started taking her out to work with me.

Each day I secured Babe to the top of my backpack and then set off, walking for miles across the rugged moorland to check my mink traps. Babe was in her element in the great outdoors, but unfortunately my backpack didn't fare quite so well and was quickly covered in bird poo. At the end of each day, we fell into the house exhausted and happy, and Babe and I stretched out in front of the fire, warming ourselves, while the sweet aromatic scent of peat-smoke filled the air. She soon recovered and the destruction of my personal possessions began again. Not that I really cared, of course, they were simply objects whereas Babe was rapidly becoming the love of my life.

In the absence of a boyfriend – and the memory of my affair with Alan was still too raw in my memory for me to be in any hurry to find a new one – I suppose Babe was filling a bit of an emotional gap in my life. I hadn't been out with anyone for over two years when Babe came on the scene, and she became my friend and someone to care for in both senses of the word. She was a very intelligent animal and almost human in her actions, so much so that I didn't really think of her as being a raven at all; in my mind she was more of a little human with a black feather coat.

As we made our daily rounds, Babe and I would sometimes stop by one of the deserted hill lochs and spend a couple of hours fishing. They ranged in size from tiny peat pools to mile-long lochs and I soon found the best ones to fish. Setting Babe on her perch next to me, I cast my line and would usually get my first bite within fifteen minutes. Reeling it in carefully, I landed a plump brown trout. Of course Babe felt it her ravenly duty to 'help' with the landing of the fish by jumping from her perch onto the flapping trout and sinking her claws and sharp beak into it. Having killed it, she would proudly present 'her' catch to me, fluffing up her feathers with pride as if to say, 'Look what I've caught, ain't I great? If you're lucky I may deign to share some of it with you.'

Brown trout made a lovely meal for me in the evenings, even if, after Babe's attentions, the fish often looked a bit worse for wear before they went under the grill. Not that Babe cared, because her meal was already taken care of. While I lived mainly on bread and pasta – and trout – I spoiled her with the finest cuts of meat: her favourites were lamb cutlet, pork loin and fillet steak. My housemates and I only earned a low wage and they were a bit sarcastic about the amount of money I was spending, but I couldn't see the problem; it was my money and whatever I might have spent on Babe's gourmet dinners, it never stopped me from paying my share of the household bills on time.

10

RAVENS AND EAGLES

After five months trapping mink on the Western Isles, I phoned Derek to find out when he needed me back for the new stalking season. It was as well I did, for he told me that the hunting company's new brochure had a picture of Rum on the front cover, with one of our Highland ponies with a large stag on its back facing Bloodstone Hill. 'There's a big spread on Rum inside,' Derek said, 'including a picture of you with your rifle on your back and two ponies loaded with stags. Listen to this: "Rum is the best stalking experience we have on offer, because it not only has the most breathtaking views of mountains and steep sea cliffs, but is also one of the last places in Scotland that still uses Highland ponies to extract the deer."'

'That's fantastic, Derek,' I said.

'You can say that again, the phone's been ringing off the

hook ever since and the stalking is already booked up for the entire stag season. So if you want your job back, Portia, you'd better get yourself back to Rum pretty soon.'

'I'll be on the next ferry. Is that soon enough?'

I began the laborious task of packing, marvelling at how much junk I seemed to have accumulated in such a short time, and after hasty goodbyes to my friends and colleagues, Babe and I left Harris on the next ferry. We arrived at the Rum pier at around one o'clock in the afternoon and I could see some of my friends waiting for me, including Derek in the 'Taliban Van'. I loaded my belongings and my disgruntled raven into Derek's pick-up and then helped the others offload their weekly food and drink supply. It was a standing joke with the ferrymen that our weekly order contained twice as much alcohol as food. Awash with beer, cider and whisky, Rum would not have been a good place for a recovering alcoholic. As we used to joke, 'There's no Betty Ford clinic on Rum. Know why? Because no one would check in.'

I was now not only working with Derek but staying at his house as well. It was the middle one of a row of three houses that had once been a coach house and a weathered sign on the door read 'Stalker's Bothy'. I unloaded my belongings and then let Babe out of her cat carrier. She hopped out, stretched her wings and fluffed up her feathers, grumbling loudly after her long period of incarceration. Then she flew onto the roof of the pick-up and, while we went inside for a cup of tea, she stood looking around, apparently awestruck at her new surroundings.

The first stalking guests, four Norwegian hunters, had

arrived on the same boat as me and we were due to start work the next day, so Derek and I hurried around making all the necessary preparations for the start of the season, including gathering in and preparing the ponies, which as usual had been running wild since the end of the last stalking season.

Rum had its own unique breed of hill pony, distinct from the ones on Highland estates like Letterewe, and kept purely for carrying home the dead deer from the hills. They are one of the native pony breeds of the Scottish Highlands and Islands and may well have been roaming Rum since the Ice Age, but were first recorded on the island in the 1770s, when they were described by Dr Johnson as 'very small but of a breed eminent for beauty'. They remained a pure breed while the Highland ponies on the mainland were being crossed with Clydesdales and other breeds to increase their size for pulling ploughs and other heavy agricultural work. As a result, the Isle of Rum's ponies are the only ones in existence preserving the ancient and now very rare bloodlines. They are tough, sure-footed and extremely hardy, thriving in conditions and on poor grazing that would starve other breeds, and – with a few notable exceptions – they tend to have a very good, equable temperament as well.

Living with Derek had one interesting benefit. In his role as local postman, Derek would meet the boat four times a week to collect and drop off the islanders' mail. The post office was the village shop which opened for a couple of hours in the mornings for us to post our letters and parcels, but since there was no sorting office and the shop had very limited space, the sorting of the mail actually took place in Derek's front room. As Derek laid out the mail in neat little piles, I would take a sneaky peek over his shoulder to see what folk had been buying. Clandestine affairs were rampant in the hothouse atmosphere on Rum. How they got away with it undetected was completely beyond me, but there was a surefire way of spotting when an affair had started because parcels with the logos of Ann Summers or Figleaves emblazoned across the packaging started arriving for the guilty party. However, I never drew anyone else's attention to that because I really shouldn't have been nosing round their mail in the first place.

Like her owner, Babe had settled in well on Rum, but while my living accommodation was in Derek's spare room upstairs, she had decided to make herself at home in the living room instead. Luckily for me the bothy had linoleum floors and wooden furniture, so any mess Babe made could be wiped up easily. The sofas were a different matter entirely and to keep those clean I had to cover them with throws and replace them every day. The washing machine was kept very busy and I often wondered how Derek put up with us.

The facial muscles of a raven have both short and longer feathers attached to them and in order to show her different emotions, Babe could raise and lower her facial feathers accordingly. When she was mildly annoyed, she would do something I called the 'eyebrow lift', when the short feathers above her eyes would stand up, making her look stern and slightly angry. When she was really furious, she would raise all the feathers on her head to make herself appear larger, her beak would gape open and she would open and close her wings to show her anger.

One day while flying around the kitchen, Babe completely misjudged her landing platform. She was aiming for the top of the cooker, which until that day had been sticky with dust and debris. However, the shop on Rum had just taken delivery of a heavily advertised new cleaning product, Cillit Bang, and feeling that Derek's house would benefit from a deep clean, I had bought some with the intention of blitzing the cooker.

When I had finished, I stepped back to admire the now gleaming surface. It was so shiny that I could almost see my face in it. At that moment, Derek walked down the stairs, startling Babe, who had been perching on the sideboard. She took flight and aimed herself towards the cooker. She stretched out her claws, intending to touch down on top of the previously stable landing pad, as she had done many times before. Unfortunately this time the Cillit Bang had done its job a little too well and the top of the cooker was now as clear and slick as an iced-over puddle.

As she landed on the cooker, she found herself skidding along the top, squawking, screeching and flapping as she went. Rolling over twice, she shot off the far end and landed with a loud thump on the floor, upside down. Righting herself, she looked around to see if anyone had noticed and caught Derek and me dissolving in fits of laughter.

She fluffed up her feathers in embarrassment but after a few seconds of watching us laugh, she could take no more and shook her tail feathers and raised all her head feathers in rage. She was well aware that we were laughing at her and in revenge she vented her fury by proceeding to attack every inanimate object in the house. Books were ripped and cups thrown off the sideboard to smash on the linoleum floor. She even threw the cutlery all over the floor, before eventually settling down on top of the bookcase, still eyeing me balefully as I set to work to clean up the mess.

As well as showing her emotions, Babe frequently demon-strated her intelligence. Every morning I would eat a breakfast of toast with lemon curd, taking great care to remove all the horrible crusts, which I pushed to the side of the plate. I must have heard the hoary old wives' tale stating that 'crusts make your hair go curly' at some point in my childhood and, since nothing was more terrifying to me than the thought of curly hair, I'd avoided them like the plague ever since. Babe always ate the crusts for me until one morning, when she refused to touch them. 'Strange, she must be off her food,' I said to Derek, who was busy making coffee. Leaving my toast on the plate, I turned around to pour myself a cup of tea. When I turned back, there was Babe eating my toast.

From that moment on, she adamantly refused to eat another crust. Watching me, she had realised that crusts were the nasty bits and the middle part was the real delicacy. So from then on I felt duty bound to prepare two slices of toast and lemon curd, one for me and one for Babe. If I didn't, she would simply steal mine anyway when my back was turned. I watched her as she ever so carefully pulled off each crust, leaving them in a neat pile on her plate before demolishing the toast. Sometimes while I was eating my dinner at night, Babe also stood on my shoulder and stole the food off my fork as I lifted it up to my mouth. The only way to stop that was to grab the sweeping brush and chase her around the house until she learned to behave herself. Before long, all I had to say was 'Brush!' and she would fly away, squawking in fear.

Most wild birds are not naturally affectionate, but I was determined that Babe would at least let me clap her for a few minutes every day. (Apart from applause and a disease you really don't want to get, 'clap' is also a Scottish word for 'stroke'.) This proved to be a slight problem since, being the vain bird that she was, Babe hated having her feathers touched. Having spent ages preening and getting her plumage just the way she wanted it, she was not going to allow anyone, not even me, to ruffle her feathers, or not without a fight anyway.

To begin with, even though I touched her very gently, she would always warn me off by pecking me with her sharp beak, but after a while, I noticed that it was actually the sides of the beak that were razor sharp. The tip, which was the part she used the most, was actually quite blunt. To avoid the sharp edges, I just had to stick my thumb in the front of her beak. Even though she at once clamped down on it, the only point of the beak that touched my thumb was the tip, which didn't hurt that much anyway and with a thumb in her mouth, she couldn't attack me, so I was free to stroke her. Keeping my thumb firmly in her beak, I buried my face in her soft neck feathers and made little crooning noises to her.

After weeks of doing this I noticed something very

peculiar. If I moved my thumb down until her head was between her legs, she would go into a sleepy trance. The pressure on my thumb would ease and I could then remove it from her beak altogether, and she would stay motionless, her head between her legs and her beak hanging open, clearly still imagining that she was holding onto a thumb that was no longer there.

In a spirit of scientific enquiry, I then started experimenting by placing small objects like coins on her back to see if she would wake and shake them off. She never did, and after a few weeks I had even graduated to using her as a feather-clad occasional table, resting larger objects like a side plate with my peanut butter on toast on her back while I turned the page of my magazine or took a slurp from my cup of tea with the other hand.

I then decided the experiment had gone far enough and stopped placing objects on Babe's back, but by now she loved receiving affection from me. With all the housework to be done, there wasn't always time to give her much attention but as I stood at the sink or sweeping the floor, Babe would often jump up and grab my thumb, trying to entice me into some affectionate behaviour.

One day, while she was behaving in a particularly needy way, she again jumped up and grabbed my thumb. This time she had a good grasp and really did not want to let go, so I swung her back and forth gently, like the pendulum on a clock, encouraging her to let go. After a few minutes of this she released her beak and landed with a soft thump on the floor but, eyes shining with excitement, she hopped straight back towards me and made another grab for my thumb. This time I swung her slightly harder and she let go after a while, landing daintily on both feet. What had I started? This went on for weeks with Babe pestering me incessantly to be swung about the room. By now I would swing her much higher and she would wait until she reached the highest point before letting go and dropping back down to the floor. A couple of bounds along the linoleum and she was attached to my hand again.

One day I wondered whether I could introduce a backflip into the stunt. Babe seemed more than up for it and I was willing to give it a go, but of course I didn't want any broken wings, so I aimed her at the sofa. Building up momentum, I swung her hard and at the last moment gave a flick of the wrist. She flew into the air, did a backflip and landed with a soft thud on the sofa. Looking from left to right and shaking her head, she paused for a few seconds, trying to decide whether or not she liked the new stunt. Of course she did, and she was back for 'seconds' shortly afterwards.

The daily power cut, that happened as regular as clockwork at about ten past four every afternoon, was another strange new thing for Babe to get used to. The village's electricity was supplied by a hydroelectric power station on the river at the base of Coire Dubh (Black Corrie) to the west of the castle. The force of the river cascading down the rocky hillside drove the water turbines inside a small generator house about the size of a garden shed. It was located in the midge-infested woods behind the castle and we often passed it as we led the ponies up to the steep corrie. Its low-frequency hum often unnerved the skittish young ponies, who flicked their ears forward and nervously side-stepped to the opposite side of the path.

The power station was supposed to supply all of the islanders' electrical needs but had never managed to do so. Most of the workers finished at four o'clock and ten minutes was usually just enough time for us all to get home, change and then switch on the kettle and toaster for a quick tea break. Since everyone had the same idea at the same time, every day at ten past four on the dot, the lights would go off, plunging us all into darkness. All islanders soon learned that this was not the best time to take a shower but when I first moved to the island, I was caught out quite a few times. There is nothing worse than standing in pitch darkness, with soap suds in your hair, freezing cold and soaking wet.

Stalker's Bothy was sandwiched between Farmhouse Bothy and Stable Bothy and the walls were so thin that you could practically hear your neighbours' conversations, so when the lights went out all you could hear were shouts of 'Oh, for fuck's sake', followed by the banging of cupboard doors and the rattling of drawers as people searched in the dark for candles and matches.

Within a few minutes, we'd see Jim the mechanic go racing past in his short-wheelbase Land Rover, heading for the hydro station. Jim drove at least twice as fast as the official fifteen-mile-an-hour speed limit but no one ever complained because we just wanted him to fix the power supply as soon as possible. Within five minutes Jim and his toolbox had arrived at the turbine shed to wage war on the faulty hydro.

There were always a couple of false starts before the power came on and stayed on. The first flicker of light would only last five to fifteen seconds before failing and plunging us all back into darkness again. Even though we all knew the drill, our hopes would still be raised – maybe this time it really would stay on – and then dashed again. The second time, it would last a little longer, perhaps a couple of minutes, just enough time to get back into whatever television programme we had been watching or make another attempt to boil the kettle, before darkness fell once more. Jim's third attempt usually worked and would normally give us power for about an hour. However, by ten past to half past five, everyone would be starting to prepare their dinner and using vast quantities of electricity to do so. The inevitable result was yet another power cut.

Babe really hated the power cuts and used to make a strange little whining noise when one occurred. Although she was usually happy to perch on top of the bookcase for hours on end, whenever the lights went off, she would try and make her way towards us, perhaps feeling there was safety in numbers. As she opened her wings and got airborne, the first thing she did was to poop, which landed with a loud splat on the newspapers spread on the floor for just such an eventuality. A raven's night sight isn't much better than a human's and flying in the dark was not one of her strong points. Having launched herself in the general direction of the table, she almost always crash-landed, and half-drunk tea and overflowing ashtrays would crash to the ground as she slid along the tabletop.

Babe very much reminded me of Errol, Ron Weasley's clumsy owl which flew into a window and crash-landed in a bowl of crisps in one of the *Harry Potter* movies. Although not the most graceful bird, Babe did provide us with entertainment when the lights went out. While she crashed around in the dark, Derek would search for candles and a lighter. Usually he found the candles quite quickly but the lighter was always more of a problem. Piles of empty lighters lay around the fireplace and table and Derek would fumble for them in the darkness and then I'd hear a flick–flick noise and see sparks briefly flashing from the flints as he tried to find one that worked.

Although otherwise useless, we kept the piles of empty lighters because they did serve one purpose: when we got really bored, we would have an indoor firework display by throwing the empty lighters onto the burning embers of the fire and waiting for them to explode – children, do not try this at home! On a remote Scottish island you had to make your own entertainment and blowing up lighters was kind of fun. Most of the time there was a loud bang, followed by a small ball of flame, which was strangely pleasing and usually made us laugh. However, on one occasion we tossed a lighter onto the fire that contained far more gas than we realised. It exploded with a bang that rattled our teeth in our heads and a large fireball of burning gas erupted from the fireplace and left scorch marks halfway up the wall. That brought a hasty end to our indoor fireworks displays.

The power cuts were so regular that in the end we stopped complaining and just waited passively until the electricity was turned back on. We were so resigned to it that when the power went off one evening as Derek and I were sitting in the living room watching TV, while our next-door neighbour was swearing loudly and stumbling around his kitchen searching for candles, we just sat there in complete silence, not moving or saying a word. A few seconds later, Babe, flying blind, crash-landed on the couch, just about knocking me out with her wing in the process, but Derek just let out a long, deep sigh and took a drag on his cigarette. A few minutes later we saw the Land Rover speed past, splashing in the large puddles of rainwater outside the house. After the traditional two false starts, the power went back on. We continued watching TV and during the course of that ten to fifteen minutes in the dark, neither of us had either moved or spoken a word.

Eventually the old hydroelectric power station was replaced by a newer and much more up-to-date version which worked extremely well and the power cuts became a thing of the past, though in a weird way I did almost miss them.

Derek was quite a skilled blues guitarist and, when not silenced by power cuts, would play for an hour or so every night. Before long Babe was joining in. As soon as he started playing, she would fly down from her perch and land on the back of the chair behind him. Puffing her feathers out, she opened her wings, threw her head back and squawked out the blues. She was out of tune, of course – she was a raven, not a nightingale, after all – but that didn't seem to bother Derek and it was great entertainment.

He was less impressed with some of Babe's other habits, particularly her destructive streak, which had never got any better. Her favourite trick was to open a book, tear a page out and then close it again, so you only discovered what she'd done when you'd read to that point in the book and turned the page to find the next one missing. More than one 'who-dunnit' remained unsolved thanks to Babe's vigorous editing.

Her hoarding also continued to get worse, particularly after she learned how to open the refrigerator. She was intelligent enough to realise that the fridge was where the most appetising food was kept and, having studied how we opened it, she got to work herself when our backs were turned one night. She perched on the dresser next to it and forced her beak in between the rubber seals on the door and the body of the fridge, releasing the vacuum, which then allowed the door to swing open. She disappeared inside, emerging a moment later with a gourmet treat in her beak. Having mastered the trick, she repeated it regularly and food began appearing in the most unusual places. One night the DVD player broke down. While attempting to fix it, Derek discovered the cause of the problem: a slice of bread had been pushed into the disc slot.

One day Derek woke up in a bit of a grumpy mood and came down early to make breakfast, only to discover that Babe had beaten him to it. She had already eaten all the bread and spilt the milk all over the floor, so Derek had to make do with black coffee, which he grumbled about profusely. Settling himself down in his favourite chair, he decided to cheer himself up by reading his new book but when he opened it, he found a large, congealed blob of flattened mince between the pages. Babe had been very careful to stash it there earlier, hoping it would never be found.

That was when Derek lost his temper. Throwing back his chair and sending it clattering to the floor, he grabbed the sweeping brush and began chasing Babe around the room, screaming abuse at her. I rushed to open the window and, seeing her opportunity, she flew out at a hundred miles an hour, with Derek and his brush in hot pursuit. Poor Babe didn't return for two days and when she did, she looked rather sheepish. She was on her best behaviour for nearly a week afterwards, while Derek grumpily ignored her.

Derek's living room had an open fireplace, a computer desk, two bookcases and an old sofa facing the TV set. In the days before Sky TV had come to the island, television reception was so bad that all that could be seen on any of the four channels – BBC 1 and 2, ITV and Channel 4 – was a fog of static like pink snow, with the ghostly figures of people barely visible in the background. However, Sky TV was now in every home and on evenings when the wind was blowing and the rain lashing down outside, we gathered around the set. The sofa had seen better days and in place of the original webbing, the underside of the cushions was held together by an old belt and some baler twine. I had been instructed by Derek to 'be careful' when I sat down on it, but being slightly absent-minded, I forgot and, slumping down, I broke the worn frame. Hearing a loud snap, I found myself sitting on the floor with my knees up to my chin.

This made Derek so angry that he started shouting at me

but, stuck fast amid the wreckage of the sofa, I had already dissolved into fits of helpless laughter and Derek's shouting only made me laugh even more. I eventually managed to persuade him to pull me out of the hole in the sofa. Had he not done so, I would have struggled ever to escape from it.

Furniture was difficult to come by on Rum and, as the state of Derek's sofa suggested, the general attitude was 'make do and mend' rather than 'let's go to IKEA'. Derek's coffee table also had one wonky leg which came off when you pushed it across the floor. If I needed to move the table, he had instructed me to hold onto the leg as I pushed it, but of course I invariably forgot and the leg would fall off, sending mugs of tea crashing to the floor and provoking a fresh burst of shouting from Derek.

Stalker's Bothy was one of the larger houses on the island, with an open-plan kitchen–living area. I loved the house and spent so much time there that I almost became part of the furniture – not just when I was wedged in the sofa – and it was a bit of an open house with a constant stream of visitors coming and going. When not working in the village shop, Norman's favourite pastime was to come over to the house for a drink. He came around most days and we would sit at the table and either drink tea or Tennent's lager while setting the world to rights.

Derek never drank much himself, other than copious amounts of strong coffee, but Norman loved his Tennent's. His terrier, Zappa, always came round with him and shot under the kitchen table as soon as the door was opened. She was the best-trained terrier I had ever met. She would lie down, roll over and offer her paw at a word from Norman, and he had also trained her not to chase or harass Derek's cat or my pet raven, but unfortunately I was never able to train Babe to reciprocate. Poor Zappa would lie completely still, with her eyes rolling in a mute appeal for help as my raven bullied her relentlessly. Babe pecked her front paws, pulled her tail and just generally upset her every time she came over. It was nothing personal on Babe's part, because she beat up Derek's cat on a regular basis too, even though the poor cat had also done nothing to deserve it.

While I'd been away in the Western Isles earlier that summer of 2006, Rum had acquired a couple of new temporary residents. Every year Scottish Natural Heritage offered placements to university graduates who wished to study for a PhD. They were sent to study the Rum wild goat herd near the abandoned crofting settlement of Harris on the other side of the island and became the only human inhabitants there, if you did not count the Bulloughs in their mausoleum.

The students' accommodation was a whitewashed cottage on a windswept green next to the mausoleum. It had no electricity and a temperamental water supply, and since there were no lights, its wood-panelled interior was pretty gloomy. There was an open fire in the living room, some seriously worn furniture and a collection of junk, most of which had come from beachcombing trips and been placed there in a largely unavailing attempt to brighten the place up. There were shells, fishing floats, pieces of bloodstone and of course a selection of goat skulls.

The first graduate to turn up that year had been Annie, an attractive woman in her early twenties from the north of England. She was joined a few weeks later by Ian, a big, burly Canadian guy with dark hair and a beard. All he needed was a checked shirt and an axe to look like a stereotypical Canadian lumberjack. They were both extremely friendly and it wasn't long before they became honorary locals. Because they were so cut off over at Harris, we helped them out by taking supplies over to them. Every time we were going over there, we loaded up the Land Rover with coal, logs, food and, even more importantly, alcohol (the staple diet of the 'Rumoch', as inhabitants of the island are called), and took it to them. Since the stalking team was usually in Harris at least twice a week, we felt it was the least we could do.

Annie and Ian studied the goats' breeding cycle and the kids when they were born. They spent long hours recording what foods the goats were grazing on, the survival rate of the young kids and the movements of the adult goats during different seasons and weather patterns. During periods of rain or stormy conditions, the pair of them simply hid inside the bothy and waited for the sun to come out again.

At weekends they always came over to the village, either walking or driving the quad bike. They would stay at the castle and enjoy a long and liquid weekend. After a few months they became a couple, which was almost inevitable, given that they were both attractive individuals and were spending so much time alone together. Within a year they had finished their feral goat studies and returned to their universities to complete their PhDs and it was a few years before

I saw Annie again, but the following summer Ian came back to the island to help Sandy the carpenter build a tea shop.

Ian often came for a swim with me, because I'd now discovered the joys of swimming in the ocean, watching the seals drifting past, and gazing down at the crab pots and the fish darting among the forests of seaweed below the surface. My parents had taken me to swimming classes when I was young, when I'd got a badge for swimming a mile non-stop. I'd been a regular swimmer ever since – in lochs and rivers as well as swimming pools – though strangely the first time in my life I'd ever swum in the sea was when I was on Rum. When I was younger, I'd just jump in the river wearing a swimsuit, but since then, especially when sea-swimming on Rum where the water temperature, though not quite as cold as the North Sea, is still absolutely freezing, I wore a wetsuit.

I'd always been a fairly powerful swimmer and the hard physical strength and endurance work that I did as a gamekeeper, ghillie and stalker had made me very fit and an even stronger swimmer. Once I'd taken my first dip in the sea I was hooked. As well as the exhilaration, tinged with just the right amount of fear, of battling the waves and heading out into deep waters, I loved the interaction with the seals and sometimes dolphins. That was something you definitely didn't get at the municipal baths.

Ian was the only person on the island who was a strong enough swimmer to accompany me when I went out in the open bay. We borrowed wetsuits from Sandy and Fliss and set off, swimming towards the pier. It was about a mile over the open water, with the sandy bottom about twenty-five feet below us. Every time we swam out there, we were accompanied by a particularly inquisitive common seal that followed us right across the bay, surfacing every few minutes for a closer look.

Ian was a little nervous about sharks so of course one day I took great delight in waiting until we had swum about halfway across the bay before announcing in a panic-stricken voice, 'I think I saw a shark fin circling us!' We were too far out in the bay to swim back quickly and no one was there to rescue us if a shark really had appeared. Poor Ian was scanning the waves frantically for the imaginary shark until I started humming the theme tune from *Jaws* and then laughed so much that I swallowed pints of seawater and came up coughing and spluttering.

Next time we went swimming, Ian decided it was time for payback. We swam out to the same point in the bay but when I pointed out an imaginary shark's fin this time, Ian was not buying. Instead he very carefully picked up a palm-sized jellyfish from the water, held it with his fingertips by the cup-shaped upper part of its body and then, grinning wickedly, he threw it at me. My wetsuit just happened to be a sleeveless one and with a wet splat, the jellyfish landed on my arm, tentacles first. It slipped off and landed back in the water with a plop and swam hurriedly away, but my arm had already started to tingle and burn as the poison worked its way into my skin and a red rash crept slowly up my bicep. I turned the air blue as the pain made itself felt, which Ian found extremely funny, but after the psychological torture I'd put him through it was probably only fair that he'd got his revenge.

As we swam the rest of the way across the bay, we picked up every floating missile we came across – strands of seaweed, algae and bits of driftwood – and threw them at each other. Close to the shore, Ian then brought hostilities to a close by diving beneath the waves and coming up again clutching a large and particularly angry-looking crab that was waving its menacing pincers at me. I hit the beach at top speed and that was the last time I ever claimed to have sighted a shark.

During the summer months, the bay rapidly filled up with yachts; during spells of good weather as many as thirty a night could be anchored there. The village shop and the café did particularly well during these times as most of the 'yachties' had plenty of money to spend. One afternoon Ian and I decided to swim out for a closer inspection of a particularly beautiful-looking yacht. Pulling on our fins, we headed out into the bay. As we swam closer to the yacht, we could see an older lady sitting in the sunshine with her feet up, drinking from a champagne glass. She must have been quite bored because she appeared to be overjoyed to see us and promptly invited us on board.

There was a small ladder hanging off the side of the boat which we had to climb in order to reach the deck but unfortunately the bottom rung was four or five feet above the water and pull-ups had never been one of my strong points. Ian went first and his muscular arms soon hauled up his fourteen-stone bulk, but then it was my turn. To reach the bottom rung, I had to swim towards the boat, dive under the surface and then leap upwards, kicking my legs as hard as I could to gain a little extra height. I just managed to grab the rung, but was then flailing about in the air like a mackerel on a fishing hook until I managed to shimmy up just enough to get my foot on to the ladder. Ian then pulled me up the rest of the way. It was a pretty undignified entrance, but at least I had made it on board.

The woman had been sunning herself on the deck while her husband was sleeping in the cabin below. 'With nobody to talk to I was feeling a bit lonely,' she said. 'I've just opened a bottle of pink champagne and of course no one likes to drink alone, so I'm glad you two turned up.' She fetched two more glasses, poured us one each and also produced some rather posh-looking crisps. After swimming halfway across the bay we were both hungry and thirsty and we proceeded to scoff the crisps like starving vultures and drink most of the champagne in one go. Luckily, she was still pleased to see us, so the pink champagne kept flowing and as soon as our glasses were empty, she refilled them.

She clearly must have been a stunning-looking woman when she was young because she was still very beautiful now, with blonde hair, perfectly manicured nails resting on the stem of her champagne glass and immaculate casual clothes: jeans, a crisp white shirt and blue deck shoes, with a pair of designer sunglasses perched on her head. She told us that she and her husband had come up on holiday from the south of England and were planning to sail around all the Small Isles and the Western Isles. So far they had already stopped at Arran, Jura and Eigg and they planned on staying a few nights on Rum.

After an hour of talking and drinking, we had sunk two whole bottles of champagne between the three of us and it was time to head back to shore before we were tempted to drink any more. She was quite concerned for us as neither of us was exactly sober and it was a long swim back. 'Don't worry,' I said, 'we're both very strong swimmers.'

We thanked her and said our farewells, then jumped off the deck into the ice-cold Atlantic. The sudden temperature change shocked me as I swam upwards and broke surface. Ian was already into his stroke and making for the shore, shooting away like he was training for the Olympics. So I gave the woman a goodbye wave and a final shout of 'Thank you!' and then set off to try to catch up with him. Swimming in the open ocean while three parts drunk was completely irresponsible, of course, but I'd noticed before that I always seemed to have the most fun when doing something that I really shouldn't have been doing. Luckily we both made it back to shore without incident and by then we were feeling hungry and thirsty again, so we headed for the shop where the nightly party was already well under way.

During the stalking season, Stalker's Bothy could get quite crowded. Various members of the stalking team lived there and shooting guests were frequently in and out of the house as well, so it often ended up in a real mess with dishes piled high on either side of the sink. We were all really busy, but tried to find time late in the evening for the household chores. Derek often filled the sink with Fairy Liquid and hot water, with great intentions of cleaning the dishes, but he often got distracted and let the water go cold, leaving the dirty plates untouched. This was Babe's great opportunity.

My raven was one of the vainest animals I had ever known. However, it takes one to know one and, as Derek never tired of reminding me, pets often take after their owners. Since I routinely spent up to forty minutes a day straightening my hair, I could hardly complain about Babe's own grooming rituals. She spent hours preening her shiny black feathers, taking each one in turn and grooming them until they gleamed like obsidian, and her daily beauty routine also included a bath. While any body of water – ponds, puddles, streams – would do at a pinch, more and more often she took to using Derek's clean dishwater filled with Fairy bubbles. Perching on the edge of the sink, she would lower her foot into the water to check the temperature, like a bathing beauty dipping a toe into the sea. Once she had satisfied herself that, like Goldilocks' porridge, it was neither too hot nor too cold, she would then launch herself into the sink, submerge beneath the lukewarm water and flap her wings frantically, covering her head and back. She wouldn't stop until her whole body was saturated and her feathers plastered to her skin. She would then jump out of the sink, shake herself hard and make her way on to the back of the chair for a lengthy bit of preening.

The whole process was extremely messy and by the time she'd finished, water would be splashed all over the walls and dripping off the ceiling, while puddles of soapy water showed the path that Babe had followed from the sink to the back of the chair. I felt very guilty, because she was my pet and my responsibility so, after cleaning and mopping up the water, I often refilled the sink and washed all the dishes as well, hoping to keep Derek sweet. He could only be expected to stand so much of Babe's bad behaviour, and I was grateful to him for letting her stay.

Derek wasn't the only one who had to put up with Babe's antics and deal with the consequences of her insatiable curiosity. One day Davy Chainsaw was preparing the stalking team's sandwiches – or 'pieces' as we call them in Scotland – in Derek's kitchen. Davy had been awarded the tea-shop contract that year and had decided to offer packed lunches for a fiver each. Derek let him use his kitchen to prepare them, since it saved him from having to do it in the village hall, which wasn't as well equipped and was also some distance away. As a result of turning his hand to what some of the more antediluvian local men still regarded as 'women's work', Davy Chainsaw had been rechristened 'Daisy Teabag' by them, much to their own amusement, if not Davy's. Many men would have folded under the pressure of the daily ribbing he got from them, but Davy couldn't have cared less. He needed the extra money to pay for a trip to Australia to visit his brother and nephew, and if he had to make sandwiches every day for a few months and put up with the constant barracking from the local blokes along the way, that was something he was perfectly happy to do.

Babe regarded the kitchen as her kingdom and while Davy was working, she was keeping a close eye on the preparation of our lunches from her perch on top of the cooker – the Cillit Bang experiment had not been repeated and it was now a safe landing strip once more. She watched as Davy carefully sliced the bread and painstakingly filled the sandwiches with salad, cheese and meat. He then stacked the immaculately presented pieces in a tower on the table and turned around to look for some clingfilm. Having been presented with an opportunity to carry out a personal inspection, Babe needed no second invitation and at once flew down, landing on the table with a soft thud.

Of course it was of the utmost importance that she tested the sandwiches before they were packaged; they simply had to receive Babe's seal of approval. Eyeing them with great interest, she stepped closer for a better look, then stood up as tall as she could and brought her beak down smack in the middle of the top sandwich on the stack, puncturing a large hole. Not content with that, she kept ramming her head down as hard as she could until the full length of her beak disappeared completely for a moment, right inside the bread tower.

I was still sitting watching her, frozen between amusement and horror, when Davy turned round and clocked my mischievous raven vandalising his culinary masterpiece. 'My fucking pieces! Get that bloody raven out of here!' he roared, pounding his fists on the table and effing and blinding for Britain as he chased Babe round the room.

That was her cue to exit. I opened the window and she scarpered quickly, pursued by another volley of abuse from Davy Chainsaw. Still seething with rage, he examined his sandwiches, then lifted up the stack and held it out for me to see. Babe's razor-sharp beak had punctured every single slice of bread right down to the bottom of the pile. Smack in the middle of each slice there was a hole like a bullet wound.

Davy wasn't about to start making a fresh stack of sandwiches. He angrily wrapped the existing ones and then fixed me with a baleful stare. 'Right,' he said. 'It's your bird. You can explain to everyone why their pieces are damaged.'

'Fair enough, Davy,' I said, but of course, since he wasn't around when I was handing them out that lunchtime, I never did and instead simply watched in silence as everyone polished them off, completely oblivious. I ate mine along with them so as not to arouse suspicion; it tasted fine to me.

When not vandalising our sandwiches, one of Babe's other favourite games was 'Upset the Humans'. To play this game correctly, at least one and preferably more people had to be present. Babe would then stroll around the tabletop, picking up objects in her beak. If you didn't react, she would simply put it down and pick up another, but eventually she would pick up something of value: a wallet, tobacco pouch or ten-pound note. That would cause the owner of the object to jump up, shouting and flapping their arms as they tried to grab back the stolen treasure. Of course this was exactly what the fiendish raven had been waiting for, and she would then set off at lightning speed, flying around the house with the object still in her beak, screeching her delight at being chased by an angry, flailing person, desperate to reclaim their property. It would only be returned once Babe had been cornered and had nowhere else to fly.

Although I'd often witnessed the game and been victim a few times myself, I still didn't always manage to play it cool enough when she fastened on one of my precious things. One day, while straightening my hair in the bedroom, I heard a familiar croak and peering out of the window, I noticed Babe landing on the roof of the next-door house. I opened the window and pushed it up as far as it would go. It was slightly warped after ten years of Isle of Rum storms, but I just managed to poke my head out and shout to Babe, who answered with a shrill cry. I called her over and she flew down and alighted on the windowsill as I carried on straightening my hair.

Sometimes when I sat on the sofa downstairs, she would land on the back of it, stand behind me and lovingly preen my hair, but today was not one of those days. Instead she was hellbent on mischief. My mother had sent me an expensive face cream in a beautiful green tube through the post a few days earlier. Containing 'extracts of ylang ylang and green tea', it looked fantastic and promised amazing results; I felt sure it would take years off me and at the price my mum had paid, it damn well ought to have done. However, the shiny green tube was too good to miss for my trouble-causing bird. Flapping over to the dressing table, she grabbed it and flew back across the room with it held firmly in her beak. She then paused on the windowsill and looked me directly in the eye, trying to gauge my reaction.

I knew that if I didn't play this correctly, I could lose the face cream forever so, mustering my best 'I really don't care' expression, I looked away from her and stared at the wall instead. However, Babe was too experienced at the game to be that easily fooled. She remained where she was, perched on the windowsill, poised for flight. I had an uneasy feeling that I was not going to win this game, but the windowsill was fairly close and I gambled that if I made a dive for it, I could simply grab the face cream, the bird, or both, before it was too late.

However, as I whipped around and lunged at Babe, one of my feet became tangled in the cable of my hair-straighteners and I tripped and fell to the floor with a crash. My outstretched fingers skimmed Babe's tail feathers as she opened her wings and took flight. I could see the outline of the tube in her beak as she flew across the bay and disappeared over the hill. She returned home some time later, empty-beaked. That was the last time that the expensive face cream was ever seen and its whereabouts remain unknown to this day.

The deer-stalking had been going really well that year and by the end of the 2006 stag season, we had shot our full quota of animals, the clients were happy and the tips were good. The hind season started near the end of October, so it was time to get stuck into that and now that the guests were all gone, we were able to go out alone to shoot. The summer visitors and seasonal workers had also departed, leaving Rum with just its permanent population.

When the winter storms were raging, the wind could be so powerful that it was almost impossible to walk into it and a sudden gust could lead to you literally being blown off your feet. In such weather the ferries didn't run and we might be cut off from the mainland for a week at a time. Even when the ferries were running, the seas were often so rough that only the most determined of travellers would brave the pitching, tossing and seasickness to reach the island. Under those circumstances, isolated from the outside world, cabin fever was always a risk and minor irritations could sometimes escalate into major rows. In spells of bad weather, spending days and even weeks trapped inside could also cause arguments to start over nothing. However, in such a small, remote community, being a good neighbour was not optional but essential. We depended on each other for mutual aid and support, so any frictions were quickly resolved and the ruffled feathers smoothed down. I was as prone to irritable outbursts as anyone else, but if all else failed, a brisk walk over the island, revelling in the landscape and the wildlife, was always enough to put everything else in perspective.

Now we only had much smaller deer culls and were working independently of SNH, we could pick and choose our stalking days to avoid the worst of the weather and gales and rainstorms usually meant a day off. The team would often congregate in Derek's front room, waiting for a break in the weather. That particular winter was very wet and it seemed as if we were trapped inside for weeks on end. Miserable, we sat drinking endless cups of tea as the wind howled down the glen, turning the torrential rain into sheets of water that crashed against the panes. When the estate Land Rovers drove by, they bucketed through the waterlogged potholes and sent jets of muddy water high into the air. Everyone paced the room, glum-faced, occasionally stopping to look out the window despondently.

One day Derek and I were driving over to Harris on the other side of the island, when the rain began coming down in torrents, lashed by a furious gale. Never in my life had I seen such rain before, it was like someone was throwing an endless succession of buckets of water over the car and even on full power, the windscreen wipers were useless against the weight of water. Unable to see where I was going, I had to stop for safety's sake. I opened the door a crack and, squinting against the rain, peered down at the road, but the water was already about half a foot deep and getting deeper by the second. The rivers had burst their banks and avalanches of water were rolling down off the mountainsides. This was my first experience of a flash flood and I was beginning to get scared; we were at the highest point of the road but there was no way to escape without going down into the floodwaters.

While I was busy panicking, Derek, who had seen it all before, calmly rolled himself a cigarette and poured a cup of coffee from his flask. When the rain finally eased, we looked down onto a completely flooded Kilmory Glen. I'd never seen such a sight before; half an hour earlier it had been dry land, but it now looked like a two-mile-long loch. The body of water was well over a hundred feet wide and had completely covered the road and the old stone croft houses. I was praying that the deer researchers down at Kilmory had not been trapped and drowned. To my relief, when we eventually got back, we discovered that they'd seen the weather forecast and stayed in Kinloch village, warm and dry.

The winter storms could lead to other problems that might have seemed trivial to some people but were practically a matter of life and death to me. As ever, milk always arrived on the Monday-night ferry, along with the bread, vegetable orders and general supplies. We would all rush to get as many pints as we could but were often restricted to a couple each, so most of us had run out again by the weekend. Luckily there was usually a freezer full of frozen milk in the barn but during the winter it was not unusual for the ferry to be 'stormed off' for several days and supplies could then run out altogether.

One Monday afternoon, the boat was due in as usual with its precious cargo of fresh milk but bad weather meant that it was cancelled and I had to go to the shop for some frozen milk. However, when I lifted the lid of the freezer, I saw to my absolute horror that there was not a single carton left because the other islanders had already rushed to the shop and beaten me to it. Grinding my teeth, I hurried back to Derek's fridge to assess the situation. It was definitely an amber alert, bordering on a red; no milk meant no tea, and even if we were frugal, our one and only small carton would barely last till the following morning.

By Tuesday afternoon the milk had run out and we were both dying for a nice cup of tea. I felt like a drug addict going cold turkey for the first time. My oatmeal-coloured mug, decorated with a stag leaping into the air, sat forlorn and empty on the sideboard. That day was just about bearable, knowing that if I could just make it to Wednesday, the boat would arrive with fresh supplies, but the inevitable happened. When Wednesday dawned, the boat was stormed off once more and with no let-up in the weather conditions, it would be Friday before the next boat arrived. In the grip of my cold turkey, I couldn't wait that long. A few hours earlier I had been over in Farmhouse Bothy next door, and I just happened to notice that they had three-quarters of a pint of blue-top milk left. Our neighbours were probably the only people on the island who still had any milk, but with ruthless determination, not to say selfishness, I set out to get some of it by fair means or foul.

It was pointless asking them for any, because even if they let me have a little, it would not have been enough, so I made the momentous decision to steal some milk. I'm not proud of it, but that was what I did. Late on Wednesday evening, I waited half an hour after I saw the light go out at Farmhouse Bothy and then, dressed in my black leggings and dark hooded top, with soft-soled trainers on my feet to prevent me from being heard, I sneaked out of Stalker's Bothy and crossed the yard.

None of us ever locked our houses so I simply eased open the door of Farmhouse Bothy. It squeaked loudly, setting my heart thumping in my chest, but after waiting a few minutes to make sure no one had heard, I edged my way into the kitchen. It was pitch black but, holding my fingers across the lens to reduce the light to a soft glow, I clicked on my torch and then opened the fridge door. Not wanting to take all the milk since, setting aside any moral issues, they were bound to notice if I took the whole lot, I'd brought a small jug with me. Filling it to the brim, but leaving enough milk for at least four cups of tea for them, I let myself out of the kitchen and stole back across the yard to Stalker's Bothy.

The next morning when I put a cup of tea down in front of Derek, he did a double take and then said, 'Where did you get the milk?'

'I stole it from next door.' I may have been a thief, but I was an honest one.

Derek rolled his eyes and made 'Tsk, tsk' noises, but his disapproval didn't stop him from drinking the tea. We soon ran out again and by the time the boat finally arrived on the Friday, the whole island was gasping for a cuppa. We needed food too but, first things first, we all bought milk and for once we celebrated with a cup of tea rather than a glass of whisky.

The worst of the 2006/7 winter was behind us when I was suddenly taken ill with a virus which had been going around the village. Not having the energy to do anything else, I lay on the sofa for four days in front of the fire. During that time, sensing that I was ill, Babe never left my side, perching on the back of the sofa and keeping watch over me. Every so often she would reach down and prod me gently with her beak to make sure I was okay.

When my fever broke, I got up and within a few days I'd regained my strength and felt able to get back to work. We still had to shoot five hinds at Papadil, a remote area in the south of the island, hidden beyond the steep, rocky slopes of Ruinsival. On a clear day, there were sea views from the slopes around Loch Papadil out across the Minch to Mull, Coll, Tiree, and Barra and South Uist in the Outer Hebrides. However, clear days were a considerable rarity on that coast.

The old Papadil hunting lodge built by Sir George Bullough was in ruins, almost smothered by the thickets of rhododendrons he had planted there, but there was a paddock for the deer ponies at Harris a couple of miles away, and we had to move two ponies over there from the village, ready for the cull of the hinds. It was a tough, three-hour walk across the island's mountainous core, so we took the ponies over there on the Friday, ready for work on the Monday morning.

Doing that in advance would cut nearly three hours off our day on the Monday, leaving us just enough time to get in and out of Papadil before nightfall.

I set off with one of the ghillies helping to lead the ponies and Babe in hot pursuit. She had been stuck indoors for days looking after me and, overjoyed to be outside again, she was singing her heart out as we set out on the long, winding road to Papadil. Babe had recently taken up horse riding and was enjoying her vantage point on the pony's back.

After half an hour we came to an area where a pair of golden eagles had built an eyrie on a sheer cliff hundreds of feet above the track. It was the perfect place for them to raise their chicks, as any predators would have had great difficulty in reaching the nest. I'd often stopped to gaze in wonder at the sight of the majestic eagles circling effortlessly on the thermals rising up the face of the cliffs, or swooping down in a screaming dive to sink their talons into an oblivious young goose or shearwater.

Now Babe chose this exact moment to show off her own fantastic acrobatic flying skills. Jumping from the back of the pony, she took off and flew 500 feet into the air, until she was no more than a black dot against the drifting clouds. Half-closing her wings, she then dived down again at breakneck speed, spinning through the air as she spiralled round and round like a corkscrew. Fifteen feet from the ground, she threw open her wings to apply the air-brakes, sailed effortlessly towards me and landed on my shoulder.

She paused for a moment as if expecting a round of applause, then took off again, soaring back into the sky. Again and again she did this, until suddenly she vanished. One moment she had been soaring and swooping through the sky, and the next she had just disappeared. I scanned the cliffs and the sky above us, desperately looking for her, and delayed setting off again as long as I could. Even after we walked on, I kept a close eye out for her, but she did not reappear. Trying to silence the fear in my heart, I could only hope that she had got bored and gone home, as she sometimes did.

Once the ponies had been safely dropped off and secured in the pony paddock, Derek collected us in his pick-up and drove us back to the village. 'Where's Babe?' he said.

'I don't know,' I said, still scanning the sky. 'One moment she was there and the next, poof, gone! But if we leave the window open, she should come back by herself, she usually does.' By now I wasn't even convincing myself.

By nine o'clock that night Babe still hadn't returned and the light was fading fast. Walking outside to look for her, I stood beside the bothy and shouted again and again, 'Babe! Come back!' but there was no sign of her. For weeks afterwards, I stood by the gate every night and morning, shouting her name and willing her to appear, but of course, deep in my heart I already knew she was not going to return. I tried to tell myself that maybe she had met a good-looking male raven and flown away to rear young of her own, and in my mind's eye I pictured her flying free over the mountains of Rum with her mate.

However, deep down I knew that there was no way she would have left me of her own accord because she was simply too tame and 'humanised'. She'd had the best of both worlds, flying free around the island but coming home in the evenings to sleep by the warm fire. The wild definitely had its appeal, but it didn't serve up lemon curd toast, fillet steak and smoked salmon. I knew that she was much more likely to have been killed by one of the golden eagles, protecting their nest site. Babe had always hated eagles with a passion. Whenever one appeared on the television, she would throw herself at the screen, pecking and cawing loudly. How else would she have known to do this unless she had had previous run-ins with them on the hillside? I never saw Babe again but even now, years later, when I wake up every morning, she is the first thing on my mind. Babe truly was the best pet I ever had and nothing could ever replace her.

11

THE MINKE WHALE

By the late summer of 2007, I'd been living at Derek's house for two years and although he had made me more than welcome, I knew I couldn't keep living there forever. I decided it was time to get my own place – though that was easier said than done on Rum, where there was a severe housing shortage. Moves were already under way to make the island community more independent of Scottish Natural Heritage. Due to the persistence of a few individuals, notably Derek, Fliss, Sandy and Ali, that eventually came to fruition in January 2009, when the islanders voted in favour of a transfer of assets in and around Kinloch Village from Scottish Natural Heritage to the Isle of Rum Community Trust (IRCT). The handover was eventually completed in 2010, providing a more stable future for people who had already made Rum their home and more opportunities for private and economic development for those wishing to move to the island.

The IRCT created and allocated three 'bare land' crofts and established several housing plots that were available to buy privately with conditions attached. Houses had to be permanently occupied for at least six months of the year, discouraging their use as holiday lets that, whatever their other benefits, did nothing to boost the permanent population of the island. The IRCT was also committed to developing a new local plan that would enable even more new houses to be built, though that might take months or years to happen.

However, in 2007 that all lay in the future and though a few island residents had moved into caravans while they waited for houses to be built, I was stumped until a friend came up with the idea of getting an authentic Mongolian yurt. Since I always have to be a bit different, it seemed like the ideal solution. If a yurt could keep its occupants safe and warm in the depths of a ferocious Mongolian winter, surely the Isle of Rum would not be too big a challenge for it.

I chose a sheltered site on the far side of Loch Scresort, a fantastic location with a view to die for right out over the whole of the sea loch and all the visiting yachts moored there. I applied for planning permission from the local council and with fingers crossed that it would not be refused, I went ahead and ordered my yurt direct from Mongolia. Six months later, in May 2008, my planning had been approved and my new yurt had turned up on the CalMac ferry, along with a pile of timber and a wood-burning stove.

Davy Chainsaw and Sandy, the local joiner who was my friend and former housemate, set to work erecting it for me. When it was finally up I was ecstatically happy. The yurt was sixteen feet in diameter, with a pure white cover laced with blue velvet patterns along the top edge and roof. The front door was bright red with an elegant flower pattern and a small window for light. The walls were made of a wooden latticework, insulated by a thick layer of wool sewn together inside a silk lining. I had also invested in six large bottles of waterproofing liquid, usually used for car hoods, and after painting the patterned cover with it, rain just ran off in little beads.

The yurt had been beautifully finished with a wooden deck outside and a solid pine floor inside. A large water butt sat on the table next to the cooker, there was a wood-burning stove, a bed, a wardrobe, a dressing table, a gas cooker, a table and a couple of chairs. I lit the place with candles and old-fashioned paraffin lamps which cast a soft glow around the place and when I lit the stove, it would get so hot that I had to open the door to let the heat out. There was only one technical issue: there was nowhere to plug in my hair straighteners, so even though I was living in my yurt, I always went round to Derek's to straighten my hair. I often took a bath as well while I was there and regularly put £10 on his card to pay for the electricity I'd used. The only exception was when his girlfriend from the mainland was staying. I then tried to keep out of their way as much as possible and was forced to resort to straightening my hair in the cold, draughty village hall.

Despite my low wages, I'd saved quite a lot of money while

I was on Rum. There were two reasons for that; one was that on Rum there was very little you could spend your money on anyway, and the other was that I'd always been a bit of a hoarder, squirrelling money away. I wasn't tight – I stood my round as often as anybody – but I didn't throw money round just for the sake of it. Now, having bought my yurt, I finally felt I had something to show for all the years of saving.

Despite its lack of bathing and hair-straightening facilities, I loved my new yurt, but it wouldn't have been a home without a yurt-warming party so, inviting all my friends over, I lit a barbecue while Davy built a huge bonfire. The party was a great success and gave me a good chance to show my yurt off to everyone. The local wildlife also gave my yurt their seal of approval. Rum had a population of greylag geese and every morning one of them would land on my roof and as it waddled across the roof, its feet would leave dents in the canvas. I watched it from the comfort of my bed, lying there listening to the sound of the waves gently lapping on the shore. When I got up, I'd open the door to be greeted by that magnificent view out over the bay.

I had a neighbour next to my yurt, a character called David, who was nominally sharing Farmhouse Bothy with Karl and Norman, but spent most of his time sleeping in a tent pitched alongside my yurt. Like Karl, David was from Wales although he was a good bit older, with greying hair and a full beard. He had worked as an engineer for many years but eventually had enough and chucked it all in. Looking for a complete change of life, he eventually found his way to Rum. If that history suggested a brooding, sad and introspective character, nothing could have been further from the truth; the locals even appointed him as the unofficial morale officer on Rum, because he was always smiling and happy, but with the soft brown eyes of a kind and gentle soul. In the six years I knew him I never had a cross word with him and nor did anyone else.

Although he sometimes did gardening for Scottish Natural Heritage, his main income came from cutting logs for the islanders, using a permanently blunt chainsaw. The islanders would hear the low hum of his badly maintained Husqvarna and instantly know it was him. David would work in all weathers and sing his heart out while he was sawing and splitting the logs, bellowing out a selection of wordless tunes that could be heard halfway across the village, cheering us all up. Even in Force Nine gales and lashing rain, he would still be out singing and smiling in his orange logging wellies and green Flexothane waterproofs.

Having surrendered his driver's licence, he rode everywhere on an old racing bicycle, held together by duct tape. The saddle was covered by a carrier bag, secured by yet more duct tape, the old worn tyres were constantly puncturing on the rough island roads and the rickety old bike was permanently being repaired, but David loved and cared for the bike like it was one of his own children. He had travelled the world on it, even going as far as India and New Zealand, and although Farmhouse Bothy was just fifty yards from the shop, he always used the bike on his shopping trips. Not content with just ringing the bell, he'd also shout 'Ding, Ding!' as he rode towards us.

Most of the islanders liked to cook but David went one step further, making absolutely everything from scratch. He baked his own loaves of brown bread, turned foraged blackberries into bramble jams and made chips from hand-cut potatoes, instead of buying frozen ones like the rest of the islanders. He mostly ate venison stews and casseroles, filled with vegetables and foraged mushrooms, but always accompanied by chips.

He liked to live an eco-friendly life and refused to use plastic carrier bags, instead loading all his shopping into a small battered rucksack, often leaving the shop with a few long green leeks poking out of the top. To mount his bike, he always stood on one pedal, pushed off with the other foot precisely three times, setting the bike in motion, and then, as it gathered momentum, he would swing his right leg over the saddle. As he rode away, we'd hear him singing happily to himself.

Although David was a good cook, his eating habits caused a lot of friction with his housemates, because he was a great believer in 'chips with everything' and used the deep-fat fryer at least twice a day, causing a build-up of fatty residue all over the walls and ceiling. Anyone living in Farmhouse Bothy always stank of chips, which greatly upset Karl and Norman, particularly as David would never open the windows to let in any fresh air. As well as the stink of the deep-fat fryer, he also hoarded food in the fridge and never threw anything away. The shelves were filled with month-old venison and mouldy cheese and when the fridge door was open, the stench of decay almost knocked you out, but since nothing was ever wasted when David was around, everything was eaten sooner or later . . . but mostly later.

Karl and Norman's protests to David were ignored, so they complained to the Reserve Manager, Ed, instead. David was then given his own fridge, which was promptly christened 'David's Laboratory'. One day I was invited into the bothy for a cup of tea, and noticed a large boletus mushroom sitting on the table, the product of one of David's foraging trips. Boletus mushrooms have to be picked and eaten while they are still quite young but this one was long past its best and riddled with wildlife. I watched in horror as hundreds of soft, white, wriggling maggots vacated the mushroom and crawled across the table, either making a bid for freedom or looking for something a little fresher to eat. When I pointed them out to David, I expected him to throw the mushroom and its occupants onto the compost heap where they belonged but no, he picked up the mushroom, casseroled it for his dinner and consumed it with great gusto.

David's bedroom was filled from floor to ceiling with junk, old papers and objects he'd collected on beachcombing trips. He had found his favourite red plastic cup washed up on the shore and carried it everywhere with him. It was so scratched and worn that it was barely recognisable as a usable object but one person's trash was another's treasure and David loved that battered cup. However, his hoarding habit was another bone of contention with his housemates and drove Ed crazy. To combat the growing mess, Ed had the farmhouse redecorated every year; none of the other houses on the island received as much attention but it was an excuse to get rid of all the garbage David had accumulated over the course of the year. A large trailer was stationed outside the house and the contents of Farmhouse Bothy were carted out by the Reserve's staff. After a token hasty paint job, the other inhabitants' belongings were returned to their rooms, but David had to watch in dismay as his precious hoard of 'treasures' was carted off to the tip and callously burnt to a crisp.

His constant hoarding made it impossible for him to sleep in Farmhouse Bothy himself because, as he acknowledged himself, there wasn't room for him as well as all his treasures. When asked by one of the locals why he wasn't sleeping there, he said his room was 'far too messy'. Instead he chose to sleep in his old green tent on the far side of the bay, sheltered behind some gorse bushes, which also happened to be the place where I'd stationed my yurt.

David was a devout Christian and said his prayers every night. He usually turned up around 11 p.m. when I would hear the zip of his tent being pulled back and it was strangely calming to hear him praising God and murmuring his thanks for all his blessings as I drifted off to sleep in my yurt. Come rain or shine, David slept in that tent. Force Ten gales or torrential rain never put him off, although he frequently took his soggy sleeping bag back to Farmhouse Bothy and hung it over the stairs to dry, creating yet more friction with his housemates, who complained that it stank out the place. Whatever the state of his sleeping bag and his fridge, David himself was always very clean, taking a shower and changing his clothes every single day, which was more than could be said for some of the people on the island.

At one point David had thought about joining a monastery. The simple, calm lifestyle – gardening, tending bees and being at one with nature – would have suited him to a tee but after looking into it, he decided not to pursue it any further as it would have required him to become a vegetarian and give up his deep-fat fryer. His love affair with that only came to an end when Ed threw it into a skip during one of the annual clear-outs of Farmhouse Bothy. The kitchen having finally been painted, it was now declared a fat-free zone, much to the relief of the other residents.

Strange habits aside, David was a popular and well-liked member of the island community. He turned up to every social event, including all the ceilidhs, and danced with all the women. For some reason there were always lots of single females on Rum, so during the ceilidhs there were never enough men to dance with, particularly as most of the men who were there spent the evening glued to the bar, but David always came to our rescue and women, myself included, would queue up to dance with him.

As well as being well liked by the locals, he also had a wonderfully calm way with the ponies. His gentle nature could calm even the most skittish pony and they would follow him anywhere, trusting him completely and growing in confidence as he led them around the hillside. As a result, the deer-stalkers were always keen to use him whenever he was available, but David preferred to work alone in the peace and quiet of his own company, so we didn't ask him too often in case he felt put upon.

One day David bought an extra-large leek from the shop,

planning to make it into a broth for dinner. He stood it up in the sink and went to cut some logs. Scottish Natural Heritage had just brought a couple of plumbers over to the island for the annual check on their properties and though nothing was wrong with the plumbing at Farmhouse Bothy, the plumbers' contract required them to take a look anyway. They arrived just as a new ghillie, Mike, a tall, well-built lad from Inverness with a quick wit, was rushing out of the house.

'Morning, we're here to check the house for any leaks or water damage,' one of the plumbers said.

Mike pointed to the kitchen and said, 'Well, I know there's a leek in the sink!'

You would have thought that a couple of time-served plumbers would have heard variants on the leek in the sink joke a thousand times before, but after Mike had gone, they proceeded to take the whole sink apart, looking for the leak. When he came back an hour and a half later, the plumbers were still fumbling around under the sink with bits of pipework scattered all over the kitchen floor. 'We checked everywhere and we can't find a leak,' one of them said.

Mike picked up the leek and waved it at them. 'No, no, I meant there's a leek in the sink.' His grin faded as he clocked their thunderous expressions and he beat a hasty retreat.

With no need for plumbers since I had no running water and no inside loo, I was living an idyllic existence in my yurt looking out over the bay. Only one thing threatened to spoil it. Over the course of the previous few months my left knee had been getting increasingly sore and painful. The work

I did, heavy lifting and scrambling for miles over rock and rough terrain, was extremely hard on the joints, but at first I dismissed it as just a bit of soreness or one of those aches and pains that went with the job. It would sort itself out with a bit of rest – whatever that was.

I cast my mind back, trying to think when the trouble had begun. I could remember complaining that my knee was hurting when I was just twelve years old, but because I was so young, it was just put down as 'growing pains', and after a while it seemed to improve. Then when I was nineteen, I was sleeping in the back of a Land Rover on a camping trip because our tent had got soaked. I'd had my knees bent double while I was asleep and was in real pain with them when I woke up, but I just assumed that it was because I'd been so cramped up.

As time went on, however, and the pain and soreness grew worse, I also developed a limp and it became harder and harder to sustain the belief that it was just a few minor aches and pains. Nonetheless, although I think I already knew in my heart that it was something more serious, I shut my mind to it and carried on doing the job that I loved, in the place that I loved above all others.

If walking was now a more difficult and painful process, the injured knee didn't seem to affect my swimming and in summer I was still out regularly, swimming across the bay in my wetsuit. By now, rather than borrowing from Fliss all the time, I had actually invested in my own wetsuit, though after my experiences when swimming in the ocean with Ian, I made sure that it had arms, to guard against jellyfish stings.

One glorious summer's day, a basking shark turned up in the bay. Although it was not a particularly unusual sight – we often saw sharks from the ferry and sometimes managed to get close to them – it still caused quite a stir. I'd always had a romantic idea of swimming alongside one. After all, people paid vast sums of money to swim with dolphins, so why not basking sharks? Feeling sure that the shark would be over-joyed to see me, I quickly tugged on my wetsuit and flippers, and padded out onto the beach. I walked out through the surf and swam across the bay towards the place where I had last seen it. However, now that I was low down in the water, the waves were blocking my view of the shark's fin. Every time I rose up on the swell, I whipped my head around, hoping for a glimpse of it, but without any joy. It must have swum away from the place where I'd seen it, but I knew it must still be somewhere in the bay because I could see loads of people on the beach pointing cameras. I turned around to face them, in the hope that someone would point me in the right direc-tion, but sadly no one did. For the next hour I swam around, searching for the missing shark but I never caught so much as a glimpse of it.

In the end, I gave up and swam back to the beach near my yurt. As I hauled myself out on to the rocks, one of the photographers came running over, waving his camera. When he showed me the screen, there was a perfect shot of me in the water with the basking shark about 100 yards behind me, but due to the angle of the shot and the lens he was using, it looked like the shark was much closer to me than that. He very kindly printed the photo and pinned it up in the village hall so although I hadn't really been swimming with sharks at all, I was still able to convince everyone that I had.

The stalking season was now beginning again, leaving little further time for sea-swimming. When the stalking clients booked their visits, they agreed to shoot the deer that we directed them to target, and those weren't always sixteen-point stags. Sometimes there were less impressive stags that needed culling for the good of the herd. Most clients understood and accepted that but every now and again we got a real obsessive trophy hunter, whose only interest was in bagging the most impressive-looking stag he could find so he could be photographed with it and boast about it to his friends when he went home.

Two guests who came over from Scandinavia turned out to be real trophy hunters. I took them over to a place called Atlantic Corrie on the far side of the island. It was a really long walk in foul wet and windy weather, with them trailing along behind me, right up Coire Dubh, over the *bealach* – mountain pass – and right down the other side. When we came down into the corrie, the wind was swirling around and the deer had shifted position from where I'd spotted them earlier, giving us an even longer walk. When we got into position, I studied the herd and singled out a stag that was perfect for culling. It had a deformed, almost S-shaped spine, and though it was only about four years old and its horns weren't that big, I knew it was the right one to take.

So I said to the client, 'Right, take that one.'

'No.'

That was a first; no one had ever said that to me before.

'Why not?'

'Because I came here to shoot a big stag with big horns and that's what I'm going to do.'

'Well, there aren't any big stags with big horns that need to be culled at this particular time. This is the stag that needs culling for the benefit of the herd. Could you please shoot it?'

He gave me a contemptuous look. 'No.'

My feeling was that if he didn't want to shoot that one, we might as well walk back down to Harris where the ghillies were waiting with the ponies, and I steeled myself for the furious argument that would erupt when he realised that having turned down that stag, I wasn't going to lead him to another one. However, as we were making our way down, there was a gap in the weather, the rain stopped and the sun broke through the clouds and, just as we were crossing the burn, I spotted an older stag not far in front of us. It was probably seven years old with a much more impressive spread of antlers, but I could also tell immediately from the way it was hunched over that something was seriously wrong with it. Its nose was pointing back towards its tail, it was panting heavily as it struggled to breathe and I spotted a trickle of blood running down its flank.

It hadn't seen us and we were downwind of it, so I dropped to the ground at once, signalling to the others to do the same, then wormed my way forward and studied it to make sure. It was clearly badly injured, probably in a fight with another stag, and was going to die anyway so, even though part of me felt the client deserved to go home empty-handed, I decided to let him take the shot. I waited until it turned broadside, which took about five minutes, then signalled to the client to take the shot and the stag fell dead as the echo rumbled across the hillside.

As well as needing to gralloch it, I wanted to post-mortem the stag to see what had been wrong with it. I took my knife out and as soon as I opened up the stag, I could see a large puncture wound where another stag's antler had gone right through its side. The antler had perforated the stag's diaphragm and without it, the lungs couldn't inflate. The stag's desperate efforts to breathe had only succeeded in sucking the stomach lining – the big bag holding the stomach – through the hole made by the puncture wound into the chest cavity. Its struggles to draw breath would have been absolutely agonising for the poor creature and it must have been close to death anyway. The Scandinavian client was happy enough, he had his trophy and we'd spared that stag further suffering, so all was well that ended well.

Living in the yurt in summer continued to be a joy, but autumn and winter were more of a challenge. Mongolian yurts are best suited to cold, dry conditions, whereas Rum was one of the wettest places in Scotland and although my yurt held up well, it was often soaking wet. As winter descended, the weather deteriorated rapidly. It had already been one of the wettest autumns on record and now the cold westerly winds were bringing in regular Force Twelve storms. My yurt held up surprisingly well, though I had taken extra care to tie it down using strong ropes and ratchet straps. Sandy had replaced my front door, so I now had a solid pine door, complete with a small window, and a large sliding bolt on each side kept the door secure from the wind and from nosy tourists. Derek had also offered me the use of his spare room again whenever the storms were really bad and I took full advantage of that. However, moving back in with him on a permanent basis was not an option, because I had grown to love my independence and my yurt far too much. When the weather was bad, I often stayed inside by the fire, listening to the canvas flapping in the wind and the rain lashing against the roof.

Before going to bed each night, I stocked up the wood burner and closed the air vents, setting it on a slow burn. Even so, by four in the morning, the fire would usually have died out and I would wake up feeling a chill in the air. I would lie there until 6 a.m., then jump out of bed, wrapped in my duvet, light the fire and jump back into bed again. I had got my fire-lighting skills down to such a fine art that I could set a fire in under two minutes and when I awoke again a couple of hours later, ready to get up, the yurt would be roasting hot and I could eat my breakfast in relative comfort. The wood-burning stove kept things nice and dry inside the yurt, but if I went off the island for any length of time, the canvas would get saturated and when I got back, it could take up to two days to get things dried out again.

Another problem with the yurt was the lack of an inside loo. Instead I was using a good old-fashioned 'pishpot', also known as a 'chanty' in Scotland. Each morning I'd open my front door and empty the contents into the bushes, but one morning when I woke up, it was blowing a strong gale. Bracing myself against the front door, I pushed hard against the force of the wind and got the door open about a foot but it required a considerable effort to keep it open and the rain was soaking my clothing as I balanced the pishpot on one arm. This was no kind of day for walking to the bushes but I figured I could just throw it straight out of the door onto the grass below and the rain would then wash it all away. So holding it in both hands I slung the contents out of the door . . . just as a fierce gust of wind blew down the hillside. The result was that the whole pot of pee blew straight back at me, covering me from head to foot. Note to self: buckets of pee and strong winds do not mix. Even more than usual, it was a relief when that winter at last gave way to spring.

I had my thirtieth birthday in February 2009 and a few months later I celebrated another milestone: my fifth year on the island. Both events required a more than usually prolonged drinking session in the village shop, when sufficient whisky was consumed to float the CalMac ferry. In the autumn of that year, towards the end of the stag season, I took an ageing guest stalking. He'd been on many hunting trips in the course of his long life but now wanted to shoot 'one last stag' before he put away his rifle for good, as he was now approaching eighty and had a very weak heart. The weather was fine and sunny and I hoped that I would be able to find him a good cull animal close to the road, so he wouldn't have to walk too far. We left the jeep in Harris and set off along the Coire Dubh path. There were a few gentle rolling hills towards the bottom of the corrie but I felt they would not tax the guest too much.

Over the course of an hour, we slowly, painstakingly, climbed the hill towards a small group of hinds, the only deer I was able to see. As it was the rut, I guessed that there would be a stag or two close by which we might get a chance to shoot. However, no sooner had we reached the top of the hill than the sea-fog began to roll in. We watched it advancing across the sea towards us like a great, white wall. The light from the sun was obliterated and we were enveloped in dense fog. This wasn't the usual light sea-mist; this was thick and heavy as pea soup. Visibility was reduced to about twenty feet in front of us and I knew that if it didn't lift, there was no possibility of a successful stalk. If we found a stag and the guest only wounded it, I would never be able to chase after it and find it to perform the final shot and put it out of its misery.

In my mind, the day was over and it was time to go home; the only question was where was the path? After a few minutes' walking, we came across a small, rocky pinnacle with two goats munching the grass. Small water droplets ran off their long, shaggy fleeces as the fog rolled by.

I had worked in mist and fog for many years, but pea soup was another matter entirely. However, relying on my fantastic, natural, inbuilt compass, I set off in the rough direction of the jeep, telling myself that providing I walked in a straight line, nothing could possibly go wrong. We stumbled around over rocks and grassy knolls for about an hour and although it did seem to be taking an unusually long time, I felt sure we were now getting very close to the jeep. Then in the distance ahead of us I saw a couple of dark objects looming up through the mist and made for them. They turned out to be a couple of goats standing next to a small, rocky pinnacle . . . just like the last one. My heart sank as I realised my mistake and I wanted to crawl away and hide under a rock somewhere.

The stalking guest looked at me in horror but all he said was, 'My heart is very frail.'

To say that I felt like a complete ninny was an understatement. I had marched the poor man around over rough terrain for an hour, doing his weak heart no favours at all, and had simply led him in a big circle. The only saving grace was that, so far at least, he hadn't had a heart attack or walked off a cliff. Since this was to be his last ever stalk, I had dearly wanted it to be a successful one and I felt I'd really let him down. Even though the weather conditions were not my fault, I still mentally beat myself up about it.

I knew that I couldn't afford to make the same mistake again; we really had to get back this time. 'Our best course of action will be to follow the coastal walk along the sea cliffs,' I said. 'The going is a little bit rough in places and it will take us a bit longer, but I assure you that it will take us home safe and sound.'

The poor man looked a bit sceptical, as he had every right to be, but he allowed me to lead him away along the top of the cliffs. After about ten minutes of walking we heard an almighty roar from a stag somewhere in front of us. He sounded like a big old boy and, due to the fog, he hadn't seen us. To be fair, we hadn't seen him either, but I knew by the sound of his roar that he was mature and the loudness of it showed that he wasn't far away. We dropped in to cover behind a rock. I was peering through the gloom, trying to spot the stag, when, as if by magic, the fog slowly began to clear and an old stag and a small group of hinds appeared out of the mist a hundred yards away. I couldn't believe my luck; it was like finding a pot of gold at the end of the rainbow.

Together we crawled into position, slithering on our bellies through the wet grass. The stag continued to stand his ground, roaring out a warning to any other stags within range, and after a few minutes, he turned broadside to us. The guest took aim and his shot echoed around the hillside as the old stag ran for a few feet and then dropped down dead. After my previous error, I had been worried that the old man had lost all faith in me but now he was singing my praises.

After I'd gralloched the stag and called up the ghillies with their drag-ropes, the pair of us sat back in the grass, beaming at each other. I can only guess at his feelings but I felt the most amazing sense of achievement too, because I knew it was his last ever stag and a moment he would now remember for the rest of his life. He was leaving on the ferry that evening and we wouldn't have time for a drink together when we got back, so while we waited for the ghillies, we shared a few drams from his hip flask instead. By the time they found us, we were both more than merry.

One of the best things about living on a remote Scottish island was the abundance of seafood. Fishing boats regularly docked at the pier with cargoes of fresh crab, langoustines, scallops and whitefish. Since he had taken on the pier master's job, Davy Chainsaw had a very good rapport with the boat skippers and managed to sweet-talk the fishermen into giving him seafood at knockdown prices. Other locals had fishing boats, sea rods, Canadian canoes and a selection of crab and prawn creels. However, people very rarely shared out their catches as the food was too tasty to part with, so I often missed out.

The only shellfish available to me were the wild oysters I found on the beach during low tide, but after a couple of trips to Accident and Emergency on the mainland, I realised I was severely allergic to oysters and had to leave them alone after that. Yet somehow I was determined to get my hands on some crabs and langoustines, so I went online to search for creels. Eventually I found a seller on eBay who sold good-quality crab pots at reasonable prices, so I ordered six and they were delivered a couple of weeks later. They were collapsible, so they could easily be transported in a boat and they were made of thick netting with a hole at one end for the crabs to get in. Baited with some rotting meat, I was sure they would prove irresistible both to crabs and langoustines. Now that the better weather had arrived, I intended to set them as soon as possible. I attached weights to them and baited them using some old venison I had found at the bottom of the freezer. Derek had very kindly offered to help me set them, so we borrowed a two-man Canadian canoe from Davy and together we paddled out into the bay.

'We should set the creels as far out from the village as we can manage,' Derek said, 'and preferably not in the path of the CalMac ferry.'

So we paddled to a far-off point, near the old crofters' village on the right-hand side of the bay, and set the crab pots in an area of deep water there, so they would be out of the way of the fishing vessels as well as the ferry. Each pot was attached to a thirty-foot length of strong rope with a large pink buoy tied to the end. I had been stockpiling the buoys at my yurt after a couple of very productive beachcombing trips to Harris. When the last one had been set, we sat back and admired our handiwork. A line of bright-pink buoys was bobbing around in the ocean, clearly visible between the gentle, rolling waves.

A couple of weeks later, I asked Canadian Ian to come and check the pots with me. Being the adventurous type, he immediately agreed and we set off together in the canoe. He was a strong rower and after a few hundred yards I was struggling to keep pace with him. The sea was very choppy that day and the waves breaking over the bow of the canoe sent salt spray into our eyes. Even though it was a fairly warm day, the cold wind chilled me to the bone and by the time we reached the first buoy, my muscles ached and I felt quite seasick.

Ian offered to pull up the first pot while I rested and tried to find my sea legs. Steadily turning greener, I watched as he hauled the heavy pot up through the water; it was clearly full of crabs. My excitement faded as he tipped the pot out on the floor of the canoe and I realised in dismay that all the crabs were far too small to eat. Most were shore crabs and velvet crabs which had eaten all my bait but weren't even edible themselves.

The next few pots were exactly the same, by which time I was cursing my luck. Clearly the bay had been overfished by the many creel boats that regularly circled the island. My boat was now full of small crabs that were scuttling along the bottom and snapping at my feet with their small pincers. The velvet crabs were the most vicious and as I sat back and pulled my knees up to my chin, keeping my toes well away from the angry crabs, I realised that, like spiders, crabs and any other creature with too many legs were just not my thing. After the last pot had been emptied and re-baited, we made the long row back to the boat shed.

A Force Nine gale lasting several days then passed over the island, leaving me unable to check my crab pots, and it was a couple of weeks later when I set out to check them for the second time. By now Ian had left the island for the winter and when I asked Derek if he'd come with me again, he took one look at the choppy sea and told me where to go. However, it was very important to get another person to help me, not only for safety's sake, but to help row the canoe. Canadian canoes require two people to paddle them and without a second person, I'd end up going round in circles.

Daryl, an eighteen-year-old ghillie hired by Scottish Natural Heritage, had arrived on the island a few months previously. He was enrolled at the North Highland College on the same gamekeeping course that I'd done and, even better, he came from Aberdeen, the same neck of the woods as myself, so I knocked on his door and asked if he'd like to come out into the bay with me. Being the young, enthusiastic, up-for-anything kind of person that he was, he readily agreed.

Down at the boat shed I clipped on my red life vest and

handed one to Daryl who screwed up his face in disgust. 'I'm not wearing that,' he said. 'Only wimps wear those.'

Reminding myself that if I fell out with him, I'd be paddling the canoe on my own, I held my tongue and led the way to the canoe.

As we rowed out into the bay, the wind picked up and the ocean swell threw our little canoe around. The waves smashed into the bow, soaking us to the skin. The first few pots were almost empty, only containing a few placid-looking shore crabs which I set free. As we kept moving along the line of buoys, I was worrying about the two furthest pots, near the mouth of the bay. Looking out to sea, I could see huge, towering waves rolling in and felt very glad that I hadn't put my pots any further out. Nonetheless as we rowed out to the fifth pot in the line, even though we were still within the relatively sheltered waters of the bay, the swell really started to pick up. The bow rose high into the air as we climbed each wave, then plunged as we slid down into the trough on the other side and the swell was rocking us from side to side as well. Water was pooling in the bottom of the canoe and sloshing around my feet.

It was at that point that Daryl dropped his bombshell. 'I can't swim, Portia,' he said, clinging to the sides of the canoe.

It wasn't the best moment to mention that for the very first time and if I wasn't worried before, I certainly was now. The ocean floor was about thirty feet below us and in this heavy swell, capsizing was a very real possibility. That didn't really bother me as I was a strong swimmer with or without a life vest and I'd always had a strange ability to float, bobbing around like a cork in the sea. Years before, I could remember telling my mother, 'If I ever go missing at sea, keep looking for me for at least four days because floating is one of my strong points and if you keep looking long enough, I'll be there somewhere.'

I had always meant to learn life-saving myself, but had never got round to doing so, something which, after Daryl's revelation, I now bitterly regretted. However, my brother was a fully qualified lifeguard who had actually saved his friend's life after he swam out too far and couldn't get back to shore unaided, and during one of our swimming sessions at the local pool, he had shown me how to tow someone who was drowning. So I had a reasonably accurate idea of what to do. Nonetheless, today was not the day I fancied testing the theory, so I quickly unclipped my life vest and handed it to Daryl. Strangely enough there were no further comments about wimps as he put it on.

We paddled out to the fifth pot but when I tried to pull it up, it seemed abnormally heavy for a fabric trap. So I stood on the side of the canoe and leaned back, using my weight to help me haul it in. As I did so the boat tilted at a 45-degree angle. 'You're mental,' Daryl said, panic etched on his face as he hung on to the canoe for dear life, and for once I had to agree with him. When I finally dragged the pot clear of the waves I found that it was not even full of crabs, but sand washed into it by the big storm. I dropped it back into the sea and went looking for the last pot. As we rowed on, I realised that I couldn't see the pink buoy marking the site. We spent a few more minutes searching, but the pot had disappeared, either stolen or, more likely, swept away by the storm.

Empty-handed, we rowed back to the shore and I've never seen anyone so pleased to be back on dry land as Daryl was that day. Never again did he volunteer to accompany me on a crab-potting trip and I can't say I blame him. My attempts to catch some crabs had been laughably ineffective and it seemed pointless to continue the experiment, so with a sigh, I gave my pots away to the manager at Kinloch Castle, who owned a speedboat and was able to set them in deeper water, further away from the village. I hoped he'd have more success than I had. After all the money I'd spent and the time and effort involved, I really couldn't believe that I had never caught a single crab worth eating.

Although I was still grieving for Babe, I had now acquired a new pet, a hooded crow I christened 'Stinky'. Some German guests, who had come to the island on a stalking holiday, had found a badly injured hooded crow and brought it to me to 'fix'. Crawling with lice and with its broken right wing hanging down, it looked a really sorry sight and I thought it would have been kinder to put it to sleep, but the Germans' pleas persuaded me to keep it, though I was more than half-convinced that it would die anyway.

Under the impression that wild animals were treated for free, I took Stinky to a vet on the mainland and was absolutely stunned when he handed me a bill for £160. As a gamekeeper who had shot hundreds of crows over the years, I couldn't believe I was now being asked to pay a small fortune to keep one alive. However, the vet was intransigent, so I had to scrape the money together. I went home the proud owner of a deloused and repaired, though still slightly wonky, hooded crow. I knew that he could never return to the wild because his wing had been so badly shattered that, although the vet had done his best, he had been unable to fix it.

I called him Stinky in tribute to the terrible smell he gave off. Hooded crows are native to the Highlands of Scotland, where there is a heavy rainfall most of the year. As a result, the birds secrete a waterproofing oil from a gland just above their tail. It works very well, keeping the crows nice and waterproof, but oh, the smell! It was a strong, sharp, musky scent which was unmistakably crow-like, but even though he stank, I still loved him. I housed him in a large rabbit run outside the yurt during the day and at nightfall I brought him inside the yurt and put him in a large dog cage, which kept him warm and dry.

However, unlike Babe, Stinky was a bad-tempered, vicious thug who took every opportunity to peck and claw me. You would have thought that after saving his life, spending hundreds of pounds on him and feeding him daily, he might actually have been grateful, but all my kindness towards him was ignored and any attempt at friendship was met with complete and utter contempt. However, no matter how badly behaved he was, I still loved him and couldn't bring myself to have him put down. He lived for another year and a half before he died, and though his bad temper would suggest otherwise, I like to think he'd been happy. I was heartbroken when he died, but being a gamekeeper meant I had to keep a stiff upper lip when in public, and I could only drop my guard when I was alone in my yurt at night, when I cried myself to sleep.

If I'd thought that Stinky's was the worst smell I would encounter on Rum, I soon learned how wrong I could be. One morning in the summer of 2009, the deer research officer on the island reported that a large minke whale had washed up on Kilmory Beach, a remote and beautiful white sand beach in the north of the island. It had died a few days earlier and was attracting every seagull within a ten-mile radius. Several of the villagers immediately staked a claim to the whale's skull as an ornament and tourist attraction, but after much argument, it was decided that, by placing it in the courtyard in the centre of the village, everyone could share in the benefits. The only problem was retrieving the skull. The whale would take two months to decompose and we simply couldn't wait that long. It would have to be decapitated immediately . . . by me of course.

I set off to Kilmory Beach with a group of helpers the next day. We had decided we would simply hack off the whale's head and drag it back a mile over the sand dunes to the waiting pick-up truck. I felt confident we would be back by lunchtime parading our whale's head proudly around the village. 'Should be fairly easy,' I thought to myself. 'How big can a minke whale be?'

After a half-hour walk along the dunes, we spotted the whale lying on the beach, though it wasn't that hard to find, as the stench had already given it away some 400 yards back. Huge flocks of seagulls sat on the rocks while others were perched on the whale's back, pecking at its tough, leathery skin. Climbing down the dunes and onto the beach, we scattered clouds of gulls in every direction. The whale had looked quite small from the dunes but up close, at nearly twenty feet long and six feet wide, it was a lot larger than I had been expecting, not that this put me off.

Not wanting to get my clothes dirty, I took off my socks and shoes, rolled up my trouser legs and tied my hair back in a ponytail. Then, grabbing my freshly sharpened six-inch kitchen knife, I climbed onto the back of the fetid whale. The sun had warmed up the rotting skin on its back and the stink close up was unbelievable. As I carefully inched along its back, there was a horrible squelching feeling underfoot, making me wish I'd kept my shoes on, as warm, rotting blubber kept squeezing up between my toes. I could only hope the whaleskin was still strong enough to support my weight, because if I fell inside the whale, I would definitely be a goner, as I couldn't imagine any of my squeamish friends rushing to save me.

Unfortunately for me, whales don't actually have a neck so, taking a guess at where the skull ended, I plunged in my knife. The skin was very tough, and it took all my strength to cut through it. As I did so a sticky green slime oozed out, giving off a stench that nearly knocked me out. I cut all the way around the head, down the sides and as far underneath as I could reach, while my friends, who were supposed to be helping, just stood around laughing and taking photos.

The seagulls were growing impatient and eventually joined me on the whale, pecking at the freshly opened carcass and squabbling among themselves. After an hour of frenzied hacking and slashing, the tide was coming in fast and I was knee-deep in ice-cold seawater. It was now or never. I clambered down from the whale and we tied a rope to its head. Then we all lined up like a tug-of-war team and began heaving on the rope, trying to rip the unfortunate creature's head off. Ten minutes later, it was still firmly attached to the whale and we were all gasping for breath, our muscles screaming, wondering why on earth we had thought up this crazy scheme. I now realised that this should have been a job for Davy Chainsaw, wielding the saw he was named after, not a kitchen knife. The whale's head was just too big and there was no way we were going to be able to snap it off. With the tide still rising, we admitted defeat and slunk back to the pick-up, feeling deflated and resigning ourselves to a couple of months' wait while the whale rotted enough for us to salvage the head.

It wasn't until we closed the doors that the smell hit me. Oh my God, how I stank! I had been careful to wash myself in the sea but it hadn't made the slightest bit of difference; a hideous, rancid smell still clung to me and we had to drive all the way back with the windows wide open. Later that night, after two showers and a bath, I still stank, and my friends kept their distance when they spoke to me for some time afterwards.

Months later, we returned to the skeleton of the whale to retrieve its skull. By then, as the whale had slowly rotted, most of the villagers had picked up whale ribs and vertebrae and put them on display outside their houses. All we needed was the skull as the centrepiece for the village square, but when we got there, we discovered that someone had beaten us to it: the skull had gone. We later found out that a man from Skye had come over in his boat and removed it, but we strongly suspected that one of the locals must have sold it to him and showed him the skull's exact location. Although we never found out who it was, the greed of someone on the island had obviously got the better of their community spirit and they were now walking around a few hundred pounds richer.

12

THE END OF THE DREAM

When spring 2010 came around, the stalking season finished and as usual, my income came to an abrupt halt. Finding work on Rum over the spring and early summer was pretty difficult, so I decided to head back to the mainland for a few months. After placing an advert in the local paper, I was offered a short contract as a lambing assistant. The farm had over 400 sheep, all of them due to give birth in the next month. It was my job to travel around the farm on a quad bike, checking the sheep and feeding them.

One morning, while I was busy checking the flock, I came across a small Shetland ewe that was 'stuck in birth' with just the lamb's head protruding. It was a common problem; the lamb's front legs had got stuck and the ewe was unable to push it out. If I'd left it much longer, the lamb would surely have died, so jumping on the quad bike,

I set off after the ewe. You would think the painful process of a difficult birth would have made the ewe easy to catch, but not a bit of it. She sprinted up the hill with the lamb's head flapping up and down behind her, but eventually she slowed down and, leaping off the quad, I rugby-tackled her to the ground as the bike rumbled on and crashed into the gorse bushes.

I grabbed the sheep's legs and tipped her over, rendering her helpless. There was only one way to deal with this situation and I gently pushed the lamb's head back inside the sheep's uterus and then, feeling my way around inside, I located the lamb's front legs and pulled them to the front of the birth canal. With a bit of gentle manipulation and a few tugs, the lamb was born, slightly the worse for wear but very much alive. The ewe seemed completely unfazed and immediately stood up and began licking her lamb.

Later that afternoon I found another ewe stuck in lamb and was stupefied when I realised it was the same one, having a second lamb. The whole process started again and once more I had to chase her up the hillside, leaving the quad bike to crash into the gorse bushes while I tackled her and helped her lamb to be born.

If the ewe's problems were now over, for the moment at least, mine were only just beginning. As I walked back to the gorse bushes to retrieve the quad bike, I heard a crunching noise from my left knee and felt an agonising pain. For the previous two years the knee had been giving me trouble from time to time, but though it had forced me to walk with a limp, it was nothing that stopped me from doing my job.

Now the crunching noise and the pain that accompanied it was something I could no longer ignore.

Three months later I had seen a succession of doctors, who all assured me that there was 'absolutely nothing wrong' with me. One particular doctor, whose bedside manner clearly needed more work, told me it was 'all in your head', and suggested I see a psychiatrist, not an orthopaedic surgeon. Luckily for me I had a good friend, Jurgen, a German doctor who came to Rum for a two-week stalking holiday with his son every year. Climbing up a hill behind me one day in 2008, Jurgen had noticed my limp. 'You are walking with your left foot turned inwards,' he said to me. 'I think you have a problem with your left knee. When it gets bad, come and see me in Germany and we will give you surgery to correct it.'

Being young and carefree, I had brushed the comment aside, imagining that, if ever, it would not happen for at least twenty years. Yet here I was two years later, unable to walk properly and feeling very sorry for myself. Not only was I in pain, but I'd had to suffer the indignity of being labelled a mad hypochondriac by my British doctors.

So I called Jurgen. He told me to fly to Germany at once and arranged for me to see a specialist. My parents dropped me at the airport for the flight and within two days I had been examined and booked in for an exploratory operation. The surgeon, Doctor Scheifer, told me that he would use a small camera to look inside my knee, assess the damage, and clean out any loose or damaged cartilage; which would help me to walk better. He reassured me that the problem would probably be quite simple and easily fixed, but when the morning of the operation came, I still felt very nervous.

When I was wheeled down to the surgery, Doctor Scheifer, masked and gowned for the operation, greeted me warmly, and Jurgen had also come to the operating theatre to offer moral support. After giving me the anaesthetic, the anaesthetist told me to count down from ten. 'Ten ... Nine ... Eight ... Seven ...' That was as far as I got. The next thing I knew, I was coming round in the recovery room. The nurses wheeled me back to the ward and I was left to sleep it off.

Later that night, Jurgen came back to pick me up and take me to his home. My leg was bound in a large Styrofoam dressing with Velcro straps, and I struggled along the hospital corridor on crutches. Jurgen helped me get into his car. He seemed preoccupied and as we drove through the winding streets of the town, he was unusually silent. Since he normally spoke non-stop, it was quite unnerving.

Eventually he broke the silence. 'Well, I suppose you want a diagnosis?' From the look on his face, I suspected that it was the last thing I wanted and I stayed silent, hoping to postpone the inevitable. 'Well I'm very sorry,' he said at last, 'but you are going to have to find a new job, because you will never be able to go back to deer-stalking again. The surgeon found terrible damage in your knee. Your cartilage has worn away and your bones are grinding together. He performed a microfracture surgery to make it slightly better for you, but it will never be good enough to allow you to climb mountains or lift anything heavy ever again. I am really very sorry.'

Trying not to cry, I bit my lip and turned my head away.

I think I had already known what was coming but it still shocked me to the core. As it sank in, I was in absolute despair.

I was staying with Jurgen and his family for a week while I recuperated and, in an attempt to take my mind off it, he had arranged a whole host of activities. Just two days after the operation he announced, 'Okay, today we are going go-karting.'

The way I felt, I would rather have been set upon by a pack of rabid dogs. All I really wanted to do was lie in bed and rest my aching leg, but having had countless holidays on Rum, Jurgen wanted to repay the favour and, not wanting to refuse his hospitality, I reluctantly agreed.

The 'go-kart' turned out to be a bobsleigh on a roller coaster which rose about a hundred feet in the air. Admittedly it was good fun, but each jerk and bump also caused me agonies. Fortunately, the other entertainments he had lined up were much less stressful and painful and over the course of the next week, Jurgen and his son showed me Bavaria. We drove through vast forests, past sapphire-blue lakes and waterfalls, all with the stunning backdrop of the Bavarian Alps, and saw capercaillie, hazel grouse, eagle owls and ravens – which of course made me think of Babe. The landscape was absolutely beautiful and I'll always be grateful to them for showing it to me.

Five weeks later, back in Scotland and staying with my parents, I developed a sudden virus which left me bed bound for nearly five months. My muscles were twitching constantly, I had numbness and pins and needles all over my body, and the worst migraine I had ever suffered. My energy levels were practically non-existent and I was convinced I was dying. However, slowly but surely, I managed to get better and by then my leg was much less painful. A year later, I had a second operation on my other knee, but thankfully that healed very well and I could now walk without too much discomfort.

After much agonising and soul-searching, I had taken Jurgen's advice and resigned from my job as a deer-stalker on the Isle of Rum. It was heartbreaking to give up my work and my life on the island that had been my home for six years, but there was no other choice. A deer-stalker who cannot climb hillsides, cross rough ground or lift a dead stag or hind onto a pony or a quad bike is no use to anybody. I had been living my dream since the moment I first went stalking with Uncle Angus and Billy all those years before, but now it was over. Nor could I stay on Rum, for there was no other work that I could do there.

So I sold my yurt to a couple of the other islanders and on my last night on Rum, I held a whisky-soaked farewell party to say goodbye to Norman, Derek, Davy Chainsaw, Sandy, Fliss and all my other friends on Rum. The next day I caught the ferry to Mallaig for the last time. I couldn't bear to watch the familiar craggy outline of the island fading into the mist as the ferry pulled away and I went below decks until I was sure that Rum had disappeared from sight, lost in the mist rolling in from the sea.

I went back to my parents' home in Aberdeen and for a few days I wallowed in self-pity, but one morning I looked myself in the eye in the bathroom mirror and told myself: 'Shape up, Portia. Far worse things happen to other people. You're still young, you're not dying, you're not crippled, you just can't walk over rough ground, climb trees or mountains, or lift heavy weights. So sort yourself out, stop pining for what might have been and decide what you're going to do with the rest of your life instead.'

I was now thirty-two, but the thought of working in a shop, office or factory – in fact any job with four walls around it – was still anathema to me, so I cast around for outside work that I could do. One day in April 2011, the perfect solution presented itself: working for the Scottish Wildlife Trust on the 'Saving Scotland's Red Squirrel Project', protecting red squirrels in their existing habitats and re-establishing them in areas overrun by grey squirrels.

Introduced to Britain in the nineteenth century in a wrong-headed attempt to add to the diversity of British wildlife, the American grey squirrels carry a disease to which they are immune but which is fatal to our native red squirrels. The greys are also larger and more aggressive, out-competing the reds for food and territory and driving them out when they encounter them. They are also far more damaging to trees and other wildlife, eating birds' eggs and fledglings, and causing an estimated £40 million annual damage to oak, beech and other native trees. There were estimated to be ten million grey squirrels in Britain and just 150,000 reds, so we faced an uphill battle to turn the tide, but it was a project I wholeheartedly supported. Furthermore, working in forests over fairly flat ground, laying traps to catch greys and helping to manage the habitat to encourage the native red squirrels, was well within even my reduced capabilities.

When we first started the Red Squirrel Project, there were four trappers, two in the city and two in Aberdeenshire. My job was to travel round the countryside of the shire and stop the spread of the grey squirrels into the Highlands. When we began work, they had already ranged as far south as Stonehaven, as far east as Banchory and as far north as Ellon, and a few stragglers had been reported even further afield, though those individuals had probably already been picked off by gamekeepers and predators without establishing fresh colonies.

I started by using ground traps, originally designed for mink. I covered them up with an old bin bag and piled leaves and stones on top to disguise the traps and make them appear more natural. I baited them with maize and never had to wait long for a catch. In the early days I often caught several grey squirrels a day and had a record catch of fourteen on one particularly sunny spring day. The city trapper, James, beat my record, managing to catch eighteen one day, although that was in the very early days of the project when they were far more plentiful.

After a year or so we were forced to change our methods, mainly because of the rising badger numbers in the area. The badgers would tear apart the ground traps to get at the maize or any trapped squirrels inside them and they became such a problem that we eventually abandoned ground-trapping altogether. With the help of our boss, Steve, the city trapper, James, came up with a new design of trap-box to put up in trees. Our traps are now wired onto a short plank of wood, covered in black plastic sheeting and nailed to the tree. That had the added bonus of fooling the general public into thinking that the tree traps were owl boxes and as a result, they left them well alone. That was a real bonus because vandalism in city parks and woodland was a big problem for us. Ill-informed people would smash up the cage traps, thinking they were providing some kind of service to the wildlife; if only they had known the trouble they were causing.

Over the years I've been able to persuade or sweet-talk most people into sharing our way of thinking and I've managed to secure permission to trap on their land from almost all the landowners in Aberdeenshire. The fact that I really believed in the project myself was a great help in convincing them. I can now trap grey squirrels practically everywhere within Aberdeenshire. It's a job I love doing and working alone suits me quite well. There are times when I feel a bit lonely and long for a few friends to work with, but I know my team-mates are all in the same boat and are only a phone call away. I try my best to call them all at least once a week to touch base with them and keep myself in the loop on any developments.

Apart from occasional loneliness, other occupational hazards include dog walkers with out-of-control, aggressive dogs and of course, the dreaded mounds of dog poo. At least once a week I tread in a big pile of it which then becomes ingrained into the deep tread on the soles of my boots. Autumn is the most dangerous time, with leaves covering the poop. It's like walking through a minefield with one misstep producing terrible consequences. If I'm lucky, I notice the dog poo before I get in the car, but often I only realise my mistake when I'm two miles down the road and have just innocently switched on the fan-heater. Cue a horrible waft, stinking out the car while I turn the air blue with swear words. After winding all the windows down for the rest of the drive home, I then have to wash the car-mats and foot-pedals.

Other pitfalls of the job include the drunks and sex perverts who tend to hang around public parks and for safety reasons I now largely avoid those areas and let James do them instead. In the course of my travels, I've also met a few animal-rights activists who have challenged me about my work. However, once I calmly explain what I'm doing and why I'm doing it, they almost always accept it and sometimes I can even convert them.

As I'm using live traps, I regularly trap red squirrels by accident. My heart melts every time I see one scurrying about inside the cage and I rush to let them out. Although most just scamper off, the ones with attitude stick around to tell me off. Jumping out of the trap, they alight on the branches just above my head and chatter angrily at me. If they're really mad, they'll stamp their feet and flick their tail in defiance of my intrusion into their squirrelly territory. This never fails to amuse me as I do love a red squirrel with a bit of attitude.

However, just as not all humans are athletes, not all red squirrels are good tree climbers. Once when I was working on a trap round in the north of the city, I caught a particularly dozy-looking red. When I opened the trap, it leapt out and immediately climbed the nearest tree. Its problem was that the tree was only about five feet tall and the poor, terrified animal clung to the top, squeaking in fright. Deciding it had had enough, it jumped back down and selected a large mature beech tree instead. Unfortunately the bark was just too smooth for the squirrel to hold onto. On its first attempt, it climbed about fifteen feet up the tree, its claws scrabbling for grip, and then comically slid back down to the bottom again.

The poor red repeated this twice more, then gave up and selected another tree, a neighbouring noble fir, and climbed to the top of it. All it had to do now was jump across to a branch of the beech tree and it was home free. However, when it made its leap, it managed to miss its target and landed instead on a much thinner branch. The squirrel's weight made that whippy branch ping backwards and launch the squirrel into the air like a stone from a catapult. It somersaulted through the air, crashed through the foliage and landed on the grass at my feet with a thump. It got up and made its somewhat unsteady way off towards yet another tree while, once I'd stopped laughing, I reset my trap, wishing the episode had been caught on camera – it would have been a Facebook sensation!

The four of us each set between twenty and thirty traps at a time in our areas and check them twice a day, releasing any non-target animals, such as red squirrels and birds, that we've caught. As by now the grey squirrels were being reduced to a very low density, we had to start upping our game. Although we still used maize as bait, we also supplemented it with peanuts, fat balls and aniseed attractant spray and even the fussiest grey squirrel found it hard to resist such a banquet. Our aim was to eradicate the Aberdeenshire population of grey squirrels altogether, but our first priority was to push them back within the city limits. In that we've been successful. Although there are still a few small, isolated pockets of stragglers, the only substantial grey squirrel population is now within the city of Aberdeen. We are well on our way to achieving our goal of culling them there as well, making ours one of the most successful projects in the whole country.

After clearing the greys out of Aberdeenshire, I genuinely believed that it would be ten years or more before the areas were repopulated with red squirrels. How wrong I was. The result was almost immediate as the reds began returning to reclaim their lost territories. Within the last two years, red squirrels have appeared in places where they hadn't previously been seen for a decade or more. That knowledge gives me the most tremendous sense of achievement and it's a great feeling when I spot them leaping through the branches of the trees above my head.

My initial contract with the Red Squirrel Project was only for two months, which was then extended to four, then six, then eight months, and after a year, I was put on a permanent contract. Six years later, I am still here. Since I was initially only working on a very short-term contract, it made no sense to sign a lease on a rented cottage when I might then have to leave the area in search of further work within a couple of months. Instead, I went back home to live with my parents.

They were amazing, helping me to readjust to mainland life and get back on my feet again, and I'll be eternally grateful to them for that. However, moving back in with your parents when you're in your thirties inevitably leads to some frictions and arguments, so when my job was made permanent, I lost no time in searching for a home of my own.

I eventually found an ideal property, a large, whitewashed cottage in three acres of land on the outskirts of Aberdeen. I was overjoyed to be moving into my own personal space again and I'm sure my parents felt the same! The cottage was a bit of a wreck when I moved in, but my mum and dad and my uncle were a great help in doing it up. My dad's engineering skills came in handy with the repairs, plumbing and electrics, my uncle did a lot of the painting, and my mum helped me to spring-clean the place from top to bottom. Within a few months the house was in perfect working order and I really began to think of it as home. Being settled in my own place has also given me a real sense of peace and fulfilment.

I'm a bit of a free spirit who has always liked to keep moving on, and I used to get itchy feet if I spent more than a couple of years in one place. Working on the Red Squirrel Project means that I'm now in a permanent job with my own permanent house and although I absolutely love my work, I do still sometimes find myself craving the freedom of my old life, when I could pack up and move on pretty much whenever I felt the urge. My uncle is a bit the same, so maybe it's a genetic thing, perhaps there's a bit of gypsy blood somewhere in our ancestry.

However, there are benefits to a settled life as well. All the moving around over the course of my life meant that I'd never really been able to grow my own food before, but having my own home has allowed me to grow my own vegetables and indulge a passion for growing soft fruit. At the side of my house is a large, lean-to greenhouse, where I grow strawberries, damsons, blueberries, redcurrants and blackberries. There is even a dwarf lemon tree; in our cold, grey northern climate it has yet to produce any fruit, but I remain ever hopeful.

I've also become a beekeeper. In the spring of 2016 I purchased two beehives and set them up with a nucleus (five frames of bees and brood). One of the queens I named Queen Kirsten, after a friend I had known since childhood. However, Queen Kirsten turned out to be a strong and ruthless leader, who mobilised her troops to go out and destroy the other hive. They duly nicked all the honey and killed most of the bees. I only noticed a week later during a hive check. One hive was particularly – and unnaturally – heavy, and the other was completely empty, save for a pile of dead bees. Having naively assumed that they would live happily together, I was forced to conclude that there is as much politics in the bee world as in our own. I now understand that they are not the placid little creatures I had imagined. Instead, war is always on their minds, but however angry my bees are and however much they sting me, I still love each and every one of them, and try to visit them regularly.

I'm very happy in my new life on the mainland, but even though I love my work on the Red Squirrel Project, I still have an ache in my heart whenever I think of the Isle of Rum – and Babe – and I often pause to reflect on my time on that beautiful island. I know that I can never go back to work as a deer-stalker and even if they set up a red squirrel project there – highly unlikely given the scarcity of trees and the fact that there are no squirrels at all on the island – the terrain is too unforgiving for someone with damaged knees to negotiate.

Although my career as a gamekeeper and a deer-stalker was much shorter than I would have wished, I still feel hugely privileged to have been able to experience that life, and prove to all the doubters that a woman really could do the job as well as a man. I often sit at home in the evening, leafing through my photographs of Invercauld, Ardverikie, Letterewe, Benbecula and the Western Isles, but above all the Isle of Rum. They stir memories that I will always treasure of that haunting, beautiful place and those extraordinary characters, the friends I was privileged to know and love in the magical years I spent on the island, the most wonderful time of my life.

Although I have lived an unconventional life, I have loved every minute of it and have no regrets at the course my life has taken. Had I settled in a boring office job, I would never have reached my full potential and become the person I am today. I've spent the past twenty-odd years working in the countryside, first in the forestry and game industries and then, for the last six years, in wildlife conservation. I loved my work as a tree surgeon and even more my time as a gamekeeper and deer-stalker, but the conservation work I now do has given me the greatest sense of satisfaction and without, I hope, sounding too pretentious about it, I now see myself as one of the custodians of the natural world. I hope to continue this work for many more years, until I finally become too old to scramble through the forests and fields, and only then might I consider taking an indoor job.

I live alone and am happy that way, but though the memory of my mother ironing Y-fronts has never left me, I'm still very open to the idea of a relationship. Just as long as whoever it is doesn't expect me to iron his pants . . . and if he could cook, that would be a real bonus!

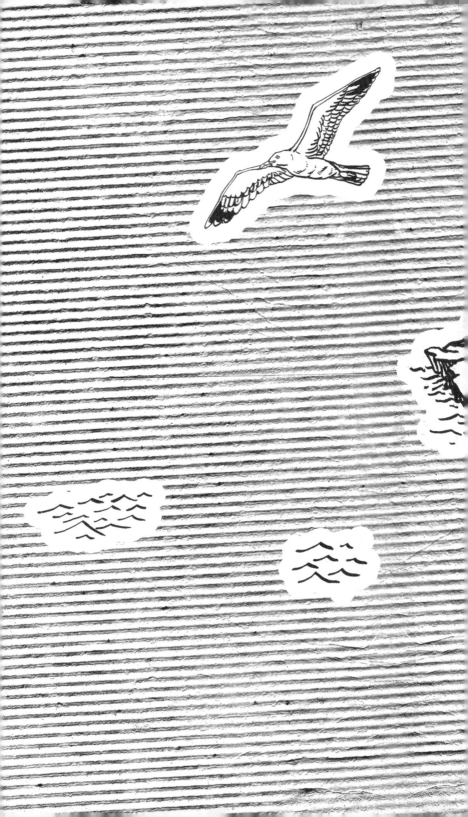